ZEN
ECONOMICS
ROB URIE

First published by
CounterPunch 2016

CounterPunch
PO Box 228
Petrolia, CA 95558

ISBN 978-0692726990

Table of Contents

Preface

IN HISTORY AND LANGUAGE THE IDEAS OF CAPITALISM AND THE capitalist 'self' entered late and required a solid century and a half of active promotion before they took on the currency of political, cultural and economic hegemony. Given the blood-soaked history of the twentieth century one might imagine that if it hadn't been for the remote geography and rapid industrial development of the U.S., the primary promoter of imperial capitalism, that Europe (and Japan) would have developed more substantially different modes of economic organization. This is to suggest that for a 'natural' system of political economy, capitalism is quite conspicuously an artifact of particular historical development.

The question at present is how to approach capitalism as it is exposited in Western economics? The challenge is that this economics has as its base premise anti-history, a theory of human 'being' that stands outside of history? A strictly historical approach can draw context around the ideas of 'nature' and 'natural system' but it can't get inside of them—it can't address them from within their 'internal' logic.

As evidence of the hold that capitalism has on the Western psyche, the question of who it is a 'natural system' for is rarely asked? On those rare occasions when it is asked the answer can be, and usually is, left undefined under the pretext of self evidence: it is a system of social organization that provides the most that can be gotten from a society's resources. But without an explicit or implied 'beneficiary' of 'the most' the statement is meaningless. The most orange things? The most swan-shaped piles of dirt? The most music and art?

What then are these resources from which getting 'the most' is a primary determinant of social organization in capitalist societies? The most fresh air, drinkable water, social relationships and freedom from violence? When put in these terms an 'appropriate amount' is likely preferred to 'the most.' 'The most' is a quantum of insatiability.

Why would one, or even 'a society,' want the most drinkable water or fresh air when having the amount necessary for drinking and breathing is all that can be drunk and breathed? The point is that there are people's, the bulk of people's in history for that matter, for whom the idea of acquisition in the modern Western sense never really occurred. History doesn't support the idea of the capitalist archetype, a singular, anti-historical 'man' that is the basis for capitalist theory.

The idea of 'efficient' economic production, the base premise of capitalism and of capitalist economics, carries with it an implied answer to who benefits from efficiency? It is the type of being who benefits from economic efficiency, from getting 'the most' from the least, goes the mythology. But this mythologized idea of efficiency has little to do with capitalist production. What is efficient in one dimension, for instance mechanized machinery, may be radically inefficient in another if it poisons the town's water supply.

With history replete with acquisitive and non-acquisitive cultures and capitalist acquisition in the modern sense of 'consumer culture' an historically and culturally locatable phenomenon, history can only answer the question from outside of the premise of efficiency. There exists no historical 'being' for whom 'efficiency', 'more' and 'the most' stands as base motive outside of history. Where this leaves capitalism is that it can be described historically, but only from outside of the terms of capitalist theory.

The second order question then is : why would capitalists and capitalist economists use an assertion of 'natural' acquisitiveness as the base premise of a developed philosophy of social organization when it is implausible when viewed against the breadth of history? What set of premises renders 'the most' in an acquisitive sense preferable to 'the smallest amount needed to get by?' This isn't to pose one against the other but rather to point to how narrow the realm of concern 'the most' embodies when considered against the broader possibilities?

Here history and language merge as that which is historical versus that which history 'records.' The smell of the air, the trajectory of light through the trees and the memories of childhood are all historical without being 'history.' The difference is history as lived experience versus history as narrative form, as recitation of 'the facts.' History as narrative form leaves out far more than it incorporates. But does this imply that it is 'truer' than what is left out? The capitalist conception of economic 'man' is an assertion. As such it occupies the space between 'fact' of history and everything else.

As is drawn out in broader detail below, the core premise of a 'natural' acquisitiveness behind capitalism and capitalist economics is static—its quickly loses meaning when it is placed in history. It doesn't describe the preponderence of historical experience that it needs to to serve as some plausible 'human core.' Left on the outside of consideration is the very possiblity of such a core? As history has it, the (metaphysical) humanism that the concept of such a core embodies is very much tied to the base premises of capitalism.

If acquisitiveness isn't a 'natural' characteristic of human being but is nevertheless put forward as the motivating factor of social organization — rationale as reified fact, then it becomes an imposition, a particular mode put forward as a universal mode. Here then is the problem: the type of being whose motivation is 'more' and 'the most,' 'acquisitive man,' either represents *the* human core or it is a cultural imposition, a static, anti-historical assertion. It may well describe aspects of some cultures. But what is doesn't do is give acquisition the 'natural' basis required to universalize it as timeless human 'core.'

The tie of history to language here is relevant. Western economics is anti-historical in the sense that it proceeds from static premises, from a timeless and universal 'economic man,' that is implausible in historical terms. In this case the form itself is imposition, a social philosophy built into Western institutions, rather than a 'discussion' amongst social philosophers. Imposition isn't a relationship of 'equals,' it is an act of domination reflecting disproportionate social power.

The static conceit that 'economic man' describes equally aboriginal and indigenous cultures ten thousand years ago and well-trained mall shoppers in Des Moines in 2014 isn't a discussion, it is a dictate. Conversely, to bring history into the 'discussion' leaves little of substance behind—without static premises the type of being who is served by 'efficiency' and whose motive is 'more' and 'the most' remains undefined, one of the infinite ways people experience life.

Of relevance is that the static assertion of 'economic man' is a taking inside of language, taking language out of the realm of communication to ossify it as an object of social power. For economic man to be a static conceit, an 'object' from a world that stands apart from time and space, doing so has to be possible. Language must be taken 'inside' to remove it from time and space. It only exists there to the extent language itself does.

This taking inside removes language from the public realm—it is no longer between 'us,' it is 'yours' and 'mine.' Put differently, art and music are social negotiation—there is no (plausible) claim to be made that there is one true meaning of artist Jackson Pollack's drip paintings or Ornette Coleman's music. These are 'living' languages and their 'record' is incidental. But 'economic man' either has particular (static) meaning or it is indeterminate as human 'core.' Capitalist theory is dependent on a very specific conception of language.

The relation of language to history in play here is about competing concepts of time. Language as social act is lived history—it exists and then is doesn't. Economic man as the primary concern and motivation of capitalism and capitalist economics is taken out of this realm of lived history. This taking out of lived history is to place it in dead history as the 'possession' of the acquirer. It is 'timeless and universal' to the same extent its acquirer is.

This concept of static language, word 'objects' taken 'inside' as possession, is both necessary premise and metaphor for broader capitalist social relations. Without economic man as primary actor there exists no required human archetype to support capitalism as political economy. Yet its historical implausibility has had no determinable impact on capitalist theory. It serves as 'its' own conclusion, as the question that is its own answer.

Philosophical shorthand for this static concept of time of capitalist theory is 'metaphysics.' A more detailed discussion of metaphysics is provided later in this book. Briefly, metaphysics, or relationships metaphorically placed 'above' the physical world, derives in large measure from the Greek philosopher Plato's theories of 'true knowledge' as existing separate from that which is 'known.' Plato's 'ontology,' or theory of how the world 'holds together,' is premised on 'timeless and universal' essences, defining characteristics that constitute 'true' understanding of the world.

This can hopefully be made clear with an example from mid-level philosophy texts. In Plato's ontology an acorn is an acorn in its essence and an oak tree is an oak tree in its essence. These essences 'unite' oak trees with all oak trees and acorns with all acorns. They also 'allow' them to be counted. Five oak trees and thirty acorns are quantums of essences, the unities in 'oak tree-ness' and 'acorn-ness' that are theorized to exist 'above' or 'apart from' things in the world.

Philosophically inclined readers can probably see the problem with this theory coming through the 'objects' of oak tree and acorn chosen. Under the right conditions an acorn becomes an oak tree. The issue isn't that at one moment an acorn is an acorn and at another it is an oak tree. A theory of time that allows that an acorn is an acorn and an oak tree is an oak tree can't account for an acorn becoming an oak tree.

An ontology that can't account for the temporal relation of an acorn that grows into an oak tree is missing a coherent theory of time, of temporal development. In Plato's ontology the idea of acorn is theorized to be 'timeless and universal' but actual acorns exist temporally and specifically. And if an acorn 'becomes' an oak tree (or rots on the forest floor) what is 'it' in its essence?

At this point this problem probably seems academic—what do theories of time have to do with capitalism? The challenge is that 'economic man,' the base actor of, and motivation for, capitalism is wholly beholden to the static ontology that supports metaphysics. If this web of premises about the world is suspect, then so are the conclusions drawn from it. To be clear, this isn't a problem that can be 'fixed.' Either the premises make sense or the theoretical frame of Western capitalism is rendered unintelligible.

A lot of philosophical effort has gone into attempts to 'rescue' metaphysics. However, in 'the world' temporal is all that there is—including 'timeless and universal' truths that, as histories of science such as Thomas Kuhn's[1] have shown, are a broad range of 'things' with none of them being timeless and universal. To be clear, no competing ontology needs to be developed to conclude that the concept of time at work in Plato's ontology is a dubious foundation for a social philosophy. This written, foundational challenges are the least concern at this point.

At this juncture the issues sketched out—metaphysics as implausible ontology and its social implications as a heavily burdened frame for understanding 'the world,' are likely obtuse to the uninitiated and contentious to those who have spent time with them. I flesh out the argument in subsequent chapters but suggest that those with an interest go to the sources[3] directly before drawing conclusions. The political implications of philosophical post-modernism that in theory draw from these sources are addressed below as well.

Plato's ontology, as it found its way through French philosopher and mathematician Rene Descartes, is fully behind the Western concepts of self-determination and choice of capitalist democracy. Without these premises, or something closely resembling them, most of what is considered self-evident about Western 'selves' is rendered indeterminate. What is developed below might be called 'political ontology' as investigation of the ideology that has grown to dominate Western understanding of the world.

Metaphysics then is the realm of these 'timeless and universal truths' that nevertheless exist temporally in the here and now. As written above, capitalism and capitalist economics are premised on the static concept of 'economic man' without which there is no theorized beneficiary, no raison d'etre of capitalism.

This is true whether writing about microeconomics that addresses 'individual choice' or macroeconomics that addresses national and global policies. Whether implicit or explicit, there is no Western economics without a metaphysical concept that ties the beneficiary of proposed policies to the type of benefit being proposed. Capitalist theory provides specific answers that have been built for two centuries into the institutions of the West.

Without a 'timeless and universal' theory of 'man' why would capitalism be expected to serve human needs? And if 'man' isn't timeless and universal then in what sense does it serve 'human' needs rather than the needs of particular persons? As basic as these questions are, there is no capitalist theory, and therefore no 'economics,' without answering them.

Introduction

THE OPENING GOAL OF THIS BOOK IS TO PROVIDE A HISTORY OF ECO-
nomic reasoning that explains the resurgence of high capitalist theory
(and fact) following its near-death with the Great Depression and its
aftermath. To do this I combine high-level history with economic ideas
to provide context to their historical development. The ultimate goal is to
provide the opening needed for fundamentally different ways of understanding and relating to 'the world.'

For reasons that will be explained in some detail later in this book, I
make very little effort to satisfy either professional historians or economists with the way that I have framed this account. Sources are provided
as needed, generally as web addresses that link to original sources. If it is
any consolation to the formalists, I spent twenty years conducting empirical research in economics and finance in close proximity to the history
and in support of the economic conclusions drawn.

The central tension at this point is in working from premises drawn
from the critique provided without first having provided it. In addition
to recognizing a personal psychological propensity toward less 'cluttered'
ways of doing things and having spent a decade and one half reading the
philosophical sources, the years spent conducting empirical research
provided practical experience with the 'objects' of philosophical inquiry
being addressed.

Brief allusion was made above to the 'internal' tension between history
as narrative form and the concept of time at work in Western economics.
This is to say that the tension between historical and economic formalisms is a function of those formalisms and not of the critique provided
here. Of relevance is the aforementioned distance between history as narrative form and as lived experience. By degree the prior finds itself on the
same side of the narrative form / lived experience divide that Western
economics resides on.

Likewise, the use of (informal) logical argumentation, to the extent it
is found below, is there because that is the 'method' of Western economics
as it descended in its broad metaphysical frame from Rene Descartes, not

because it is a preferred narrative form. The effort is to argue from 'inside' the given language rules when necessary while providing the broader context needed to demonstrate that the rules themselves derive from the ideology being critiqued.

So, on with the show.

By the middle of the 1970s the New Deal[5] crafted during the Great Depression to provide political stability and save American capitalism from the threat of wholesale repudiation ended with barely a whimper. There was no announcement that such was the case and it started with Jimmy Carter, a Democrat from the Party of Franklin Roosevelt whose administration had crafted the New Deal, in the White House. A high capitalist revival began in response to the theorized 'failure' of the Keynesian economics that had supported the New Deal.

'Deregulation,'[7] the coded policies intended to 'free' capitalist enterprise from the burden of social accountability, began with the removal of government constraints on airlines and railroads with the goal of making them profitable. The capitalist virtue of profit gradually replaced direct social purpose in national economic policies. Banker economics returned with a vengeance when Mr. Carter appointed Paul Volcker Chairman of the Federal Reserve. Mr. Volcker immediately set about crashing the U.S. economy[9] to protect bank profits from the ravages of inflation.

This capitalist revival had two reversals in public perceptions of state-economic relations going for it. The first was the discrediting of 'government' through the increasingly unpopular War in Vietnam. Until the waning years of the war the military draft sent American youth to kill and die in a war that the U.S. political leadership had concluded was a lost cause a full decade earlier[11]. Adding to this growing disenchantment was the 'war on drugs' that placed a significant proportion of younger Americans on the wrong side of government power.

The second reversal was the economic effects of the recurrent oil crises of the 1970s and the relative decline of U.S. industrial might due to the rebuilding of the industrial economies of Europe and Japan that had been destroyed in WWII. The turn against 'government' was used by well-funded right-wing 'think tanks'[13] to conflate the economic policies of the New Deal and recently enacted environmental regulations with both government 'incompetence' that had led to the 'loss' of the widely detested

War and with government regulatory overreach blamed for rising inflation and unemployment.

This misdirection was both effective and near complete—the role of
Western industrialists in perpetuating the Vietnam War to profit from
it, in creating oil crises to raise the price of oil[15] and in pushing the 'war
on drugs' to retain monopoly control over drug production for Western
pharmaceutical companies was kept well out of sight. And the much-de-
rided environmental regulations had been drawn straight from the basic
'market' economics of forcing capitalist enterprises to bear the costs of
their production.

The election of Ronald Reagan in 1980 gave retrograde voice and added
form to the shift in Western political economy then underway. Mr. Reagan
launched his campaign for the Presidency in Philadelphia, Mississippi[17]
to gain advantage from residual Southern white resentment of the civil
rights movement as he blamed declining economic circumstance on the
racist caricature of the 'welfare queen' to deflect attention away from the
industrialists and bankers responsible for the decline. With his appoint-
ment of banker Donald Regan as Secretary of the Treasury the modern
epic of finance capitalism was set into motion.

Through the contrived Cold War 'competition' of ideologies Mr. Reagan
began resurrection of the U.S. military, the most extractive and expensive
imperial military in world history, and with it the hold the military and
associated industries have exerted over Western political economy. In the
context of recurrent economic crises, wars to secure economic resources
(oil) and the wholesale takeover of Western 'democracy' by a small group
of ultra-wealthy capitalists, Western economics since the 1980s was con-
signed to writing footnotes for this capitalist revival.

In part by replacing debate over political economy with a cultural left-right divide this newly ascendant capitalism proceeded largely
unchallenged by economic and political theorists in the West. In the U.S.
the liberal-progressive 'left' took its point of departure as fundamental
acceptance of capitalist revival ideology as it toyed around the edges with
cultural issues and the contrived misdirection of 'Party' politics. Some of
the most enthusiastic proponents of this capitalist revival and 'free-trade'
globalism were self-described liberals[19].

There are a number of cultural, historical and philosophical reasons
for the ease with which the New Deal and its related 'managed' capitalism

were so easily replaced with a more insistent version of 'market' capitalism. The conflation of ideology with historical circumstance and with the particulars of geography, culture and history found willing acceptance of the dubious assertion of the relation of capitalist democracy to the wealth of the West following WWII.

This isn't to imply that the 'wealth' so much in evidence wasn't 'its' product, but rather to associate its detriments in the two most destructive wars in human history with imperialist land-grabs in part undertaken to feed the nascent industrial economies of the capitalist West. Prior to WWI much of 'the world' was divided amongst the European and American imperial powers. A close look at past and current trade relations finds an historical persistence based in this imperial past. And the residual tensions expressed in war debts go far in explaining the genesis of WWII[21].

Additionally, war is a profit generating enterprise for Western industrialists and the bankers who funded the not-so-great wars of Europe and the Pacific. Alternatively, 'ideology' as it is presented below ties almost exclusively to capitalism as 'its' deeply instantiated set of premises about the world. Once these are understood it becomes clear why dissociation of capitalism from 'its' product more broadly considered, including wars for resources and environmental catastrophe, is so difficult.

In the West capitalism and democracy, capitalist democracy, are put forward as systems of political economy that provide people with 'what they want,' the freedom to choose how to live and how to best organize 'their' societies. This conception of freedom comes with a particular set of assumptions about the nature of human beings: conceptions of the 'self' doing the choosing, of the nature of society and of the realm of 'free' choice.

These assumptions about 'man,' and here capitalist metaphysics re-enter the story, in turn serve to 'naturalize' capitalist democracy, to situate it as the product of 'true' understanding of the natural order of the world. As it is applied to the whole of 'humanity,' capitalism is an ideological imposition put forward as 'free' choice.

Deference to nature, to natural order, locates capitalism and democracy outside of human interests as adherence to the will of a secular god against which other political economy, that which exists in opposition, is by degree mistaken, the result of misguided understanding of the 'laws' of nature. In turn the very idea of an 'oppositional' ideology ties to the

concept of freedom as freedom to choose between 'externally' given existents, between that which is put in front of Western 'selves.'

To its inhabitants the Western 'self' is indubitable, what else could the
fundamental unit of concern be? The delineation of 'self' from 'the world'
is likewise self-evident, the internal dialogue that serves as its proof shares
space with no one and nothing else. This 'self' is the 'self-evident' unit of
Western political economy because only 'it' knows what it wants. Political
economy that denies it the 'freedom' to pursue 'what it wants' is an affront
to 'nature,' to the natural order on which capitalist democracy is premised.

That the 'self-evidence' of the Western 'self' derives from a particular historical-philosophical worldview does little to affect how it 'feels.'
However, it does relocate it from the realm of nature and natural order to
that of history and culture. As the basis—the fundamental unit, of capitalist democracy the precepts of 'freedom' and free 'choice' are recontextualized as cultural imperatives, as bounded concepts that within their own
terms have particular meaning but outside of which are a historically and
culturally specific set of beliefs put forward as universal 'truth.'

Capitalist democracy as the political economy of 'freedom' is tightly
circumscribed in 'the world,' the 'choices' of 'free choice' are overwhelmed
by 'natural' constraints on possibility that are better described as social—
political and economic. Contrary to the Western frame, 'nature' doesn't
send the bills, establish the boundaries of 'property,' start the wars or build
the schools.

And the unbridled 'self' confronts developed political economy that
draws a tight circle around the 'freedom' that is its theorized basis. Against
this social-material basis, 'freedom' is a psychic artifact, the 'feeling' of
detachment of self from the world that informs its reaction to it. 'Freedom'
as psychic artifact is to choose from among the available alternatives, not
to create them.

The 'stuff' of capitalist democracy finds an established order of boundaries, property with clear title and an array of institutions to 'protect'
it, whereas its broader consequences fall on 'the unfortunate,' those for
whom the natural order of the 'self' is on the outside of political economy
that is posed against it as a fact of nature, as a true expression of the will
of a secular god.

This can be clearly seen in Western views of unemployment when there
are no jobs to be had. Here the rigorous logic of rational economic cal-

culation fails second-grade arithmetic: when there four unemployed for every available job it is mathematically impossible for three of the four to find jobs. Recent experience in the U.S. had seven unemployed for every available job.

On the other side of Western consumer goods is their reciprocal in economic production, a 'vortex' of garbage the size of Texas floating in the Pacific Ocean[23]. Climate change that is the product of industrial production and its artifacts in Western 'consumer' culture is warming the planet at a faster rate than the most aggressive climate models of a few years ago predicted[25]. And the planet is currently undergoing the sixth mass extinction of plants and animals in world history[27].

Rising sea levels that are a direct result of global warming are threatening coastal cities with gradual submersion and their inhabitants—tens of millions of people, with dislocation and the social strife that goes with it. Wars for economic resources are being 'rationalized' into permanent strategies of technocratic slaughter where 'drones,' murder robots, directed from thousands of miles away are used to kill people without warning or reason.

The West is currently experiencing the residual effects of the third financial calamity in as many decades. The resulting immiseration is hidden behind the visible prosperity of a tiny plutocracy that controls Western political economy[29]. The 'logic' of social resolution is to provide an ever-increasing share of social wealth to those who need it least. And technologies that didn't exist only a few decades ago are being used to create the most intrusive surveillance state in human history with the citizens of the West as its target.

This and other evidence of radical social dysfunction is being put forward by those privileged to speak from authority, the broad technocracy of accredited experts trained in their respective 'rationalities,' as unrelated events—what could drone murders in Pakistan or Yemen have to do with rising long term unemployment and immiseration in capitalist economies or an 'out of control' surveillance state?

Each of these social and environmental catastrophes has the temporal circle of 'event' drawn around it, as something that happens in time and then doesn't happen—the unfortunate consequences of political, economic or national security contingencies, the silos of Western institutional complexity, that are 'rational' within their realms but collectively suicidal in their aggregated expression.

As global warming, the technologies of mass slaughter and the rapid consolidation of economic 'wealth' suggest, these contingencies are more trajectories than events, the accumulation of a unifying tendency across time in history. As history before the rise of global capitalism suggests, this unifying tendency is historically and culturally locatable in the capitalist West. What had been a trajectory of seemingly 'manageable' social and environmental problems turned exponentially upward with the capitalist revival begun in the 1970s.

The rapid acceleration of the most destructive elements of global capitalism is coincident with the reemergence of a theocratic form of radical capitalist theory that harkens back to the century before the Great Depression. This reemergence is related to the epic of finance capitalism now three decades on that is eerily similar in intent, structure and capacity to the system of political economy that culminated in the Great Depression.

With public policies from 'both' political parties in the U.S. and their rough equivalent in the 'center-right' ruling parties of Europe as evidence, the 'lessons' Western economists and politicians learned from that earlier epic is how to save the system of global finance. The overwhelming preponderance of efforts to 'save the economy' have been to save Wall Street at any cost without either reconsidering its role in the recurring economic crises of more recent vintage or its relation to the reconstitution of capitalist political economy globally in its most ideologically 'pure' form.

The disparity between the factual consequences of this radical capitalism, its catastrophes of increasing scale and scope, and its ongoing reconstitution in the institutions of global political economy, is the inevitable result of the internal logic of capitalism. This logic derives, perhaps still implausibly at this point, from an ancient ontology that claims a divide between the temporal world we exist in and that of 'knowledge.' But where precisely would this 'knowledge' reside if global warming ended human existence?

While the main topic of this book is 'economics' broadly considered, the theoretical 'frame' of capitalism is deeply instantiated into Western political economy as an approach to 'the world.' The same economic theories that reduce the state-market machinations and coercive social relations of international trade to 'market' exchange abstract Western 'individuals' from the world we inhabit and from each other.

The visibility of capitalism's 'products' exists in stark contrast to the invisibility of its products more broadly considered—the intended 'unintended' consequences of its technologies of catastrophe. The U.S. is both the preeminent capitalist political economy in 'the world' and the largest maker, seller and 'user' of the weapons of war. In 2014, with no competing 'superpower' on the horizon, the U.S. is spending one trillion dollars to rebuild the largest nuclear weapons arsenal in the world[31].

The logic of weapons production flows from the profit motive of capitalism, from the technological view endemic to its premises and in its tendency toward controlling economic relations. From bases in New York and London international finance is capitalism's 'smart bomb' that leaves 'property' relocated into the hands of financiers and entire nations economically devastated. And behind these 'markets' lies state 'interests' devolved from the same otherworldly logic that acts on / in the world with little concern for broader consequences.

For those as yet uncomfortable with assertion of intent, allow for the intersection of the deeply embedded worldview of capitalist democracy with capacity—the capacity for global annihilation by means of nuclear weapons dates from the mid-twentieth century. And while global warming has been two centuries in the making, its world-threatening acceleration is mere decades old.

These capacities have emerged from the same 'pragmatic' rationalism as capitalism—from 'progress' in the sense of material accumulation and from an instrumental relationship with 'the world' that is the result of a particular set of premises and type of inquiry into how 'the world' 'works.'

The inability to eliminate nuclear weapons despite the theorized end of the Cold War; the unwillingness to reverse global warming through reconfiguration of Western political economy and the rapidly rising consolidation of social wealth despite the 'promise' of capitalist democracy that it would be broadly shared are put forward as unfortunate coincidence, as human folly unrelated to the technological capacities that have been developed in each of these dimensions.

It is no accident that these capacities have emerged in their most pernicious forms in the capitalist West. The antique ontology of capitalist theory posits hierarchy, otherworldliness and anti-history that frames mass annihilation as unrelated inconvenience, as the hand that points and fires the gun but that is never responsible for where the bullet strikes.

The American political / economic / moral conceit of 'exceptionalism' joins it in fact to an imperial history that precedes it by millennia. This imperialism has long, inglorious history in genocide, slavery and wars for economic resources. The Western innovation is deference to the secular deity of economic 'system' that knows how but that never asks why? Where precisely does this system reside outside of human interests to make it 'exceptional?'

The self-evident 'solution' to this history is to assign a 'why,' to rationalize away capitalism's destructive tendencies and keep the parts that satisfy human wants. However, this 'solution' assumes that its constructive and destructive elements are dissociable; that its underlying premises are 'true' in that they capture and facilitate the essential characteristics of human being and that potential 'solutions' can come from within its internal logic.

History tells a different story, one where theorized benefit is tied inexorably to realized fact. Much capitalist wealth 'generation' is more accurately described as imperial wealth relocation—its 'constructive' benefits accrue to one group while the costs accrue to another. This can be seen in sequential wars and political machinations in the Middle East to control oil and in Central America to assure cheap labor and agricultural imports through U.S. led coups, wars and campaigns of terror.

The same is true of the 'exceptional' nature of capitalist democracy where its 'fruits' are used to take the capacity for self-determination away the 'un-exceptional' on the other side of the imperial divide. The history of the U.S. is overthrowing democratically elected governments to install brutal dictators when economic interests are at stake. And 'technical' fixes to the catastrophes of capitalism assume a unity of interests in the 'search' for solutions that the logic of capitalism assures will never arise—these fixes might be 'rational' but there is a reason why they never come to fruition.

Western economics (for present purposes the 'space' that must be explored before alternatives are possible) is an exposition of capitalist ideology put forward as scientific explanation of the economic 'aspects' of social life. This will no doubt read as gross overstatement by Western economic practitioners given the diverse 'movements' and schools that have long histories of enthusiastic disagreement. The unifying factor is the metaphysical humanism of 'economic man' without which this economics has no implicit or explicit goal. As is addressed in greater detail below, this is true no matter how deeply buried the conceit is in economic models.

This economics is also 'an economic approach to analyze social issues[33]' as Nobel Prize winner in economics Gary Becker put it. 'Economic man,' the metaphysical humanism of capitalist economics, is both the 'rational' actor of economic method and the fundamental unit of capitalist political economy.

As metaphysical 'object' s/he 'exists' in 'timeless and universal' ether and in life as reconstituted in capitalist political economy. As an artifact of Western ontology this metaphysics serves jointly as an implausible premise for capitalist political economy and as an implausible framework for Western economic methods.

While criticism of Cartesian metaphysics is generally presented as methodological critique, the critique presented here places metaphysics in the realm of 'political ontology' raised above as the central hegemonic force at work in the Western 'worldview' —a hidden governing ideology as the term 'hegemony' was put forward by the Italian political theorist Antonio Gramsci[35]. The archetype that economic man is has political content as both the theorized actor of capitalist economics and through its stance toward the world.

Criticism of capitalism can only be effectively rendered from outside of 'its' internal logic because of its deep instantiation in the Western worldview as it has been reconstituted in capitalist social institutions. From within this logic only 'its' conclusions are possible. This content-logic lies at the very heart of the Western worldview, from perceptions of 'individual' and 'society' to the Western concept of 'truth;' from the theorized purpose of scientific inquiry to who 'we' are as people and to the nature of 'nature' itself. As it is reconstituted in political economy this worldview is in full collision with 'the world' because 'its' set of contingent 'wants' and priorities are the means and logic of environmental and social catastrophe.

The social practices of 'the West,' broadly considered, are an historically iterative reconstitution of this metaphysical worldview—'understanding' of 'the world' forms the guiding premises—both form and purpose, of Western institutions from political economy to its particular political, military, scientific, technological and academic expressions. And this worldview lies behind existing social hierarchies inasmuch as they find explanation in theory and / or as they have been historically embedded in the institutions of Western political economy.

The argument can be easily made, and quite often is, that the premises of capitalist democracy and 'its' facts are light years apart. This is one of the chief claims of neo-liberal policy makers in their quest to build ever '-purer' forms of capitalism into Western institutions. So while much of this book is dedicated to exploring the philosophical premises of capitalism, they are socially relevant to the extent they have been reconstituted in the institutions of Western political economy. And over the last one hundred and fifty years these institutions, largely American and European corporations, are responsible for creating the vast preponderance of social and environmental ills emanating from capitalism.

It is this hegemonic nature of capitalist theory that must be addressed before the distance between theory and fact has meaning. The nature of hegemony in the Gramscian frame is of a social apologetics that takes its form from existing social order. The capitalist 'reframe,' to the extent it is such, puts a 'natural order' in place of Gramsci's social order. A 'natural' social order, the role that capitalism claims to fill, requires 'true' understanding of the relationship between an invariant—timeless and universal, human 'self' and the 'form,' structure and content, of society that best serves this 'self.'

What is constructed here is a humanist theology, an interwoven set of premises about the 'nature of man' that takes as its 'structure' what philosopher Martin Heidegger, following from Kant, called 'onto-theology' meaning a related set of beliefs about the 'nature' of the world. The 'self-evidence' of the Western 'self' addressed above is evidence of the hiddenness, the theological nature, of these interwoven premises.

This hiddenness, when related to a social order believed to reflect natural order, is hegemonic in Gramsci's sense of deeply instantiated premises that serve to legitimate an existing social order. Of interest is that most Western economists spend little to no time considering the archetype at the center of their social philosophy.

The perceived distance between capitalism in theory and in fact is perpetual by design; it results from the metaphysical nature of capitalist theory and 'closing' it renders visible that these exist on irreconcilable planes. Ultimately it is factual political economy that is socially relevant. But the political part of political economy requires addressing the base perceptions that give capitalism its plausibility as mode of social organization. In this way taking these philosophical premises apart is a necessary step toward the social relevance of the critique.

Metaphysical hegemony is more than 'mistaken' practice, even as reconstituted in its 'pragmatic' institutions. It is an arrogance premised on the 'special access' to 'the world' that derives through history and metaphor from hierarchy in Cartesian metaphysics, from the privilege of thought over broader experience of being and from the separation of the metaphysical 'self' from 'the world.'

Western science is the most visible embodiment of this metaphysics as social practice. Science is described / understood as the method of gaining 'true' knowledge of 'the world'—knowledge that stands outside of time, space and human interests. Its basis in Cartesian metaphysics lies in the idea of 'truth' as atemporal object and in its methods of demonstration—scientific research as it is related 'back up' to its metaphysical 'object,' as mode of proof.

As geographical metaphor, its problem is of the coincidence of temporal and atemporal objects—timeless and universal 'truths' that nevertheless exist temporally. This can be framed perhaps more intuitively as the difference between 'knowledge' and physical existence. It can be found in 'external' references made by academics as what 'we' know. The unity of knowledge with physical existence can be recovered by considering where this knowledge would reside if all of the knowers were no more. One can speculate on laws and rules that 'govern' 'the world,' the very definition of metaphysics, but without a knower nothing is 'known.'

This concept of knowledge as 'external' truth can be found in its political incarnation as capitalist hegemony. The web of beliefs that places economic man in a 'natural' social order that lies at the intersection of humanist and onto-theological precepts provides an 'external' basis for social organization. But given its genesis as social metaphor, as social explanation that serves an existing order, its form and 'content' reflect this order. Most fundamentally, its special status is as a tool of social domination and control that is 'legitimated' through deference to 'nature,' to 'the world' outside of human interests. As such its base stance is arrogance toward 'the world' premised on its place in this natural order.

Arrogance here isn't meant as personality quirk, but rather as the presumed hierarchical relationship of metaphysical 'truth' to 'the world' that lies behind the social dysfunction and environmental catastrophe of capitalism from its birth in European imperialism to its modern incarnation as totalizing political economy. The theorized benefits of capitalism are in significant measure, most likely in preponderance, its opposite, largely because its premises and conclusions are otherworldly—theorized to exist in unlikely ether, while its results are in 'the world' in which we live.

This metaphorical 'distance' leaves the capitalist calculus capable of 'counting' only its theorized product while 'the world' is forced to accommodate its reciprocal in social and environmental catastrophe. By placing 'economic man' in the metaphysical ether capitalism is a highly developed identity put forward as 'freedom.' Economic man is the actor who acts on 'the world' without living in it, the tourist without a home to return to.

In this theorized 'ether' there exist multiple 'mans:' biological man, historical man, philosophical man, technological man—and on and on ad infinitum. Of some relevance is that each of these 'mans' has scientific analog—reconstitution as 'objects' within the institutions of Western political economy. But none of these other 'mans' exists as their basis—as their form and purpose. In opposition to the 'idealist' proposition that all of these 'mans' are equally probable, economic man embodies the metaphysical metaphor that is the base object of Western capitalist democracy.

'He,' or some analogous metaphor—'rational man,' is the actor who embodies the methodological requirements of Cartesian metaphysics. As the idealized embodiment of an historical existent—the burgeoning European industrial economy as Western 'economics' was being developed, methodology is tied to the 'type' of object that was needed to build the bridge between this metaphysical 'self' and 'the world' as it is frozen 'for all time.' 'Economic man' is the methodological contrivance that has been iteratively reconstituted in the social institutions of the West to the point where 'he' has been made its central character.

To invert the point, in capitalist political economy 'freedom' is to act on the instantiated identity of economic man as it is reconstituted in Western institutions—to be 'free' to be externally circumscribed. This isn't to back into an implied humanism, 'socially-constructed' man, nor is it an allusion to the 'truly free' man hallucinated in the metaphysical ether. It is to identify the character of economic man in its particulars—in its hegemonic identity-act as reconstituted in the Western institutions of capitalist democracy.

This identity-act is to forego the agency long put forward as the core of the Western 'self' through the metaphysical alienation of this 'self' from 'the world.' Economic man is everyone and no one, the no one in everyone. The metaphysical approach requires a theoretical 'someone' to gaze out at 'the world' and economic man is the chosen actor.

That capitalist political economy is reconstituted in his / her image has turned this methodological contrivance into the instantiated identity of Western 'individuals' as social actors without society and as free choosers whose realm of 'choice' is that which is put in front of them. The metaphysical 'method' proceeds from this latter premise.

A consequence of economic man's separation from 'the world' is that the fundamental constituents of capitalist political economy, wars for economic resources, radical social alienation, environmental catastrophe and ultimately, the social incapacity for reconciliation in any of these dimensions, are put forward as existing outside of, as incidental to, core capitalist activities.

What this factual dysfunction illustrates is the implausibility of the metaphysical construct—the lines of division theorized to exist in the ether that find no analog, no such clean lines, in 'the world.'

In social terms this division is illustrated through the capitalist tendency to see the human catastrophes it causes as 'psychic' artifacts, as the failure of those doing the suffering to competently negotiate the distance between self and world. Political economy that sees its core constituents, its dysfunction expressed in social pathologies and environmental catastrophe, standing outside of itself can only find resolution through being rejoined with the world.

The collision between the mental objects of capitalist theory and the facts of capitalist production occasionally finds voice in metaphor. 'Externality' is the Western economists' term for the 'internalities' of capitalist production that are claimed to be incidental to it—environmental devastation and the social catastrophes of unemployment, poverty and social exclusion that don't fit into the perceived goals of capitalist production and are therefore excluded from the 'internally' circumscribed realm of consideration.

'Externalities' are put forward as critique from 'without,' as unintended consequences that can be managed from 'within' through more and better capitalism. However, the coincidence of these externalities with capitalist production illustrates the metaphysical blind spot at work—from effect on / in 'the world' capitalist 'intent' is indistinguishable from its unintended consequences.

Recognition of this visible / invisible divide could in theory force humility, a care-reticence to act on what is visible alone for fear of the consequences of that which remains invisible to it. But through the metaphysical divide the factual consequences of capitalism can never challenge its mental objects because they are perceived to exist on different planes. Western economists can't 're-think' capitalism because it is all they have.

'Historical' challenges to capitalist economics have had limited impact by design. The temporal / atemporal divide of its metaphysical 'construct' is bound by the constraint of the theorized atemporal realm. The often made 'historical' claim that capitalist democracy is the 'end of history' is more revealing by posing it as the 'beginning of history.' Capitalist metaphysics posits a directional relation of knower to known; of Western 'selves' to their knowledge and desires, which renders history 'impossible.'

As 'end of history' capitalism is placed in historical development that can't be accounted for from within 'its' internal logic. If less intuitively plausible, capitalism as the 'beginning of history' necessarily follows from this metaphysical atemporality through infinite regress, the 'historical' starting point of capitalist theory. This incompatibility of economic theory with historical narrative takes us back to the different theories of time at work. The ideological implications of a theory of the world that always begins in the present should give pause.

Catastrophe Finds a Theory

HISTORICAL ACCOUNTS, PARTICULARLY OF THE CAPITALIST ESCAPADES of the last two centuries, better illustrate the 'facts' of capitalism than does philosophical argumentation. But they are irrelevant within the closed logic of capitalist theory—they simply cannot be accommodated. This is one of the reasons why capitalist theory has been so remarkably resistant to its facts. With the ultimate goal of this book being to create a 'clearing' where alternative political economy can be considered, the historical accounts offered below are largely related to economic theories and their consequences.

The Great Depression of the 1930s offered a distance between capitalist theory and fact so great that those on the receiving end of its 'market' outcomes couldn't be ignored. As with current circumstances in the West, the decades leading up to the Depression witnessed high capitalist revival following the tempering tendencies of the 'Progressive' era.

The misery created by the Depression was of depth and breadth that those whose lives were thrown into chaos and destitution threatened political-economic rupture, repudiation not just of capitalist theory but also of the very premises of Western capitalist democracy.

To the rescue of capitalism came economist John Maynard Keynes who found paradox[37] in the metaphysical relation of economic man to economic 'system.' Keynes was a logician with an understanding of paradox—the tendency of logical constructs to be self-contradictory. The Keynesian 'fix' to the Great Depression was through deference to system over the simple aggregation of economic men / man acting rationally.

But Keynesian economics eventually fell prey[39] to the internal logic of the earlier capitalist metaphysical frame. By the 1970s paradox had once again reared its head through 'stagflation,' the coincidence of high inflation with falling economic production, and Western economists pulled economic man back out of the closet and gave him a job on Wall Street.

This idea of 'system' is one of the fundamental conceits of Western thought. Cartesian metaphysics is a 'system' of deductive logic that is theorized to be relatable to 'the world.' 'The world' is a 'natural system' whose 'truths' that 'stand outside of it' give purpose to the project of Western science.

The belief that logic and mathematics more broadly, are 'natural' systems of thought, a 'universal language,' lies behind the special privilege they receive in the 'Western worldview.' By inserting the complication of 'paradox' between the 'system' of capitalist political economy and its actors Keynes' produced a break from the capitalist theory that preceded it, a disjuncture.

To be clear, the idea of economic 'system' had more than a century of precedence in Western economics before Keynes shifted focus back to it. However, his economic 'paradox' is the proverbial fly in the ointment, the 'question' that once asked can't be taken back. Keynes' argued that particular types of economic paradox had to be resolved from 'outside' of the 'natural' system of 'the economy.'

He called on government to do the resolving, to provide the resources needed to fill the space that paradox had created in the Great Depression. However, Keynes' 'paradox' raised the larger question of metaphor—in what ways are logical and 'natural' systems related? This question points directly to the temporal / atemporal divide that renders capitalist metaphysics so deeply implausible.

The 'logic' of Keynes' logical paradox evolved from metaphysical method—from the 'rational' bridge between the temporal and atemporal realms of capitalist theory. The narrow problem is that 'rationality' as both psychic capacity and operational method is either unitary or relating it 'up' to economic system is theoretically disjointed.

In the Keynesian frame paradox doesn't stand 'outside' of logic—it is intrinsic to it. Implied is that resolution is to work 'around' paradox, not to 'fix' it. Keynes' 'paradox of thrift,' the circumstance where in an economic depression 'over saving' produces an additional fall in economic production, backs into the idea of this 'individual' rationality that produces systemic 'irrationality'—the 'paradox' is retained.

Conversely, to 'fix' it requires reconciling this system with its 'constituents' by 'changing' either one or the other to eliminate the paradox. Otherwise, the 'natural' system of capitalist political economy is rendered indeterminate—'its' premise as system doesn't follow from the 'nature' of its actors. This was framed earlier as the intersection of the humanist-theological concept of economic man with the onto-theological concept of a 'natural' social order. Together they create a coherent, if implausible, belief system.

'Fixing' capitalism would be incoherent without presupposing a particular form for these actors, its metaphysical humanism—who precisely would Keynes be saving capitalism for if not for economic man? However, 'working around' this paradox has the same implications. A rough analogy would be fixing a tractor for a dog: the act of making the tractor 'function' as a tractor is logically unrelated to any possible purpose the dog will put it to.

Capitalist democracy is premised on this specific conception of 'man' without which there is little basis for asserting that capitalism and / or democracy are 'natural' modes of social organization. Within the classical frame of Adam Smith the 'invisible hand' is the 'natural' system that relates the acts of rational self-interest of its economic actors to the production of social wealth[41].

This economic 'system' requires that people act in a specific way—'economically,' to earn a wage or profit. If people aren't economically calculating in their actions the 'system' of capitalism doesn't 'work.' Likewise, if there is no economic 'system,' acts of economic self-interest don't aggregate to produce social wealth. The decaying monarchies of Europe in Adam Smith's time were prime examples of this latter propensity.

Keynes' 'paradox' was that in some circumstances people acting in their economic self-interest doesn't benefit the 'system' of capitalism. In fact, with his 'paradox of thrift' people acting in their own self-interest can cause collective economic harm. Keynes imposed his 'paradox' as an 'object' of logic onto capitalist theory. Inferred was that by isolating it to 'special cases' the relation of economic actors to capitalism could be kept 'intact.'

However, as a determined pragmatist what Keynes probably understood but chose not to address is that capitalist theory is a metaphysical imposition in its totality—the relation between economic man and the 'system' of capitalism is wholly 'logical.' This logic either ties in a determinable way to 'the world' or it is ultimately theological.

This formulation has the actual genesis of this set of beliefs backwards. Economic man was wholly deduced and the idea of natural system in some cases was deduced and in other cases was borrowed as metaphor from the 'natural' sciences. In either case paradox is an impassable breach, not a theoretical inconvenience. Keynes' pragmatics implies a notion of social virtue every bit as insistent as that of capitalist theology.

Ironically, both with and without this conception of paradox capitalist democracy as the 'system' of political economy that derives from and facilitates 'self-determination' is incoherent in 'its' own terms. Economic actors needn't just be rational, their rationality must take specific form across the breadth of time, space and humanity or there is no unity of worldview to aggregate to 'rational' economic 'system.'

'Irrational' people acting in a rational system would produce 'irrational' outcomes. Alternatively, if some proportion of humanity is 'rational' and some proportion isn't then the economic failures 'identified' by Keynes as the result of 'paradox' could just as well be a function of this ratio—of an outsized proportion of the 'irrational' gumming up the system of capitalism.

To be clear, in this case the 'natural' basis for capitalist democracy is wholly circular, it is the natural basis for those who 'possess' a particular type of 'rationality.' And there would be no theoretically coherent rationale for capitalism that doesn't simply assume the superiority of 'rational man' over its residual in the world.

This latter tendency has found its 'real world' expression in capitalist imperialism, in the imposition of a 'natural' system where 'nature' hasn't seen fit to bestow it. The inference back 'down' from 'system' is that social 'success' results from careful adherence to its dictates, a notion of 'freedom' with analog in some of the more savage parodies of capitalism found in history.

Capitalist theory is a closed logical system through the historical premise that it is both method to and repository for economic 'truth.' As repository 'economic man' is its circular embodiment as well as its primary actor, s/he is simultaneously everyone and no one. If her economic 'aspect' is insignificant in relation to other aspects there is no reason to believe 's/he' would be expressed in the proportion needed to render Western economics, and with it capitalism, theoretically coherent.

To question the construct, to argue that rational man isn't rational, leaves neither premise nor method remaining. To accept the premise leaves only method as entry point for critique within the frame. The 'internal' debate of the nature / characteristics of 'rationality' is wholly circular—how is it demonstrated without presupposing it?

Alternatively, who is to determine rationality who hasn't already 'demonstrated' her / himself to be both rational and to possess the method to such determination? The 'solution' quickly devolves into infinite regress. It is this characteristic that renders Cartesian metaphysics and its 'application' in capitalist economics and political economy 'totalizing,' either 'accepted' or rejected based on the willingness to remain within the confines of 'its' circular logic no matter what the consequences.

The circularity of capitalist theory already assured that economic man never 'transcended' the metaphysical ether—never had the opportunity for even a brief visit to 'the world.' The paradox that Keynes found in 'rational system' assured that within the ether 'things' were more complicated than had been imagined. And within the self-given task of truth determination, of what value is metaphysical 'truth' if paradox renders it too 'paradoxical' to draw clear inference?

While Keynes alluded to 'animal spirits[43]'—the occasional 'irrationality' of 'rational' beings, he did so without forcing the assertion through the logic of capitalist democracy. By doing so Keynes 'saved' capitalism without having a 'rational' basis for doing so within the capitalist frame.

Capitalism as it has been reconstituted in the institutions of political economy of the West is similarly totalizing—if economic man isn't plausible as both primary actor and 'rational' in the operational sense of capitalist metaphysics then both capitalism as political economy and capitalist economics are theoretically incoherent within the terms put forward by their proponents.

To be clear, outside of these terms there is plenty to discuss. But that discussion proceeds from the point where no theoretical support for capitalism as 'legitimated' political economy exists and where the modes of discourse are 'flattened' to the level where non-'experts' have as much say in the matter as do the self-appointed possessors of economic 'truth.'

This isn't to confuse theory with political action—there is little possibility that ideological capitalists and their apologists in Western economics will be swayed by the 'internal' incoherence of their beliefs. Nor will they voluntarily give up the social power they wield to consider alternatives to capitalism. The recurrent crises of capitalism and their related political calamities point the way to the most probable rupture that will open social possibility back up regardless of the depth and breadth of the mechanisms developed to shut it down.

And if the thesis presented here has bearing, this rupture will represent the reciprocal of capitalist political economy that was always already present. The impending environmental catastrophe of global warming is the product of the metaphysical worldview that divides the same act—capitalist production, into intended and unintended consequences and then only 'counts' those that are nominally intended—capitalist 'wealth.'

To be clear, this is a fundamentally different point from the distinction within capitalist theory between earned 'profits' and unearned economic 'rents.' The institutional infrastructure needed to distinguish 'legitimate' capitalist profits from profits earned through expression of economic and / or political monopoly power, 'rents,' would require a separation of economic from state power that has never existed and will never exist.

Burning down the metaphorical house to bake a loaf of bread 'produces' both more and less than a loaf of bread. Not only are the 'frictions' of economic imperialism—unemployment, poverty, internal and external social repression and social exclusion 'internal' to capitalism, its totalizing nature frames these social failures as personal failures in a perfectly ordered universe that isn't.

The question of what would replace capitalism as an economic 'system' is the wrong question—it keeps all possible answers in the metaphysical ether—in psychic opposition to a question with only one answer, its own. If inference from the trajectory of any of a growing number of social and environmental catastrophes informs it, capitalism is already in the process of ending itself by ending 'the world.'

Within metaphysics 'holism' as integrated 'relatedness' is put forward as possible reconciliation with 'the world.' But holism retains the same distance, the same dysfunctional construct, that finds analog in Keynes' deference to 'system' as resolution of paradox that was itself ultimately undone by the paradox conceived within its own limits. Holism is ultimately the arrogance of Cartesian 'truth' applied to 'the world.' It faces the same challenge of transcendence, of bridging the distance between self and world, which capitalism does.

Moreover, like Keynes' economics, metaphysical holism is conceived as 'system,' as a set of knowable relationships that can be managed from the 'inside' of atemporal space. It is this same division of 'inside' and 'outside' that makes capitalism incapable of reconciling its theory with its facts. As a theory of 'system' holism is incoherent outside of metaphysical construct. And it is without apparent irony that capitalist holism—the reconstitution of global political economy in the image of capitalist theory, is being sold as the 'solution' to its own catastrophes.

It would seem that within metaphysics there isn't much interesting to say and outside of it there isn't much left to say. But outside of the implausible and totalizing nature of metaphysical 'truth' there is everything to say and everyone to do the saying. The incoherence of the metaphysical construct is only at issue because its 'internal' requirement is coherence to support the 'truth' claims made for it. The incoherence of capitalist theory on its own terms is a potent metaphor for the broad results of capitalism as it is reconstituted in political economy.

However, this is the failure of its 'own' project—of the 'will to truth' of its proponents, not of the possibility for the overwhelming residual of existence to be realized. Any broad read of Western economics finds its 'timeless and universal' truths are particular and largely divergent theories—no metaphysical 'unities' there. And the same is true of Western science. The threat posed by 'flattening' truth claims is in exposing their role in strategies of social domination and control, not as threat to 'truth' as discursive object in embedded experience.

To be clear, theoretical incoherence poses no factual threat to capitalism because of its embedding in Western social institutions. 'External' assertion of capitalism's facts will far more likely pose this challenge through social rupture, not through academic debate. Putting forward a competing totalizing system as alternative political economy seems a less than promising proposition—if capitalist metaphysics remain plausible there seems little point in endlessly revisiting the question because it is designed to offer only one answer—its own.

The Western 'self' of capitalist democracy is 'its' own 'logical' outcome given the frame. And if not, why create a competing totalizing 'system' at all? The inability of capitalism to either correct 'itself' or to be corrected due to its totalizing nature is its central defect. Alternative political economy that stands a chance of producing different outcomes would 'flatten' the hierarchies of metaphysical reasoning to reconcile 'self' with 'the world.'

This 'flattening' is to remove the contrived partitions of capitalist metaphysics; it isn't to 'force' flatness nor is it to pose an oppositional metaphysics. The social conditions required for this flattening are the material conditions for economic and political 'democracy' as factually reconstituted metaphor outside of metaphysical conceptions of the 'self.'

Alternatively, Western capitalist democracy is imperial imposition, its 'own' insistence. Removing imperial imposition isn't to replace it and the clearing created is the possibility of reconciliation with 'the world' and not forced reconciliation. To be clear, this isn't to 'oppose' the capitalist construct through oppositional metaphysics; it is to shove it to the side by creating the material conditions that render it irrelevant.

And opposition to capitalist political economy will be found in 'its,' in capitalism's, oppositional relationship with this world. Capitalism won't be voluntarily abandoned—the entirety of the institutions of Western political economy is dedicated to its perpetuation. But through relating its precepts to its catastrophes social clarity can be found around its true 'product.' And with this social clarity comes the possibility of creating real alternatives to it.

Economics as Social Explanation

THERE IS A LONG-STANDING TENSION BETWEEN POLITICAL, CULTURAL and economic explanations of social relations. All are reductive forms, internally delimited modes of explanation as social negotiation over the relations being explained. Western economics has particular form evolved from its basis in Cartesian metaphysics that proceeds from deductive 'first principles' and relates them through logical methods to 'social' objects that are likewise deduced. Cultural explanations have tended to either tie closely to artifact—e.g. the Sharia prohibition against paying interest on loans, or to devolve quickly into antique racist blather, e.g. the 'Arab character' in Western narrative.

The tension between political and economic explanations relies on a different dynamic. Political power and economic power are both forms of social power. But as the saying regarding the Western academic practice of separating economics from politics has it, 'economics only deals with solved social (political) problems.'

As reading of capitalist economics has it, the structure of its fundamental premise is (1) we are all in this economy together (economic 'system') so (2) whatever arrangement of circumstance produces the most income / wealth / 'utility' is best regardless of how it is distributed. As might be imagined, this theory of 'unity' in economic outcomes requires a developed apologetics to keep those on its losing side amenable to the 'unity' thesis.

The starting point relating capitalism to broader political economy is to distinguish between capitalism in history versus theory. This isn't to argue 'the facts' within the capitalist frame; rather it is allusion to the history of the practice of Western economics where practitioners have tried to reconcile theory with observed political economy.

Capitalism as it has been related to history comes with a large and intrusive institutional structure needed to keep political economy capitalist. In fact, the accumulation of capital produces the political power to push institutional constraints out of the way. This tendency was well understood until it was conveniently 'forgotten' by the theorists of capi-talist revival in the 1970s.

The tension between these two capitalisms, between 'pure' theory and historical attempts to relate it to existing political economy, is rough analog to the modern Keynesian / neo-liberal divide. Like the celibate religious sects of the sixteenth and seventeenth centuries, free market (neo-liberal) capitalism—that without the developed institutions needed to 'manage' it, tended to last for one generation, two at the most, before concentrated political-economic power shut the door on subsequent 'market' compe-tition and internal contradictions created crises that couldn't be ignored.

Recognition of these tendencies was behind the anti-monopoly reg-ulations and forced de-consolidation of industries in the Progressive era and in the broader attempts to regulate capitalism coming out of the Great Depression. The current era represents the later stages of one of these recurring epics of consolidation of political-economic power in the hands of a tiny economic elite.

The political analog here is that attempts to impose the institution-al framework necessary to keep capitalism capitalist pits its theologians against its pragmatists around the vestiges of the New Deal and around the environmental regulations designed to force industrialists to bear the costs of their production.

The metaphysical structure of capitalist economics makes 'pragmatic' reconciliation of 'its' theory and 'the facts' as they are broadly understood paradoxical—the rationale for capitalism is rendered incoherent by 'prag-matic' adjustment. Capitalism is either a 'natural' system, in which case pragmatic adjustment is to second-guess 'nature,' or it is ideology posed as the 'will' of nature for the benefit of those doing the posing.

The distance between the theoretical object 'system' and the factual existence of those doing the existing—those on the losing end of social and environmental catastrophe, broadens the Marxian idea of 'class' to reunite capitalist political economy with 'the world' more broadly con-sidered. Put differently, the calculus of 'benefit' to the 'system' of political economy depends very much on who is doing the calculating.

The inherent tension of 'system' is illustrated in the distance between cost and benefit—benefit without cost, the base notion of capitalist 'self-in-terest' and its mechanisms of social production predictably produce its inverse, cost without benefit, in the social and environmental catastrophes that capitalism creates.

Left unexplained is the locus of this 'system', even as geographical metaphor, and its precise tie to human relations. Implicit in capitalist theory is benign production, the social relations where 'doing well' is not directly related to others 'doing poorly.'

In Western economics this is accomplished by simply assuming away social power, the power of some to 'do well' by making others 'do poorly.' This idea of 'system' is to capitalist production as human wants are to needs, the infinite ether versus material relation. Without apparent irony the 'proof' of capitalism is material—the abundance that fills known and heretofore unknown wants without relation to needs.

At this point a fickle nature is exposed, amorphous wants for an interchangeable set of imagined and as yet unimagined things and desire that subsumes all others, a pornography of things. The goods and services that never before existed pose a temporal challenge, an imposition into the atemporal realm of 'self-determined' desires that puts 'history' back into the determination of this Western 'self.'

Want of the new requires knowledge of it and this knowledge implies that what is wanted is already 'known.' The distance between it and its 'objects' requires that it reside in the ether unrelated to its material 'proof.' This knowledge is want as psychic quantum, stuff-lust unrelated to actual 'stuff.' And the re-imposition of history, of temporal existence with the power to reach into the timeless ether of the Western 'self,' renders the relation of capitalist 'system' to 'its' participants indeterminate.

Nineteenth century critiques of capitalism, including that of Karl Marx, saw historical development unbounded by the environmental limits now increasingly in evidence. Marx wrote at a time of nascent industrial reach—the capacity for aggregated environmental catastrophe was limited. The century-and-a-half since he wrote saw rapidly aggregating environmental consequences—the result now evident in climate change and the potential for near-instantaneous apocalypse through nuclear annihilation.

In the contemporary era the totalizing reach of electronic communications / surveillance and the intermediation of an ever increasing proportion of social interaction by capitalist corporations is reconfiguring the Western social 'environment' into relations of the dominant to the dominated.

Creation of a 'suspect' class under the guise of protecting 'freedom' is consigning all who aren't a part of the political-economic elite and its immediate circle of functionaries—the police, the political establishment and the state apparatus, to the outside of social power. In this new environment all dissent is considered a threat.

The central debate that Marx addressed was between the capitalist contention of capitalism as the end of history, as 'natural' stopping point, or as a place in historical development. Left unconsidered was whether capitalism could produce its fact in social and environmental catastrophe, the product of capitalist production as economic taking until all is taken or destroyed?

The relevance of Marx here is in the locus of concern, political economy premised on metaphysical distance versus actual social relations. Capitalist 'system' to which deference is made is the aggregation of 'economic man.' By shifting focus to the actual persons of social relations, not as the 'objects' of capitalist humanism, Marx reframed 'economic man' as metaphysical improbability.

In this space the social and environmental catastrophes of capitalist production leave no distance between their facts and the persons who live them. Lived social and environmental catastrophes have no 'offset' at the level of system, no redeeming virtues that can be pointed to as justification. By closing the distance between actual social relations and the 'system' of capitalism any alleged benefit to 'system' lies in factual distribution. If some people benefit and others are made worse off there is no metaphysical 'space' in which to hide this social fact. And the division need not be so precise. Even the beneficiaries of capitalism suffer from social and environmental catastrophe, if only by degree.

When history is brought back in, the relation of 'wealth' to 'its' facts in history makes clear that the theorized unity of 'system' hides 'its' facts of wildly disproportionate social outcomes. The capitalist conceit / apologia that the social basis for political economy is premised in psychic artifact—in 'want' or some related psychic quantum, requires this abstraction of 'system' to provide the amorphous space between its theory and its occasionally inconvenient social facts.

Crude Western economic explanations of social relations such as Nobel Prize winning economist Gary Becker's 'utility maximizing' choice of spouse / partner are clearly devoid of history, culture and political context. But explanation outside of context is the goal of this economics—to posit theories that apply, however implausibly, across time and space, geography and the particularities of embedded circumstance.

The Depression era economics of John Maynard Keynes brought social life back into the picture in the sense that Mr. Becker's utility maximizing individuals produce collective outcomes that are different from the mere aggregation of individual economistic 'satisfactions,' sometimes catastrophically so. However, to the point argued above, the distance between Western 'individuals' acting individually and capitalist social 'organization' begs the question once again of whom capitalist 'society' is organized for?

If 'local' 'rationalities' don't aggregate to 'global' rationalities then in what way does a 'system' of political economy 'managed' to global rationalities—Keynesian economics, 'serve' its constituents? As current circumstance in 'the West' has it, Keynesian economists offer more plausible explanations of social-economic relationships in capitalist economies than do cruder versions of base capitalist ideology like neo-liberalism.

But again, the question left eternally unanswered is whom it is that economic policies are intended to serve? The premise is of self-interested wants driving behavior within a benevolent natural system. J.M. Keynes identified circumstances where self-interested behavior makes visible a malevolent 'system.' Mr. Keynes' 'paradox of thrift' isn't 'external' to people acting in their own self-interest, it is directly related to it. The social and environmental catastrophes linked to capitalist production also make visible this malevolence.

With deference to history, this modern era of economics in the West—the revival of pre-Keynesian capitalist theory, and the changes in political economy that both led to it and grew out of it, began in the mid-1970s with 'economic' explanations of geopolitical events. The challenge for Western economists was that 'political' actions had economic consequences that they could only explain within their existing frame—it was / is the only one that they have.

Explanation was necessary for the continued viability of Western economic practice—if economists had to step outside of their existing frame to explain events then its limitations would be visible and the broader 'project' brought into question. Actual argumentation was rococo with 'endogenous' (internal) and 'exogenous' (external) causal differentiation.

Without deductive 'first principles' capitalist theory had nowhere to go outside abandonment of the broad project. The theoretical and conceptual problem lay in part in in 'scaling' the economic impulse. If 'political' decisions drove economic outcomes then what was left for the economists? More directly, if outcomes were 'economic' then how were motivations not economic?

The answer in part is that 'political' decisions that had economic outcomes like U.S. orchestrated coups in Honduras and Iran were about control of economic resources (labor, bananas and oil). Political control is the social power that Western economists have assumed away. The effort required to explain 1970s 'inflation' and unemployment in terms that avoided their genesis in cartel economics involving state actors effectively closed the 'profession' to all but the truest of believers.

The economic orthodoxy that grew out of the 1930s was premised on technocratic management of the recurrent crises of capitalism that had culminated in the Great Depression. The compromises forged between the West's residual plutocrats and the broad populace faded with the institutional memory that recalled the regular economic catastrophes that preceded it.

The political upheaval around the globe of the 1960s led to the challenge from the left that Keynesian policies had maintained capitalist imperialism and from the right that by constraining capitalism a benevolent natural order had been rendered ineffectual. The facts were that capitalist imperialism had hardly been constrained and the compromises that had produced relative economic stability had left the fundamental political and economic tensions of capitalism intact.

The proximate circumstances that led to rupture, to the shift from Keynesian managed capitalism to the revival of the crudely ideological capitalism of the late nineteenth century, were framed as geopolitical when their basis lay in corporate-state imperial strategies.

The sleight of hand that rendered these strategies opaque was the long history of 'the West' using state power to further economic interests. The recurrent oil 'shocks' of the 1970s and the effect of the particular structure of agricultural subsidies in the U.S. produced economic outcomes that needed to be deflected away from their bases in capitalist production.

This practice had long history in the imperial pillage of the nineteenth and twentieth centuries up to today. Overseas 'involvement' in South and Central America, the Middle East and Asia for the benefit of connected capitalists was hidden behind Cold War rhetoric and political 'emergencies' either partially or wholly created by Western governments.

The practice of economists labeling the effects of state predations in the interests of connected capitalists 'exogenous' was to serve self-imposed modeling constraints, to 'pretend' that expression of state power in the interests of particular capitalists and capitalism broadly considered nevertheless produced outcomes well explained by 'economics.'

Rough variants of imperial capitalism were behind the growth of industry in the West and it is the primary military / non-military user of oil by design. As the fuel that drives capitalist production, oil was integrated into Western political economy through cartel machinations and through government subsidies that made it available for less than the true costs of production. The strategic economic importance of oil to capitalist economies is integrated into its geo-political importance in that a 'functioning' economy is needed to build the military materiel of geo-politics before the threat of modern warfare is plausible.

The oil shocks of the 1970s were sold as geo-political in nature with the first in 1973 even called the 'Arab Oil Embargo[45]' even though Iran, then still a U.S. client state, and Venezuela, were the main OPEC members in favor of embargo and both had little quarrel with U.S.-Israeli relations, the alleged geopolitical rationale for the embargo. And it was multi-national oil companies based in the U.S. that were the primary actors holding oil off of world markets to raise the price.

What was demonstrated with the embargoes was the effect that suddenly limited access to oil had on Western industrial economies that were structured to be wholly dependent on plentiful supplies at relatively low cost. Again, this 'structuring' of oil dependence was intentional, not an accident of history.

Cartel lobbying by U.S. industrialists from automakers to tire manufacturers to the oil companies themselves 'engineered' oil dependence by collectively fighting against less energy dependent technologies. Additionally, U.S. military force was used to instantiate oil into Western economic production by separating the military costs of securing it from the 'market' costs borne by industry.

The oil 'embargoes' of the 1970s produced swift, steep recessions and the paradox within Western economics of rising prices coincident with falling economic production. The modern storyline of U.S. energy dependence / independence was borne here and the last embargo in 1979 resulted from oil-rich Iran declaring its independence from the U.S. And the hard turn right in Western academic economics evolved from the seeming economic paradox of 'stagflation.'

The net economic effect of the shocks was to increase profits for oil producers as it reduced economic production in proportion to the oil dependence of specific industries and industrial economies. Additionally, rising oil prices fed into broader inflationary pressures. In this context the combination of higher oil prices and the suddenly limited supply of imported oil on industrial production produced 'stagflation,' the coincidence of economic weakness with rapidly rising prices.

For economists raised on technocratic expositions of Great Depression era economics the dual incidence of inflation and economic weakness was a paradox—the received wisdom allowed for one or the other, but not for the two together. In the unfolding historical context this perceived paradox provided the opening crude capitalist revivalists had been waiting for.

In their search for 'pure' explanations of economic outcomes like inflation and falling economic production Western economists had to look past the explanations that don't fit their models. Leaving the 'exogenous' causes of inflation and falling economic production out of 'economic' consideration effectively hid the role of the capitalist-state in these outcomes. Doing so may not have been directly intentional despite the ideological predispositions of most Western economists—economics doesn't suffice as explanation when state and cartel power determine economic outcomes.

It is the metaphysical 'structure' of capitalist economics that makes it reactive and anti-historical. 'Market forces' always negate the capacity of existing economic power to affect future distribution in the ever-present 'current period' of capitalist economic models. Even when 'time' is 'added' to static models it is metaphysical (static) time—time that is carefully structured to produce only the outcomes economists are looking for.

By the 1970s Western academic economics was decades into the separation of economics from political economy. Even those mainstream economists who may have seen the relation of 'political' policies and events to economic outcomes lacked the 'toolbox' to incorporate politics into their economics to provide broader social explanations. Again, this was / is largely a constraint from the metaphysical structure and premises of capitalist economics.

Without the time-invariant actor of economic man and the motive of economic self-interest there is no self-determination to give a 'natural' basis to capitalist economics. This economic self-determination requires clear partition of the economic 'self' from 'the world' and from other social realms. If 'the political' impinges on the realm of the economic then economic outcomes are rendered indeterminate.

The theory supporting this orthodoxy was developed through logical deduction, the fitting of theory to 'the facts' as they were perceived and undertaken through the filter of economic abstraction. Within this abstraction all of the particulars of catastrophic events like the Great Depression are shoved to the side in favor of the tiny residual that might share 'cause' with some other event.

With respect to inflation one 'abstract' explanation had it that spending more of relatively fixed incomes on oil meant spending less on other things leading to falling prices of those other things. Were this the case rising oil prices 'couldn't' account for the broad inflation being observed in the 1970s. A related explanation had it that the economic weakness associated with the oil shocks led to rising unemployment thereby reducing incomes and the capacity to buy things. In both theories inflation that was in fact rising should have been falling.

And in fact, a complicating factor was that the agricultural subsidies leading into the 1970s were designed to support agricultural prices by limiting production—paying farmers not to grow crops. When the combination of poor harvests and increased export demand led to rising prices for agricultural products these farm subsidies were restructured to increase production with minimum guaranteed prices—the supply of agricultural products was no longer limited by the subsidy system[46].

The 'political' goal of restructuring agricultural subsidies was to reduce food price inflation which is an 'economic' outcome with political consequences. By restructuring the subsidies the basic economics of agricultural production were reconfigured to support industrial food production. Industrial food production is to Western economists capitalist food production. Given the subsidy system it is better described as state-capitalist enterprise. It was political considerations expressed in government policies that altered the agricultural economy, not market forces.

Shifting agricultural production from family farms to industrial agriculture was the articulated goal of the American political leadership, the Nixon administration—it was only a 'market' outcome to the extent that markets reacted. The exclusive and reactive nature of capitalist economics treats these iterative relations of political economy in a way that postures doing so as politically 'neutral.'

Given the complicated simplicity of the orthodox economic models and the sudden withdrawal of the key ingredient from industrial production—oil; 'stagflation' seems an entirely plausible result irrespective of the ability of conventional economic theories to explain it. An in fact oil prices tracked broad inflation measures like CPI (Consumer Price Index) quite closely throughout the 1970s. The studied insistence by economists that the facts staring them in the face required elaborate explanations when multi-national oil companies behaving badly would suffice suggests that ideology was driving their theories.

In the broader sense this 'failure' of Keynesian economics to 'explain' stagflation was the opening capitalist ideologues had been waiting for since the New Deal was first implemented in the1930s. The New Deal was a pragmatic amalgam of slightly fettered corporatism and social guarantees that took the rough edges off of Western capitalism in order to save it from its most 'internally' destructive tendencies. Ideologically determined 'proof' that Keynesian analytical precepts were implausible was needed to dislodge it from academic convention.

From the 'outside' replacing Keynesian economics with the crisis-prone capitalism that had led to its rise in the first place seems a large step backward within the Western narrative of 'progress.' From the 'inside' of capitalist economics there was no other choice—the circularity of capitalist theory leaves only internal resolution or the broader project is brought into question. A new era of 'deductive' economics proceeded from the high capitalist premise that people are rational in a specific 'operational' sense and that we make judgments based on the same theories about how the world 'works' as the economists pushing them.

Keynes had added the complication of 'paradox' to the deductive 'content' of Western economics. By pushing Keynesian economics to the side, as the capitalist revivalists did, the 'burden' of addressing paradox was placed there as well. This freed newly resurgent capitalist economists to explore the infinite iterations of narrow ideology without annoying intrusions from 'the economy.' The use of increasingly complex mathematical models was directly related to the implausibility of the economics being put forward. The hope apparently was that if the content wasn't convincing the package might be.

This was / is true of both the political-economic 'left' and 'right' that worked within the internal logic of the Western economic frame. The 'empirical' proofs offered for these theories were raw ideology in the form of mathematical models of varying degrees of 'sophistication' designed for their alleged logical rigor, not for relevance to that which they were purported to describe. This revivification of antique ideology could be discounted as a 'mistake' of history had the cartoon theoretics that emerged not found their way into the wholesale remaking of Western political economy.

Despite that the premises and 'proofs' of capitalist revival economics resided in the realm of dubious logic, its 'facts' informed the public narrative to 'demonstrate' that management of the economy was misguided, if not outright counterproductive. Such efforts would be offset, went the theories, by rational people running capitalist-revival theories about how 'the economy' works through economic models in their minds to counteract the effects of government policies.

For instance, a government works program to put the unemployed to work would be understood by 'rational' citizens to have to be paid for through increased taxes either now or in the future. The increased taxes would reduce net income by the amount of the tax increase and force people to consume less thereby offsetting the benefit of putting the unemployed to work.

The utter implausibility of non-economists having any notion of this arcane economic theory was countered with the conceit that these theories 'of the world' are available to everybody by way of their representing true knowledge of it. People are 'rational,' antique economics is rational, and therefore people act rationally in accordance with the precepts of this economics.

Implausibility aside, these theories require near complete ignorance of how a modern money system with fiat currency 'works.' The relation of government expenditures to tax receipts is a convenient fiction, not an economic truth. This misunderstanding points to the flawed premise of 'rational expectations' economics in that even were people 'rational' in the way that economists claim we are we would still have to share their flawed understanding of 'the economy' to behave in the ways that they predict.

The historical circumstance that was argued to support this revival was the post-War prosperity of 'the West' that found little explanation in the free-market principles that neo-capitalists espouse. Capitalist economists of the 1970s carefully parsed the 'successes' and 'failures' of Western economic history to fit their ideology.

In addition to the relative 'internal' economic stability provided by progressive taxation and social insurance programs like Social Security, Medicare and state unemployment insurance schemes, the nations of the West had used the 'public' sector, the military and related industries, to develop much of what modern industry has commercialized in its own name.

The 'success' of Western capitalism, to the extent it can be called that, was the result of a government-industry hybrid in which government played the role of key innovator and imperial enforcer in the interests of connected capitalists. Neo-liberal 'market' economics do little to explain the convergence of endowment, history and social accommodation behind this prosperity.

The social dislocations of the 1960s and early 1970s were global—as prevalent in 'socialist' Europe as in the capitalist U.S. They had articulated basis in the history of Western capitalist imperialism, in internal economic dislocations from reconfigured industrial bases, in residual and contemporaneous racial tensions from the history of slavery and its unrelenting grasp, in the hugely unpopular war in Vietnam and in the 'drug war' that targeted global youth to maintain monopoly control over drug production for Western pharmaceutical companies.

The falling rate of corporate profits that economists claimed to be responding to was in large measure the result of oil cartel extraction—the higher price of oil ended up in the pockets of cartel producers as well as those of the oil industry that had engineered the early embargoes. Near instantaneous petro-fortunes were parts of the scenery in the West in the 1970s.

To conclude that the economic dislocations of the 1970s were the result of failed Keynesian policies, as the capitalist revivalists did, makes little sense in the historical context of repeated oil shocks on oil dependent economies, the end of the post-War dominance of the U.S. in global industrial production and the preceding decades of relatively crisis-free economic performance.

Behind this neo-liberal renaissance was the heavy hand of the residual plutocracy that effectively ran U.S. foreign policy in its own interests for the prior century. At the height of their influence Keynesian economists were at most the technocrats charged with maintaining economic stability in the service of capitalist imperialism. What had been saved by the New Deal was a wealth divide that constituted a 'shadow' plutocracy by the very rich.

As the threat of the wholesale replacement of 'managed' capitalism by the competing political economies of socialism or communism receded this plutocracy was emboldened. By the 1960s it was funding 'think tanks[48]' where capitalist 'intellectuals' were fed and housed in exchange for putting forward renewed rationales for pre-New Deal economic policies.

Going into the political turmoil of the 1960s radical capitalist theory had remained marginalized by its past failures. But the combination of the mistrust of government coming out of the Vietnam War, the 'war on drugs' that put a generation of citizens on the wrong side of government power and the seeming inability of Keynesian economics to explain the economic turmoil caused by repeated oil supply 'shocks' provided the opening the capitalist revivalists were looking for.

Keynesian economics was 'pragmatic' in the sense that it smoothed the edges of the crisis-prone capitalism that had produced the sequential economic depressions of the prior century. But it did so at the cost of the theoretical coherence of capitalism. 'New' and 'neo' Keynesians largely bought into the most radically incoherent theories of the capitalist revivalists and they did so without answering the fundamental question of whom precisely, they were 'saving' capitalism for?

Without the 'economic man' of older capitalist theory there is no self-determined 'self' that capitalist democracy serves and with 'him'

Keynesian management of the economy is theoretically incoherent. 'Pragmatism' either has some fundament of concern, a 'care structure,' or it isn't pragmatic.

Following the 1970s variations on high capitalist theory were divided in their application to global political economy. The West has taken the market-theological approach of foregoing much of the former 'guidance' of 'the economy' in favor of 'market' outcomes while building out the machinery of economic imperialism in the form of the most expensive and destructive military in world history.

The ascendance of 'finance' capitalism has left Wall Street in charge of reconfiguring Western political economy through their socially-given capacity to create money in the service of capitalist enterprise—mainly their own. The seeming paradox of crude market ideology backed by the economic and military might of Western political economy has aggregated to an opportunistic, predatory capitalism that favors markets when doing so provides advantage and government 'intervention' when it provides advantage.

The multi-trillion dollar bailout of Wall Street in 2008 goes against every 'market' principle capitalist ideologues ever put forward. But it finds wide precedence in the strategies of economic imperialism implemented overseas by the IMF (International Monetary Fund) in the service of Western banks and bankers for the prior fifty years.

Current U.S. machinations in the Middle East and Africa are part of a global grab for 'economic' resources that is eerily reminiscent of the global imperial order that preceded the first of the great slaughters of the twentieth century, WWI. And rabidly ideological capitalism is currently being reconstituted in Western political economy through increasingly intrusive 'trade' agreements and through the corporate takeover of public institutions. The seeming paradox of capitalist democracy devouring itself is addressed in subsequent chapters.

In contrast to the Western approach 'the East,' China in particular, has taken the managed capitalism route in ways that both pre and post date the revivified market theology of the West. Through heavy state guidance, participation and resources a group of Asian nations has produced remarkable simulacra of Western prosperity along with much of the social and environmental dysfunction of industrial capitalism.

China has used developed trade policies including a managed currency, a targeted export strategy, state banks, the build-out of integrated infrastructure and an iterative notion of economic development to produce several decades of sustained economic growth. Within the capitalist frame and set of virtues China has been a remarkable 'success' story. This current success brings history back into Western 'economic' explanations of the 'demise' of central planning, and with it, communism.

This isn't to argue that China's mercantilist strategies are close analog to central planning, but rather that China should have had no 'success' with 'state' capitalism if the neo-liberal theories of Western capitalism are 'correct.' It also reframes the relative success of Keynesian 'managed' capitalism away from the market-theological contention that it places undue limitation on the 'natural order' theorized to produce 'prosperity.'

Within the Western frame China and much of the rest of Asia have demonstrated success by explicitly not following the Western model. Left unanswered, much as Keynes left it unanswered, is whom precisely this prosperity is being created for? The 'self-evidence' of the answer requires a generally analogous actor to 'economic man' as well as the capacity to not see the associated social and environmental catastrophes that are as much its product as the 'goods' now found on store shelves. And to step back from the ether-space of 'system,' the social distribution of this total product—intended and unintended, is its fact, not the polished goods in store windows of the few offered as evidence.

Caveats are needed before this global capitalist renaissance can be properly considered. (1) The first is of sustainability both within the internal logic of capitalism and without as political economy that generates serial social and environmental catastrophes. From within capitalist theory the question of who it is that capitalism serves needs to be answered. A quick observation is that its social fact offers plausible explanation in the distribution of social wealth—it serves the wealthy.

(2) However, this criticism comes from 'outside' of capitalist theory. Without the cartoon humanism of 'economic man' capitalism is a social imposition, a forced identity that has no basis outside of the theories of a few thousand ideologues in the West. The history of capitalism is of narrowly distributed booms followed by widely distributed busts, the recurrent 'crises of capitalism' that threaten to 'end' history in ways other than those imagined by its proponents. These social and environmental

consequences are indissociable from capitalist production meaning that as capitalism encompasses the globe so do these effects.

(3) The internal logic of capitalist 'competition' has in history been magnified as imperial conquest—competition amongst nation-states for the resources needed for industrial production and to provide the level of prosperity required to maintain internal political stability. The regularly recurring and increasingly destructive military entanglements undertaken to secure economic resources is the major source of geo-political instability.

(4) The tendency of capitalism to consume itself through the consolidation of economic power so much in evidence in the West today produces untenable social divisions that eventually produce social rupture.

(5) The technocratic proficiency that is the hallmark of capitalist production has no 'internal' limitation—it can be used to produce the 'better' doomsday machine (nuclear weapons) and the mechanisms of total social control.

(6) The virtues of capitalism that are typically put forward emerge from its specific internal logic, not from 'nature.' Its perceived 'benefit' is socially, culturally and historically locatable. This places Western economics as social explanation in the service of existing social relations and not as the realm of social possibility that its proponents claim it to be.

Capitalism Hits the Skids

THE ECONOMIC AND FINANCIAL CALAMITIES IN THE WEST OF THE mid-late 2000s are the broadest and deepest since the Great Depression and in significant ways they share genesis with it. The theoretical-philosophical backdrop to both epics—their 'public' explanations, evolved from technocratic expositions of base capitalist ideology.

Political economy premised on it—'market' capitalism with a large financial component, was widely understood to have failed the overwhelming majority of the citizens of the West for as long as it took the generation that lived through the economic disaster of the Great Depression to pass on.

The 'economy' that briefly produced spectacular and highly concentrated wealth ultimately imploded from its own weight in both epics. The central difference in the current epic is the response of the political classes. In the absence of polities ready to force political action in their favor the political classes have mildly accommodated populist cultural issues while wholly reviving the political economy of catastrophe.

The accommodations that 'saved' capitalism in the 1930s are nowhere to be found today. And the proposition has been put forward in each of the periods between the crises of the last thirty years that 'the problem' has been solved while each subsequent crisis has been more severe and has reached deeper into steadily declining circumstances.

The political response to the recent crisis was to deploy all available social resources to the rapid resuscitation of the system of global finance capitalism that produced the crisis. Wall Street and the corporate executives who gained wealth and power through the financialization of the economy together created an economic doomsday machine through the combination of financial leverage, an arcane web of cross liabilities and broad economic disenfranchisement that can bring the economies of the West to the point of crisis in a matter of days.

It is the combination of the structure of global financial relations and their deep embedding that turned recent epics of financial fraud and theft into catastrophe for the larger economy. The compensation of culpable

Wall Street bankers was higher immediately following the crisis than it was before while the fate of the large numbers of newly unemployed was left to the vagaries of 'market forces.'

The subsequent measures of economic 'progress' put forward by official sources and the 'liberal' and 'conservative' economic technocracy—GDP (Gross Domestic Product), Consumer Spending and Household Income, treated the rapid revival of the architects of catastrophe as if their 'good fortune' were of equal benefit to those left to now demonstrably dysfunctional market forces.

Since those panic-ridden days two related strains of unlikely assertion have been made across the political 'spectrum' of Western technocracy. The first, the assertion typically put forward by Western economists that 'more is better' regardless of how it is distributed, faces the challenge that the wholesale revival at public expense of the architects of economic catastrophe reflected in these growth 'measures' has empowered them to further reconstitute political economy for their own benefit against the interests of everyone else.

The social wealth that accrued to bankers, financiers and corporate executives has come through business practices that actively harmed tens of millions of people—the economic looting of the housing bubble and related financial frauds and the decades of the pirate capitalism of 'investment' banking that shifted economic resources into the pockets of financiers while leaving the liabilities to be borne by the formerly employed workforce in the form of looted pensions, looted health care funds and greatly diminished prospects.

The bankers and corporate executives whose fortunes were revived by the political classes in the West were directly responsible for the immiseration of those whose fortunes weren't revived—the rich became richer by making a lot of other people poorer. In this sense economic 'growth' can hardly be the unqualified good that even the political 'left' has in recent decades suggested it is.

This point is also made through the recent public policy 'debates' of the Western economic technocracy between 'expansionary austerity,' cutting public expenditures under the theory that doing so boosts market 'confidence' in the fiscal probity of nations and thereby lowers interest rates, and Keynesian policies of increased government expenditure to bridge 'temporary' declines in 'the economy.'

The most vocal advocates of economic austerity are the bankers and financial managers who benefited, and who continue to benefit, from transfers of public resources to them in the form of bailouts, subsidies and guarantees. Austerity policies benefit banks and bankers to the extent they cause falling prices—banks have their loans repaid in more valuable dollars. The bank bailouts left bankers with the political clout to push these self-serving policies.

The financial 'sector' also benefits from the low interest rates that austerity makes 'necessary', the 'cost' of money to the banks that they lend out at higher rates. Under the auspices of the IMF (International Monetary Fund) policies of economic austerity have long histories of devastating local and regional economies so that Wall Street bankers are assured repayment of their loans no matter what the social costs.

It is no great surprise then that the bankers and financiers whose fortunes were revived with public funds and whose wealth remains a function of government guarantees and subsidies used their power to force policies of immiseration onto others. This is the nature of the corporate-state 'free-market' capitalism that the West has been promoting for decades now.

The environmental catastrophes aggregating at the end of the last millennium and the start of the new—global warming, increasingly destructive methods of resource extraction and irreversible loss of interrelated ecosystems are the direct result of the growth of capitalist production and its associated consumer culture. The regularly made contention that global warming and the other environmental catastrophes are evidence of market 'failure' doesn't go far enough—it is the failure 'of' markets, not 'in' them.

The relation not generally made is that it is the joining of this production to the system of finance capitalism that enhances the ever-present imperative for catastrophe, the debt based money that carries with it the terms of coercive extraction and the time-structure of well-regulated environmental destruction. The 'solution' eternally put forward by capitalist ideologues that 'more markets' will solve market failure is a confidence game of infinite duration as the climate warms up.

As with the distribution of the benefits of economic 'growth,' capitalist production 'rewards' capitalists for dumping their costs onto others. The same capitalists doing the dumping have purchased the political capture that leaves all social recourse short of political-economic rupture and replacement a distant possibility. By increasing the social power of capitalists economic 'growth' is the problem, not the solution, to current and future social and environmental problems.

The Western idea of social 'progress' is beholden in significant ways to increasing material wealth, the theorized 'product' of economic growth. Capitalist economics is designed to assert that people are 'better off' even if added wealth is accompanied by a broad increase in economic insecurity and social and environmental catastrophe—the detriments of capitalism that are only rarely deducted from its broad calculation.

This view derives from the calculated instantiation of unlimited acquisition as social 'virtue' and the creation of the material conditions of social fragility that immediately threaten calamity when the incomes and wealth of the ruling plutocracy appear at risk. The frame of interest is always 'now' and the measure of success the future because failures remain perpetually and insistently unrelated in social explanation to the mechanisms of capitalist production.

Economic 'progress' is to make the poor and the historically marginalized more 'like' the wealthy in terms of income, wealth and the things they buy. That this 'progress' could in theory be partially accomplished by redistributing existing wealth falls prey to its initial distribution put forward in capitalist theory as natural and rightful when its history is of imperial power being used to take it. This idea of 'progress' tied to existing wealth distribution is the ideology of the perpetual 'future,' social struggle put on hold for the vague promise that someday someone, somewhere will do better than in the present.

Left largely unsaid is that the wealth of current ambition accrued through the economic distance now theorized to be converging. Progress in the realms of race and gender are measured as decreased dispersion in economic outcomes, as 'closing' the 'gaps' in income and wealth. The measures are always relative and 'oppositional' —black to white, female to male, high school dropouts to college graduates, to avoid questions of capitalism's 'rewards' so narrowly concentrated that no conceivable relationship to social utility produced is plausible. The 'best' and / or 'natural' strategy for 'developing' nations is to become 'developed,' to develop cultures of Western abundance.

The cynical assertion that seven billion people could under any arrangement of circumstance drive Sport Utility Vehicles and live in large Western houses collides with existing mal-distribution in capitalist economies and the social and environmental catastrophes of capitalist production underway. More pointedly, the capitalist 'virtue' of 'more' can be seen as ideologically motivated imposition, as vague 'promise' made to benefit those doing the promising. Political and economic debate centers on the best ways to make new and historical 'out' groups more like the wealthy, to increase their material 'well-being.' Left unstated is that both content and structure of Western political economy is arranged to assure that this will never happen.

Within this storyline of 'progress' the premise that 'more' is 'better' and the nature of the social mechanisms of wealth accumulation are left largely unexplored. Capitalist theorists have worked for nearly two centuries to 'naturalize' insatiable material want as a base characteristic of 'human' being and to pose the naked taking of capitalist imperialism as divine distribution, the 'natural' reward for the power of subjugation. This want is used to justify economic imperialism, the conditions of coerced and / or stolen labor and of lives lived as appendages to the technologies of economic production created for distant consumption.

The 'comparative advantage' of capitalist theory and the 'labor arbitrage' of business strategy are used to legitimate the fortunes of Western capitalists produced under conditions of engineered coercion and immiseration. These capitalists—'high tech' barons, the pirate financiers of Wall Street and retailing 'giants' like Wal-Mart, hide their accumulated social power behind arcane theories of 'free market' economics to create and exploit conditions of engineered immiseration and dependence, the 'state of nature' that capitalism is always there to 'solve.'

As somewhat more than mere coincidence, the geographic locations of these regions of 'misfortune' overlap substantially with two centuries of imperial conquest much as the unfortunate to be saved are the residual of empire existing in their 'natural' state as current or former imperial subjects.

The tradeoff at 'home' is the wholesale disenfranchisement of the 'middle' class under the ruse that the newly immiserated benefit from stolen labor as it is reconstituted in the low priced goods available to those whose incomes remain. An engineered 'consumer culture' more than a century in the making sees no relation between the 'bargains' it buys at the mall and the 'bargains' it produces at work, between the discount it pays at the store and the discount it now receives in its paycheck.

The 'iron law of wages' of antique contrivance left out of its explanation the one percent of the population that takes over twenty percent of the income and the top ten percent that takes over fifty percent[50], the 'bargain' now found in the paychecks of the newly immiserated as special thanks for 'consuming' itself. Facilitating this process is Wall Street whose skills at metaphysical conversion translate two centuries of labor into digital entries on the balance sheets of those whose total social contribution is shifting what others produce into their own pockets.

To the extent the products now filling the shelves of Western stores were ever viable as 'market' goods the labor that produced them could be paid its share of the revenues but it never is. The claim always and everywhere is that the coercion and immiseration of today will produce the benefits of capitalist accumulation for future generations. The fact is that those doing the coercing and the immiserating are receiving these benefits in the form of visible fortunes in the present. The capitalism claimed in arcane theories to produce 'more' left unexplained the 'who' and 'what' of its theorized bounty.

While history is replete with coercion, exploitation and immiseration not directly related to capitalist production, the 'innovation' of capitalism is to reframe them as virtues. Capitalist theories of 'human nature' attempt to 'naturalize' exploitation, to internalize it by placing its social pathologies in theories of a 'natural order.' Whereas modern consumer culture was consciously 'constructed' from without, 'economic man' as the aspirational striver of capitalist 'system' actively seeks 'self-exploitation,' to participate in economic production knowing 'his' product will accrue to a narrow plutocracy to be used against 'him.'

In modern circumstance acting in one's interest as economic 'producer' is to act against it through 'voluntary' self-expropriation. The temporarily broadened income distribution of the New Deal provided the illusion of a 'system' of self-exploitation that gave something back—for just long enough for its genesis in economic catastrophe to be forgotten. The illusion was accomplished through contrived circumscription, through the division of 'us' from 'them' with national boundaries and history to confuse economic production with its imperial relocation.

To the question of material need, Western economics proposes that want is all there is—that need of food, shelter, health care, education and social relations are of similar magnitude and nature as the wealthy person's want of a fourteenth television set for 'their' third house. This want may be scalable—cardinal versus ordinal, linear versus exponential, but never is it relatable to the need that separates the well fed from the hungry and the well housed from the homeless. Capitalist 'want' is for economic pornography, its objects explicit, isolated from social context, time and history.

'Consumer' products contain no residual of the circumstances of their production, their packaging part delivery device and part added inducement to trade want for judgment. This pornographic quality is essential—the mothers, fathers, sisters, brothers and neighbors of capitalist production are unwanted encumbrances when associated with their product, the displaced rural workers leaping to their deaths in Chinese computer factories and the eleven-year-old children making tee shirts for Americans in sweatshops in Haiti. Only in this isolated state can want—stuff lust, be boundless, mere psychic artifact innocent of all charges against it. And only through feigned ignorance facilitated by well-conceived strategies of abstraction and social alienation does this pornography find an audience.

As theory of social relations capitalism is more precisely a theory of anti-social relations. Its created / contrived 'wants' are used to legitimate the use of social power by the already wealthy to take from whomever they can by way of the creation and use of asymmetrical social relations, military force, police powers, laws written for and by the rich and judiciaries established to benefit the rich.

As a theory of human nature capitalism is put forward as the basis for the Western 'self' that places its results, its social pathologies and social and environmental catastrophes, in nature, in the realm of the unavoidable, the inevitable and the necessary. Its theory of insatiable wants is reunited with its factual history in a finite world with finite resources that was only in recent decades reintroduced to its global imperial ambitions.

History is replete with warnings of impending catastrophe only to see them resolved with technological 'solutions' that further instantiate the singular logic of capitalism as historical imperative. Left unstated is that these solutions were to problems created within the trajectory of this contrived imperative, the firefighter who arrives to put out the fire s/he started, the assassin who, for a price, will sell us the antidote to the poison s/he administered.

Western 'faith' in the benevolent structure of nature's 'laws' as an invisible hand guiding market exchange places social relations in an opaque netherworld of determined self-determination, of 'freely' chosen bondage. The 'natural' basis of economic coercion in material need is placed against the socially created imperatives of property, laws and existing relations to posit 'markets' as locus of implausible equivalence, the entirety of history reduced to 'want' of the wanted in an eternal 'present.'

Left unconsidered is the before and after, the circumstances of culture, history and broader social relations that take back this market equivalence and then some. Capitalist markets are the meeting place of empire and imperial subjects, the 'free' exchange of asymmetrical social power in the service of imperial extraction. Their façade is the 'brand' of capitalist democracy, the slogan put forward as its explanation. It is hardly an accident that Wall Street creates the 'fluid' of equivalence in market exchange; the thing-act of money whose exchange 'proves' it is freely undertaken.

As social fact money is the metric of inequivalence, the distance between the terms of capitalist production and the price of goods in market exchange. The question of how much an ocean, a forest, or even 'the world,' is 'worth' provides the illusion of possession and implies the right of annihilation. The hypothesized 'solutions' to its catastrophes always and everywhere exist in the same time-space as equitable distribution in some future period that never arrives.

The central 'political' impediment to resolution is Western state power expressed in the service of particular capitalists and 'their' enterprises. The imperial dimension finds global expression in the power to force its harms—its social and environmental catastrophes, onto the same people whose wealth as expropriated labor and resources has so contributed to imperial power. If capitalism is capable of 'solving' its catastrophes why are they accumulating at such a rapid pace and the theorized solutions so implausible?

As theory of 'nature,' the question of why capitalism's wisdom has been so tightly circumscribed in culture, history and geography places it far more probably as cultural imperative, as totalizing imperial ambition put forward to convince its subjects and beneficiaries alike that it fulfills a grand design not of their making, of an all-knowing nature handing out the paychecks and demerits by degree of obedience to 'its' laws. Were this humanism not reconstituted as the basis of social life, as the institutional object provided the 'choice' of conforming to its narrowly circumscribed dictates, this objection might be mere abstraction.

As reified 'object' reconstituted in Western institutions economic man is imposed identity, the metaphysical 'core' of Western being against which its reciprocal in embedded being is material imperative, the distance between life as it is and its wholly implausible explanation in the service of an existing social order. And were capitalism's facts of political economy merely inconvenient then dissension could be kept to the level of academic debate. But in each of the dimensions laid out below capitalism is catastrophe with increasing impact.

As mode of social organization, capitalism is a catastrophe generating mechanism that places its catastrophes outside of human actions. Its tendency toward consolidation of economic, and with it political, power produces asymmetrical social power. This asymmetry is self-perpetuating and self-reinforcing; producing the economic 'freedom' to keep like 'freedom' for itself, in the few hands that got 'there' first.

As history, this social power has been used through its brief centuries to perpetuate itself—to put forward institutional rules and context as advertising slogans that hide the imperial relations at its core. This concentrated power is used to force its attendant catastrophes, the intended 'unintended' consequences of capitalist production, onto those who lack the social power to resist. The profit motive is incentive for the 'efficiencies' of cost shifting, for pumping and dumping the toxic excrescences that are its product onto those who can't say no.

This tendency can be seen the in regularly recurring wars for control of economic resources where large numbers of people who have little relation to capitalism are tortured and killed, in global environmental calamities where those most affected never 'benefit' from it and in the restructuring of political-economic relations where doing so is designed to benefit the already wealthy against those whose lives are radically affected by forced changes. Political economy where some benefit from the immiseration of others is a social catastrophe by design for those so immiserated.

Where it exists, the visible prosperity of Western capitalism is put forward as advertisement for the social relations that are purported to have brought it into being. However, on those rare trips to the realm of the 'political' little apology is made for related imperial reach or for the layer after layer of surveillance and military bureaucracy dedicated to 'protecting' the Western 'way of life.'

The strip malls, car lots and grocery stores of capitalist abundance are the visible topside of political economy where military conquest and imperial domination are combined with 'production' to relocate the resources put forward as capitalist 'creation.'

'Government' in the service of Western capitalists is framed as incidental, as unavoidable annoyance / irrelevance that diverts 'resources' from the 'private' economy.

More precisely, these public-private bureaucracies *are* capitalism—they are the 'outsourced' back offices of multi-national corporations, the military enforcers of resource 'extraction,' the financial managers of pirate investment banking, the 'research and development' departments that created the telecommunications, computing, pharmaceutical, agricultural and military infrastructures that the dim heroes of capitalism put forward as 'their' own, as the products of 'their' special genius.

Self-serving rants against 'big government' are rhetorical device, the public statement that they—the self-appointed 'heroes' of capitalism, and they alone, are responsible for everything good in life and deserve to be 'rewarded' for it as they have already 'rewarded' themselves.

Increasingly in evidence is the declining ability of social institutions, including those of the developed political economies of the West, to respond in any constructive way to the forces of this social and environmental destruction. The financial catastrophe begun in the West 2008 is the most destructive in an escalating series of financial crises with no substantive changes in the destructive power of Wall Street evident or apparently possible.

The political incapacitation to act against the most destructive forces of capitalism is by design—the high-capitalist program of neo-liberalism put forward by Western bankers and capitalist ideologues is now four decades into shifting power from 'nations' to multi-national corporations owned by a shrinking group of international plutocrats. Western state power is now openly and conspicuously dedicated to consolidating power in the hands corporate titans and their masters in the plutocracy.

There is no 'political' paralysis when military 'intervention' is needed to secure the resources important to capitalist production or when 'markets' need to be opened by force to increase the reach of neo-liberal predation. To those who perceive a problem, it is of capitalist democracy being implausible cover for Western states serving the interests of connected capitalists. It is not of political incapacitation through a 'competition' of interests.

The crises of capitalism increasingly in evidence result not only from the consequences of capitalist production but more broadly from the approach to 'the world' that derives from economistic reasoning—the manipulation, control and domination of all aspects of life in the name of economic 'efficiency' in the service of the Western 'self.' The 'efficiency' of capitalism is, and has always been, an accounting gimmick, a merging of the 'unintended,' the coerced, the contrived, the destroyed and the temporary with the 'produced.'

But only the 'produced,' capitalist product, is credited in the social accounting. What system of social accounting lists the 'credits' of political economy without its debits?—the very same one that allocates social wealth by these credits, that makes it the 'property' of particular capitalists while letting the 'debits' in the form of social and environmental dysfunction and devastation accrue down the path of least resistance.

Global warming and its potential catastrophes is an aggregation of these debits, one whose scale and scope make it visible as both fact and metaphor. It is metaphor for the uncounted, uncountable local catastrophes of capitalism, for the toxic violations, the contaminated, the poisoned, the immiserated, the irradiated, the dislocated, the exiled and the abandoned. With two centuries of capitalist production and Western 'consumer culture' to 'thank' for global warming, to whom should the bill for its rectification be sent? With history as a guide payment will be extracted from where it always has been, from those who lack the social power to resist.

The point is sometimes made that political and economic instability runs counter to the interests of capitalists, the inference being that the desire for profits provides a 'natural' check on the historical tendency of capitalist states to go to war at the drop of a hat[52] and to keep fighting for years or decades after the possibility of achieving geo-political goals has passed. The idea of 'instability' at work is the product of active imagination filtered through the contrived misdirection of 'shared sacrifice.'

If one group, let's call them capitalists, can thrive at the expense of others, the subjects / victims of capitalist imperialism, from where precisely does the threat to profits arise? The same system of social accounting that credits economic 'product' to the bank accounts of particular capitalists while letting its debits fall where they may provides the twin ditches used in the cost-benefit calculation of imperial conquest. American industry has thrived because of the global instability that the American state has so reliably produced, not in spite of it.

The ready, pliable work forces of capitalist industry didn't one-day fall from the sky. Their history is of socially created circumstance, of the catastrophic regional and global wars of mixed provenance supplied on every side by for-profit arms manufacturers and financed by the same bankers who subsequently and quite mysteriously come into possession of the residual political economies of the 'victors' for whom they have near endless 'helpful' recommendations. Instability, catastrophe and disaster are the pillars of capitalism, the misery, the devastation and want that add the luster of necessity to its product.

The Western economist's theory of instability requires a quaint notion of capitalism akin to antique Scottish economist Adam Smith's petite bourgeois shop-keeps fearing they would lose business if the rabble chased good paying customers away. Left out of this calculus is that if the 'rabble' burned these businesses to the ground it would all have to be built again—the buildings, the inventory and the infrastructure. Even if particular shop-keeps suffered loss of life and 'property,' the 'system' of capitalism would have its best year in decades.

On the one hand the formal calculus of Western economists that sees benefit in catastrophe and destruction is an artifact of honest effort at social accounting from within their very own wholly implausible premises. On the other hand, the system of political economy they are selling sees actual benefit in catastrophe and destruction, the dividing line between its visible and invisible products existing outside its purview.

Wall Street—finance capitalism at its inglorious best, regularly uses economic power backed by the threat of state power to insert itself into political economies around the globe to arrange economic production for its own benefit. The great 'mystery' of economic austerity, the draconian cuts in public spending in the midst of ongoing economic depression hoisted onto the economies of the West after the Wall Street induced financial-economic catastrophes of 2008, is straightforwardly the same creditor's view of corporate accounts—the banker's view used in 'work-outs' of corporate debt, now applied to national accounts.

Capitalist imperialism isn't the mutually beneficial system of trade between equals of Western economic theory—the IMF (International Monetary Fund), the supreme private-state tool of finance capitalism, has been one of the most economically and politically destabilizing forces in world history for some six decades now.

Even if Western capitalism were populated by Adam Smith's shop keeps opening their doors in the morning and waiting for customers to come in and transact for a modest profit, the 'system' of capitalism, its social component that produces collective outcomes different from the simple aggregation of its parts, is fundamentally destabilizing. In recent decades Wall Street and the corporate West were provided with wish lists in terms of the freedom to conduct business as 'they' saw fit.

Wall Street was effectively deregulated, allowed to increase leverage, to shift risks (within the system of finance and without) and to engage in predatory practices that actively harmed 'its' customers under the ratio-nale that business leaders know what is best for business. By 2008 Wall Street had hung itself with the rope it had constructed[54] and had hung the economies of the capitalist West with it. Of relevance is that the crisis begun in 2008 is but one of the regularly recurring crises of capitalism that go back two centuries or more.

This more recent crisis was particularly potent in part because of the depth of the reconstitution of radical capitalist theory into Western politi-cal economy. The economic 'leverage' of finance capitalism was integrated into broader economic relations to an extent last seen in the lead up to the Great Depression. The economic and financial leverage that is Wall Street's business magnifies economic instability to the degree it is instan-tiated into it. Wall Street got exactly what it claimed would be good for business and economic catastrophe was the result.

But this catastrophe neither diminished the fortunes of its central protagonists nor did it result in any major 'rethinking' of capitalism. The same Wall Street that so magnified the long-understood economic disas-ter generating mechanism of predatory lending was rapidly restored at public expense while the 'real' economy was left to 'its' own devices.

In much the same way that capitalist economic relations have been reconstituted in global economic production in ways that make their sudden withdrawal economically catastrophic and therefore politically untenable, Wall Street has instantiated its corrupt, extractive business so deeply into Western political economy that sudden withdrawal of its debt based money means instant catastrophe.

The seeming mystery of why Wall Street bankers suffered no loss even while 'their' businesses were kept alive at public expense gets to the heart of why its business of leveraging economic instability is 'allowed' to persist. It also explains why the newly immiserated have been left to bear the consequences of its engineered catastrophes. Capitalism is a system of engineered dependence that forcibly replaces sustainable political economy with its recurrent, and therefore predictable, instability.

The visible prosperity of Wall Street's bankers is imperial product— Wall Street is rich because its powers of economic extraction lead to immiseration through engineered dependence; 'it' is rich because it makes others poor. Were 'banking,' rather than particular bankers, essential to 'the economy' of the West the protagonists of recent catastrophe would have been fired and replaced by people with greater competence at banking at a fraction of their cost. But the 'system' of leveraged instability was left intact; its engineered dependence its 'product' and the rolling catastrophes it creates its raison d'etre.

Meanwhile, Western economists pose as neutral observers, as technocrats using the tools provided them to develop solutions to the catastrophes they work so diligently to create. That Western economics is technocratic exposition of base capitalist ideology is hidden behind the premise that 'the world' is ahistorical object; that two hundred years of capitalist ideology reconstituted in political-economic relations has no bearing on its current constitution. This leaves economists the task of 'discovering' the very same facts that they create, the logical circle that proves capitalist democracy ever more 'correct' even as its catastrophes render it less plausible.

History finds no welcome here because temporal outcomes complicate the realm of atemporal theory. As 'science' these economists admit only truths as relevant to life on other planets as on their own, their timeless universality ready substitute for coherence, relevance and admission of culpability for 'the world' that now bears their likeness. Recurrent catastrophes are 'addressed' wholly within the mode of reasoning that produced them, the 'natural experiment' that asks how many times related catastrophes could plausibly be claimed to bear no relation?

The 'solutions' proposed by the mainstream economic 'left' to recurrent financial-economic crises proceed from the premise that the system that produces them should remain substantially intact and that the 'work' of Western economists is to clean up the catastrophes that capitalism creates. As with the number of angels that fit on the head of a pin, hypotheses of the number of entirely unrelated catastrophes finance capitalism has produced in recent decades range from a few to the infinite depending on the definitions of 'angel,' 'head,' and 'pin.'

As the 'free market' in irony has it, the political economy Western economists have so faithfully served has ever less use for them as the rich and powerful feel the need to explain the social wealth now accumulated in their own pockets in inverse proportion to its quantity. This leaves the social apologetics of the economic 'left' with the patina of 'dissent' needed to fill the distance between the greatness of capitalist democracy and its inevitability as fact of nature.

Hidden behind innocuous sounding 'free-trade' agreements, glittering new technologies and the 'resolution' of recurrent economic crises is that through the institutions of capitalist imperialism, in particular Wall Street and the IMF (International Monetary Fund), the antique capitalism of the nineteenth and early twentieth centuries has been re-imposed along old imperial routes.

Over the last four decades the political and economic architecture of global capitalism complete with developed institutional frameworks and infrastructure have been forcibly re-imposed on much of the world, non-compliant governments replaced and indigenous economies destroyed so that what remains of Western political economy is domination and control by radical capitalist ideologues.

At the level of global 'system,' the capacity for resolution of systemically destabilizing events through existing 'political' channels has been handed to global corporations and their capitalist owners who benefit from environmental destruction, wars for control of economic resources, the replacement of indigenous political economies with those dependent on capitalist extraction and the declining circumstance of 'labor.'

After NAFTA (the North American Free Trade Agreement) was passed with 'bi-partisan' support in the U.S. subsidized industrial American corn flooded Mexico and destroyed substantial portions of the peasant agriculture[56] that had sustained peasant farmers for generations. Their livelihoods destroyed, those 'freed' from the land either went to work in Maquiladoras[58], factories established by multi-national corporations in Mexico to exploit cheap labor, or they migrated to the U.S. in search of work[60].

A similar process has taken place around the globe with indigenous populations driven from lands they inhabited for centuries to facilitate capitalist 'resource' extraction that left functioning ecosystems in ruins and recently exiled populations to find new ways of existing in a world now tightly circumscribed by capitalist 'property' relations. The destruction of sustainable indigenous economies and their replacement with unsustainable industrial agriculture and newly 'freed' labor adds to the environmental catastrophe of global warming and to the human catastrophes of economic disenfranchisement and dislocation.

The 'efficient' model of industrial agriculture being imposed by Western capitalists is a major contributor to global warming through heavy dependence on fossil fuels, it poses unknown health risks through the genetic modification of crops, it replaces localized economic risk with systemic economic instability and it forces tens, if not hundreds, of millions of people into labor 'competition' in rigged labor 'markets.' And by replacing functioning indigenous economies with international dependencies imperial capitalism becomes totalizing political economy. The capacity to say 'no' requires viable alternatives that these capitalist institutions assure will never arise.

At present there are no viable, or even vaguely plausible, plans being put forward by persons and governments capable of bringing the scale of political-economic reconfiguration needed for resolution of global warming and other aggregating environmental crises. The capitalist West is the main hindrance to resolution. This leaves functioning indigenous economies, in particular low carbon footprint agriculture, as the only 'fallback' to the radical dysfunction of capitalist production. Maintaining less 'efficient' indigenous economies may seem impractical in the modern view. But it isn't the 'primativists' who are creating the circumstances where there may well be no alternative—it is the capitalist West.

The Parable of Citizens United

In 2010 the Supreme Court of the United States made a ruling in a case popularly known as 'Citizens United' that corporations as 'persons' have the right to 'free speech' through the (nearly) unrestricted expenditure of money to influence 'political' issues[62]. The primary issue put forward was the 'distribution' of political speech with corporate money being the mechanism of distribution.

Seen in broader context the ruling joins the trajectory of the consolidation of political power through the consolidation of economic power in the West. The ruling was widely decried as 'anti-democratic' because it visibly transforms power from the realm of the economic to, in the words of George Orwell, make 'some pigs more equal than others' in the realm of the political.

Western corporations have hierarchical management structures and senior managers were already in the position to 'speak' for themselves through 'their' corporations. Through the Supreme Court decision wealthy capitalists and corporate managers can place their interests in monopoly positions in the 'marketplace of ideas' of Western fantasy.

The 'Citizens United' ruling is considered one more step toward total corporate control of Western political economy. But the basic idea of concentrating political power through the designation of personhood dates to the United States' Constitution when slaves were designated 'three-fifths[64]' a person to accrue political representation to slave 'owners.' It is telling that the U.S. legal precedent that corporations are persons dates to the immediate aftermath of the Civil War that ended the formal institution of slavery.

Money is the ultimate reconstitution of capitalist metaphysics in 'the world.' It is the thing-act that unites intent with capacity, the social 'fact' that comes into being as act through 'its' expenditure. In the realm of the economic money is the mechanism of economic man 'reaching out' to act in / on the world. As 'thing' money exists as paper, coins or digital entries. But it only 'becomes' its social fact through exchange.

Likewise, corporations are thing-act, a particular mode of social organization designated through legal charter to be a whole that is theorized to be more than the sum of its parts, a 'thing' that is socially realized through its 'acts.' Outside of legal charter corporations are 'persons' in the same sense that a home mortgage is—there are actual persons who are its referents but the mortgage itself is no more a person than are other social creations like a pogo stick or a dump truck.

The alleged rationale for the designation, to give corporations the ability to enter into legally enforceable contracts, reconstitutes the metaphysical 'self' of economic man as a bodiless mind, the 'brain in a vat' of Cartesian philosophical speculation. That actual people reside inside these bodiless 'minds' is the point of incoherence, multiplication through reduction of the 'self' of metaphysical self-determination. The 'method' of corporate 'persons' then is money—the mechanism that converts 'thought' into action in 'the world.'

As method money is the 'physical' expression of metaphysical 'will,' the wants and desires of 'persons' as they are reconstituted in the world. The social act of 'spending' implies a 'person' doing the spending and the logical circle is completed. While the legal precedent that corporations are 'persons' was established long ago their recent reconstitution as capital 'P' persons appears to derive from confusion, deliberate or not, over the Cartesian metaphysical concept of the 'self' doing the speaking as it has been reconstituted in Western political economy.

To the extent that the corporate and 'personal' politics of corporate managers don't directly overlap 'Citizens United' designates corporations to 'speak for themselves.' This is implausible on its face—corporations are social institutions and any 'speech,' in the form of funded politics, will emanate from actual people. What 'Citizens United' further abstracts is existing political economy from its alleged constituents.

Before the ascendance of corporations modern nation-states were put forward as representing analogous abstract interests, those of 'the nation.' Nations can create and enforce laws, enter into contracts and serve the narrow interests of 'their' 'leaders' as general analog to the newfound place of corporations as socially defined persons. However, Western capitalist democracies drew 'their' social legitimacy, however implausibly, from the 'will of the people.'

The Citizens United ruling formally replaces the 'people' of Western capitalist democracy with corporate plutocracy through the asymmetrical distribution of income and wealth to be expended in 'politics.' To be clear, the political philosophy and theories that asserted such was ever not the case are the same premises from which capitalist democracy was reconstituted as political economy—the conceit is put forward as a legitimation strategy, not as either description or intent.

And the 'power' of nationalism was always through reifying the historical, cultural and social contingency of 'nation' much as designating the wholly contrived entities of corporations now is. Executives acting in their corporate capacities could in theory act against their 'own' interests by pushing corporate costs such as environmental destruction off onto themselves as citizens. However, unlike for the rest of us, the difference would find its way into their very own paychecks. And only people who perceive themselves to be immune from negative consequences would do this.

Capitalism is in theory a 'system' of economic allocation—economic 'democracy' in the Western frame is the 'right' of economic participants to differentiated outcomes that are in theory determined by economic contribution. The political analog would be the right of political participants to differentiated outcomes based on their political contribution—hardly the 'one person, one vote' of the advertising slogans for Western democracy. But it is a base premise of 'representative' democracy.

If, in the terms of the metaphysical conception of the Western 'self,' capitalism were the political economy of 'just' economic distribution because it (in theory) allocates economic resources based on economic contribution, why would the distribution of political power be fundamentally different? The central difference in 'outcomes' is the quantum of measure—income, wealth and profits are 'concrete' as reified economic virtue, the circular 'proof' of economic contribution.

The political power that accrues from winning elections is the 'political' analog of this economic virtue. The Supreme Court could in theory have ruled that no money may be spent on political issues and (implausibly) separated the realms. But by designating political expenditure 'speech' the Supreme Court 'freed' this quantum of economic virtue to be used to influence the realm of the political. What the Supreme Court didn't do is 'free' the expenditure of 'political capital' to influence capitalist enterprise.

And in fact the Western conceit is that economic 'efficiency' is served by leaving capitalist enterprise relatively unencumbered by political influence while capitalists are granted increasing power to determine the realm of the political. This can be seen in 'trade agreements' where the goal is to 'free' corporations from governance by civil authorities.

Either the money whose expenditure is political speech has genesis in social virtue—the just distribution of capitalism, or it is straightforwardly a corruption of politics. Likewise, in the theories of representative democracy political power has virtuous genesis as 'the will of the people' or it is illegitimate. Put differently, why would those who possess money, wealth, be perceived to have more insight into the realm of the political than those who possess political power would have into capitalist enterprise?

To be clear, this theoretical incoherence in the service of capitalists and capitalism is all within the frame of capitalist democracy—it isn't critique from the 'outside.' To assume fundamental difference between the realms of the political and the economic misses the basis for the 'legitimacy' of capitalist democracy as it is derived from 'nature' in Western metaphysics. It is the political economy of 'freedom,' of 'free choice' by self-determined 'rational' selves—the economic choice between 'work' and 'leisure' and the political choice between this candidate and that.

Those who choose-act wisely accrue social virtue as power and wealth and those who don't aren't rewarded. This is the basic premise of the 'structure' of capitalist economic distribution. 'Wealth' accrues through 'natural' endowments, e.g. 'intelligence,' and hard work in the service of capitalist enterprise. Within this logic what 'rational' political system would put those who lack endowments and / or are lazy on equal footing with the 'intelligent' and 'hard working' in wielding political power? This very argument fitted prominently in the 'choice' of representative democracy over more direct forms in the founding documents of the U.S.

Here possession is 'its' own demonstration, the backward induction that wealth and power found 'their' rightful places because 'nature' allocated them. While utterly implausible when viewed through the lens of history, the theories of capitalist democracy are in this way used to legitimate the existing distribution of political—economic power. The rich and powerful are that way because that is how 'nature' distributed power. Citizens United reunites the political with the economic in the political economy of capitalism. Working to 'reverse' Citizens United and the ascendance of corporate power while retaining capitalist political economy misses the only theoretically coherent target there is—capitalism.

This logic of capitalism and its 'proofs' outline the broad modes of social differentiation in 'the West.' That this 'logic' as mode of demonstration is wholly circular within 'its' own argument—it is 'logically' its own criteria, ties to the circular social apologetics of its 'proofs.' How does capitalism measure the relative economic contribution of people? By how much wealth they have accrued. As broad historical metaphor slave 'masters' were credited with capital accumulation through 'ownership' of the means of production—slaves, and through their social capacity to take the product of slaves for themselves.

The United States was 'founded' by rich white slaveholders who allocated political power in the 'newfound' 'democracy' by these very theories. Slaves weren't given three-fifths of a vote in accordance with their partial designation as 'persons,' they were 'chattel' property and this designation and the political power that accrued with it went to the slaveholders. This is the historical basis of capitalist democracy. Why would rich white slaveholders put forward developed theories about the 'natural' basis of democracy as the 'Founding Fathers' did?

The answer is that capitalist democracy is the circular 'legitimation' device for social privilege, for its alleged basis in the laws of 'nature.' What then was the starting point of this capitalist democracy, the time when the existing distribution of political and economic power played no role in its subsequent distribution? Never. When were the 'freed' slaves put on equal footing with the rich white men who had stolen their labor—made 'free' to 'compete' as 'equals' without hereditary disadvantage? Never.

The political economists Adam Smith and John Locke[66] put forward wholly deduced 'histories' of an 'earlier' period as the basis for the 'fresh' starting point capitalism needed to suggest it ever wasn't a rigged game. This history versus its related mythology illustrates the otherworldliness of life in the metaphysical ether—the wholly imagined universe of capitalist theory that backs into the 'just' distribution of existing political economy through empty logic. This is the history that the Supreme Court continues to codify with decisions like Citizens United.

But surely 'the present' is the time when political economy is distributed irrespective of prior distribution, outside of the accumulated fortunes of slavery, executive machinations for self-enrichment, financial gamesmanship, military aggression in the service of capitalist enterprise and the imperial predations that divided and organized 'the world' to assure access to economic resources and pliable work forces. 'Citizens United' explicitly grants political-economic power to capitalists over 'their' workers and over labor more broadly by magnifying the political imperatives of capitalism and of the particular capitalists who are its beneficiaries.

Any analysis of modern 'outsourced' manufacturing finds it fairly recently relocated to the ancient imperial routes from which so much Western wealth 'mysteriously' accrued. As far back as the time of Adam Smith there existed public understanding that capitalists used 'combines[68],' collective action, to exert power over labor to keep wages low and working conditions 'cheap.'

The current high concentration of wealth in the West came through imperial predations hidden in corporate profits, through stock options dubiously granted corporate executives by captive Boards of Directors and through 'free-trade' agreements that place the rich and their managers in direct competition with 'labor' for share of corporate revenues.

The power over 'state' policies that 'Citizens United' codifies makes a mockery of the capitalist contention that economic wealth accrues on the basis of economic contribution rather than on existing political-economic power. And the focus on 'corporate' power places a layer of abstraction between the real actors—capitalist owners and senior executives of these corporations, and their being held socially accountable for the actions of 'their' corporations.

In the realm of the political 'Citizens United' makes a mockery of the Western notion of political 'self-determination' through 'democratic' participation. In opposition to the mythology, the 'representative democracy' of the United States is exactly as it appears—representative of the interests of the already rich and powerful. 'Citizens United' didn't create this circumstance—the concentration of political-economic power to levels not seen in modern history preceded the ruling by a decade or more.

But it is clear evidence that the broad institutions of capitalist democracy like the Supreme Court no longer feel the need for misdirection, for maintaining the pretense that it is a 'system' of economic and political self-determination. Existing economic power is being used to buy political power to perpetuate 'itself,' to arrange circumstance just as wealthy capitalists have always done. Citizens United but formalizes this relationship, puts it out there for all who have eyes to see.

Capitalist theory puts the rich forward as the creators of their own circumstance. Where precisely did all of the 'real estate' regularly being transacted in the U.S. come from—what was its genesis as 'property?' Where did the accumulated wealth now put forward as 'speech' come from? Corporate power and improbable 'market' relations derive social legitimacy from the instantiated theology of metaphysical 'self-determination' that places all outcomes in the realm of 'nature.' History places them social relations, in factual political economy, not in improbable deduction about the nature of the world.

Money is only speech in metaphysical equivalence—in theory, not in the world. And corporations are only 'persons' in a metaphysical sense—the metaphor exists in the realm of metaphysics, in thought, not in the world. Speech requires a speaker and corporate charters do not speak. Expression of will requires someone with a will to do the expressing.

The idea of a 'person' in thought but not in fact is at the core of the Cartesian metaphysical conceit. Lost to the Supreme Court is that its genesis with Descartes was tied to the Christian idea of a soul. The Citizens United decision isn't simply a 'mistake,' it is an extension of the 'logic' of capitalist democracy, paradox and all. Were the Supreme Court to rule that corporations have souls the logical circle would be completed.

How to Kill a Planet Without Really Trying

A BASIC PREMISE OF CAPITALISM IS THAT IT IS A FORM OF ECONOMIC production that produces more than it consumes. This idea is rooted in the genesis of capitalist economics. The 'surplus' that remained when more agricultural 'output' was produced than was consumed by the farmer formed the base element of capitalist trade and the base metaphor for 'profit.'

Driven by the profit 'motive,' capitalist production is claimed to transform the elements that go into it, 'inputs,' into more than the sum of the parts. This is in theory achieved through 'efficiency,' through the 'rational' allocation of inputs, the materials and processes, of economic production. Economic efficiency is the process of creating more from less, the alchemy of economic rationality applied to 'the world' that produces 'surplus,' the excess of output over input, that finds its 'worldly' expression as 'profit.'

The overwhelming presence of the goods that capitalism 'produces,' the stores full of consumer goods, the materiel of capitalist militarism, the car lots, air travel and theme parks—the stuff of consumer culture, lends credence to the perception that it is nature's bonus for right living, the treasure awarded the ciphers of nature's law for correct interpretation of 'the rules' of 'the world.'

Global warming, wars to control economic resources, recurrent economic and political crises and the forced instantiation of the political and economic mechanisms of capitalist imperialism detract from its fact, but not necessarily from this perception. What capitalism does unequivocally do is occupy space as political economy. By occupying this space its fact is presented / perceived as inevitable, as the existing order that can only be replaced within 'its' rules of legitimacy. Who could rightly object to an economic order that produces so much stuff?

In a narrow sense the physical detritus of capitalist production, environmental degradation now accumulating to global warming and the social pathologies of imperial social relations, is considered 'externalized' cost, the unfortunate and largely unrelated coincidence of capitalist 'wealth' production. In the global sense this accumulated social and environmental degradation is a totalizing force, the imposition of the costs of producing the 'stuff' of capitalism forced onto 'the world' by those to whom its 'benefits' accrue.

This abstraction of capitalist 'product' from the broad circumstances of its production is a / the central characteristic of 'profit' extraction, the intended unintended by-product of this production that simultaneously finds its way into the town water supply as toxic waste and into the capitalist's pocket as 'profit.' There is no 'information' to be found at the level of 'product' that both toxic waste and 'profit' are its co-products.

And more to the point, at the point of exchange particular 'consumers' are unlikely to bear either the burden or the benefit of these co-products. The capitalist alchemy behind 'surplus' production can hardly find demerit in the vagaries of the climate or the toxic runoff that washes onto the neighbor's fields—that is the realm of 'nature.' That the neighbor, and more broadly 'the world,' has no capacity to right the wrong goes without saying by the fact it occurred. And the 'consumers' of system lack both knowledge of the broad circumstances of production and any direct interest in them.

When considered in coincidence with wars for control of resources and the imposition of modes and methods of social control to facilitate capitalist production and wealth extraction, the contention capitalism produces more than it consumes depends very much on limiting the scope of the costs considered in the calculation. As with the alchemy of yore, if capitalism produces environmental and / or social crisis that substantially harms 'the world' its product in 'stuff' becomes mere coincidence, evidence of the mistake that never should have occurred.

The rhetorical starting point, the posture, of capitalist political economy is as accomplished fact, the arrangement of circumstance that 'everyone' contributed to but for which no one is responsible; to be taken as given before constructive engagement can proceed. When the economic relations and practices that are theorized to produce global warming are discussed the starting premise is that potential solutions must be carefully considered so as not to produce 'unintended' consequences that interrupt the existing economic order, this when no such care was put into the development of the political economy that produced it. When alternative energy and alternatives to energy are discussed the starting premise is that the energy 'needs' of the global industrial and consumer economies are established fact that must be met and bested before material effort is put into the development of 'alternatives.'

In recent decades 'the world' has been so arranged that reversing global warming and rethinking the role of 'energy' in political economy require challenging the base premises and institutions of capitalism. Inferred in its 'fact' is that 'the world' capitalists have created is indubitable. But this is a rhetorical device designed to end consideration of real alternatives to it, to delimit potential solutions to the self-serving logic that benefits those responsible for its most destructive consequences.

Put forward in real and implied defense mechanisms is that the potential to change 'the world' ended when modern capitalism rebuilt it in 'its' image. Also implied is the totalizing and anti-historical contention that only capitalism can change the world. The ideological frame used to explain these destructive consequences is 'unintended;' the self-serving division of benefits and detriments into 'intended' and 'unintended' products as if they are divisible.

If they truly were divisible the 'solutions' would be simple—produce the 'benefits' and forego the detriments, the social and environmental destruction, which capitalism produces. But because these 'unintended' consequences are indissociable from their 'products' their toxic effects are as much 'intended' product as are Sport Utility Vehicles, Credit Default Swaps and margarine. And herein lies 'the problem:' because these adverse 'products' are indissociable from those theorized to be desirable, there are no 'solutions' from within the system of political economy that produces them.

Capitalism is put forward by its proponents as the necessary and 'given' starting point for addressing its social and environmental consequences because all other solutions require the radical reconsideration of it as sustainable political economy. Conversely, 'solutions' from outside of the closed internal logic of capitalist theory challenge the entire frame by illuminating the realm left unconsidered by it—if 'efficiency' isn't efficient then how is it 'efficient?'

The answer lies in the way that metaphysical reasoning parses the realms of consideration—'local' efficiency has capitalists profiting by forcing others to bear the costs of their production through polluting. But the costs are borne by others making the production inefficient in the larger sense. The point is that local efficiency isn't just a sub-set of the realm of possible efficiencies; it is in terms of looming environmental catastrophe antithetical to 'global' efficiencies. In this sense capitalist 'efficiency' is one of the worst ideas ever conceived.

And were these detrimental environmental and social consequences displayed as 'its' product with equal fervor, if different purpose, would it be considered viable? The premise that capitalist democracy produces what people 'want' collides with its fact that it also produces what people don't want. And this leaves aside the engineered 'wants' resulting from a century of advertising as capitalist propaganda.

The 'solutions' eternally put forward derive from this same internal logic of capitalism. Predictably, the first is 'more' capitalism, 'market-based' solutions such as tradable pollution 'rights' that operate under the premise that reframing 'unintended' consequences as market 'products' affects their metaphysical conversion from 'unintended' to 'intended' consequence.

The base premise of tradable pollution 'rights' is that capitalist production is given fact with a 'growth rate' of toxic pollution thrown in for good measure. Missing from consideration is that capitalist 'profit' is the product of forcing costs of production onto others. Any 'solution' that takes capitalism as its premise is destined to react after social and environmental harm has already been inflicted. From the capitalist perspective 'incentives' not to pollute are incentives to threaten ever more pollution.

It is hardly an accident that Wall Street banks are the central proponents of 'financializing' the 'unintended' products of capitalist production. These banks earn trading profits from pollution rights and they benefit from the ability of corporations to force the costs of their 'unintended' production onto others through the credit 'enhancement' benefit of doing so. In the thirty years since tradable pollution 'rights[70]' were first proposed the quantity of greenhouse gases entering the atmosphere has increased exponentially[72].

These 'rights' are created to promote the fiction that putting a 'market price' on environmental destruction will limit its production when the fact of its existence is already as a failure of markets under the relevant economic theories. Creating a secondary market system to 'correct' the 'inefficiencies' of the primary system is tacit admission that the base premises are flawed. For all that has been written by economists on economic 'incentives,' the base incentive of capitalism is to force others to bear the costs of capitalist production. A different way to frame this is that capitalism is a race to destroy the world by design.

When capitalists are gaming the secondary system through proposing fictional projects that will be 'foregone' with the granting of more pollution 'rights,' through public unwillingness to fund the costs of effective international oversight, through the unwillingness of sovereign governments to allow their regulatory capacities to be overridden by external 'private' interests and through legal machinations designed to get around the prohibitions agreed to, will a tertiary system be then proposed? It is neither ironic nor 'unintended' that proponents of 'more capitalism' are also working through 'free-trade' agreements to limit the capacity of civil governments to forcibly constrain corporations from increasing the quantity of toxic pollution they produce.

The second type of 'solution' to environmental catastrophe being proposed from within the capitalist frame is to develop technological 'work-arounds' such as to radically reconfigure the oceans to absorb greenhouse gases or to develop nuclear energy for which there exists no plausible / feasible way of safely disposing of the resulting nuclear waste.

These 'solutions' and multitudinous others are derived from the same reasoning that produced the 'unintended' consequences of capitalist production they now are being proposed to ameliorate. This reasoning in all cases proceeds from the premises that capitalist production is given and eternal fact and that additional layers of capitalist technocracy are preferable to simply limiting or ending entirely the production responsible for the socially and environmentally toxic consequences.

The ultimate purpose and likely effect of doing so is to further instantiate capitalist technocracy into global political economy. The 'carrot' being offered is that 'the world' can continue to benefit from capitalist production, albeit with exponentially increasing complexity and with the number of people experiencing its 'benefit' shrinking steadily. The 'stick' used as defense mechanism is the theorized economic catastrophe that will result from ending this toxic production.

The frame put forward is that 'nature' requires capitalism to meet 'our' material needs when in fact existing capitalists are using engineered economic dependencies to hold 'the world' hostage to their strategies of economic extraction. Current circumstance of social and environmental catastrophe is the outcome of the earlier instantiation of capitalism into

/ as Western political economy. The strategy is to eternally 'up the ante' under the illusion / delusion that today's failure is always just one step prior to tomorrow's 'success.' The premise that leaving those who created the problem 'in charge' of choosing / developing solutions is collectively suicidal.

As a practical matter the scientific evidence in favor of catastrophic climate change is to a large extent produced in the countries of the West most resistant to political-economic resolution of it. Science as 'solution' apparently exists on the wrong side of capitalist profits. And once engineered dependencies are accounted for the argument against radical reversal of capitalist production and its associated dysfunctions is the trade of trinkets, gadgets and toys for 'the world.'

These engineered dependencies are real in that political economy of the West, and increasingly of the global East and South, is built as crisis-generation machine—any slight interruption in intent and / or fact of capitalist production is designed to cause mass social dislocations. The paradox of these dependencies is that they fail to take into account the intended unintended consequences of capitalist production—the increasing complexity and interrelatedness of Western political economy is the proverbial bottomless pit of related dysfunctions.

A glimpse of the power to create near instantaneous catastrophe was seen in the economic and financial collapse begun in 2008 in the West. The 'recovery' from that event was for its malefactors alone[74]. The contingencies for climate change currently being undertaken are to 'manage' 'its' consequences much as economic recovery was engineered for a few hundred wealthy families with the rest of us left to our own devices. To be clear, the 'plan' in the West is for new layers of complexity, and with it, ever more engineered dependencies.

The U.S. in particular is in the process of establishing regional 'centers' to 'advise' businesses affected by climate change on how to 'adjust' to predicted changes. Undoubtedly the next step is to 'privatize' the effort. Finally, the ongoing build-out of the mechanisms and strategies of social control that can be seen in surveillance technologies, in laws that give latitude to 'authorities' to address social contingencies as they see fit, in the militarization and privatization of the police and in the abandonment of social purpose in political economy together approximate admission by Western powers that the plan is to continue on existing trajectories at all costs.

Fracking Made Easy

THE PRACTICE NOW BEING USED IN THE U.S. AND RAPIDLY SPREAD-ing around the globe of hydraulic fracturing, 'fracking,' to release and capture 'trapped' natural gas, provides an object lesson in how capitalism relates to environmental devastation. The basic technology of fracking is to drill holes deep into the earth to force a witch's brew of chemicals under high pressure into rock formations to release embedded natural gas.

The fracking 'fluid' being injected into the ground is composed of dozens of different toxic chemicals that are used in 'proprietary' combinations[76]. The fracking fluid is patented to prevent easy relation being made between it and the toxic contamination increasingly found in water tables and in and around fracking sites. With water tables resting far above the rock formations being fracked, lining the fracking holes to prevent fracking fluid from contaminating water supplies might make the practice less environmentally catastrophic.

But lining the holes is prohibitively expensive—fracking only makes economic 'sense' when its costs in terms of toxic contamination are forced onto others. And in the U.S. National, State and local parks and lands are being 'released' for use in fracking, a transfer of public resources to private interests at little to no cost to them.

Many fracking companies are financed with borrowed money setting in motion the imperative that natural gas be produced quickly to make debt payments. Forcing others to bear the costs of fracking through environmental contamination serves two purposes—it reduces the costs borne by the fracking companies making debt repayment more likely. And doing so increases the likelihood of earning a 'profit' that now includes covering the cost of interest payments on borrowed money.

To be clear, the imperative of both debt and 'profit' is to cut / shift all costs, not just foregoing lining the fracking holes to protect groundwater. This tendency can be seen across the U.S. where mines, factories, and in some areas entire mountains ranges, are simply abandoned once resources have been extracted. Debt based financing creates a hierarchy of liabilities that places banks and debt-holders ahead of the people who are poisoned and whose land is destroyed.

This provides the motivation for 'smash and grab' business practices where maximum environmental devastation is produced as quickly as possible so that creditors are repaid before the companies creating the devastation become buried in lawsuits. Having then taken all assets of value out of the companies they file for bankruptcy leaving nothing for those they have harmed to claim against the harms. The fracking company principals then form new corporations and start the same process over again.

Fracking is sold as a way to bring prosperity to rural areas. People who 'own' land sell the resource rights to fracking companies for initial, and sometimes residual, compensation. In parts of the U.S. State and local governments use the 'right of imminent domain' to seize land from those who won't sell in exchange for modest compensation. Land that may have had sustainable, if modest, potential for agricultural production is poisoned by fracking to the extent that it is unusable for decades, if not centuries thereafter.

The fracking companies earn 'profits' until the natural gas supplies are exhausted. Initial academic research funded by the oil and gas industry claimed that virtually inexhaustible supplies of natural gas could be extracted using the technology. Subsequent experience found that it becomes un-economical, even with cost shifting, far more quickly than initially estimated.

Those whose land has been destroyed by fracking can abandon it. But in many cases as owners they still have liability for cleaning up the residual toxic waste created by the fracking companies. And property lines do not bind water tables—water flows across and under them. The water supplies of people who said no to fracking have been poisoned with fracking fluid by its migration. Land without clean water is worth far less than land with clean water. This poisoning of unrelated water supplies constitutes is economic taking by fracking companies.

What Western economists count as economic production is the natural gas produced from fracking. There is no deduction made for the land and water that is destroyed. The people who need medical care because they have been poisoned also count toward the 'product' of fracking.

The 'profits' that accrue are theorized to 'signal' to other capitalists that fracking is 'efficient' allocation of capital and new capitalists will in theory begin fracking until profits decline. Because existing fracking companies earn profits through cost shifting new capitalists entering the fracking business will also have to shift costs to be 'competitive.' Those who fail to do so will be relatively unprofitable and risk having 'their' assets seized by creditors and new managements installed who will shift the costs needed to 'earn' profits.

As is current practice in a growing number of U.S. States, fracking companies use their economic power to get State and local laws passed granting them virtual immunity from lawsuits and from criminal prosecution for environmental crimes. Additionally, State resources are used to build and repair roads used for fracking, to spy on, infiltrate and disrupt fracking opponents and State lands and waterways are used as dumping grounds for toxic waste that can't be dumped on 'private' lands.

Fracking isn't a 'special case' of capitalist production—it is entirely typical. Through debt-based financing and equity monetization this type of production ties directly to the 'clean' capitalism of Wall Street and international banking. Bankers wearing thousand dollar suits sit in luxury offices arranging financing for fracking companies without ever getting their hands dirty.

Fracking industry capture of 'government' provides it with infrastructure at public expense, legal cover for socially and environmentally catastrophic business practices and state power to take land, waterways and resources as needed. And the same economic accounting that counts the near total loss of a major U.S. city, New Orleans, to a hurricane as an economic plus counts the toxic devastation and destroyed lives of fracking as beneficial capitalist production.

This arrangement of circumstance is what makes 'market' solutions to environmental devastation so radically implausible. By the time a secondary market in pollution rights has been established the smash-and-grab business practices of capitalist production have already smashed and grabbed. The way to stop environmental destruction is to stop environmental destruction, not to inveigh antique economic theories that assume it doesn't happen.

Catastrophe-nomics

Copper mined in Chile finds its way into products in the U.S. and Europe under the explanation it got there through 'trade.' It is dug out of the ground by means of giant machines leaving behind land that is poisoned and barren. The process of converting the raw copper into its 'purer' form puts tons of waste into the air and renders rivers of water undrinkable.

The trade relations that bring the 'product' in its various stages and forms to 'market' evolved historically through imperialist predations, through the slaughter and displacement of indigenous populations and through the overthrow of popularly elected governments and the subsequent installation of brutal regimes that crushed political opposition to both the destructive character of copper mining and to the system of international trade that makes it economically viable.

Mining and moving the copper requires raw materials and fuel acquired through similar international machinations—through the division of the world into economically 'rational' pieces by imperial powers that were the 'victors' in the most destructive wars in human history. The 'market' price of the copper is a function of over a century of political and economic conquest. No evidence of this history remains when the copper changes hands in international markets.

The alchemist's conversion of complex social processes involving thousands of people into the commodity of copper that has purity, weight, quantity and form exchangeable at a market price assumes the market price to be its own justification, a 'backward' purification process that legitimates the social-historical process that brought the 'product' to market.

The act of exchange in 'free' markets is assumed to transmit commensurability 'down' the production process—either its totality was also 'freely' undertaken and its byproducts in the form of poisoned land, water and air, directly compensated or their benefit is conferred to the breadth of humanity through the lower market price of the 'product.'

History disappears from this process for a reason—the engineered dependence, coercion from heavily armed 'security' forces, forced relocations, corrupted political processes, poisoned resources and broken social relations are either justly 'compensated' or no transaction—no product exchanged at market price, would have occurred according to the internal logic of capitalism. All 'exchange' is 'free' according to this totalizing logic.

In introductory economics textbooks Western economics is put forward as 'the study of the allocation of scarce resources' or some other such simplistic implausibility. While hardly informative, it isn't necessarily intentionally misleading—ignorance of the genesis of Western economics is partly the result of its hegemonic character. Its base premises are deeply embedded in the Western psyche through the totalizing worldview of capitalist political economy and its institutions, through the Western understanding of the 'self' of capitalist democracy.

It is also the result of generations of specialization, the capitalist 'division of labor' applied to the study of ever-smaller pieces of capitalist ideology as it is tied to the broader Western metaphysical worldview. As such this economics has become 'its' own object, the act of political economy that is also its 'explanation.'

'The world' seen through 'its' lens exists within a closed logic as both source and result. Market exchange is 'free' because it takes place—it is 'its' own 'proof.' History is irrelevant to these truths because time stands outside of them—the 'allocation' of 'scarce resources' was always and will always be 'its' goal whether human beings exist or not. This economics has as its product 'truth' that is alleged to stand outside of the social interests from whence its questions spring.

Most Western economists would take forceful issue with the characterization of their economics as ideology. The perception from the 'inside' is of rigorous study of the major issues at the core of national economies. But from its fundamental premise of rational, self-determined individuals as the primary actors of political economy to its methods theorized to tie theory to fact; Western economics is *the* prime example of the Western intellectual tradition of Cartesian metaphysics.

And the dilemma is that this metaphysics is 'constructed' to answer its own questions. It is a closed circle of dubious propositions that through history have become so deeply instantiated that its base premises are invisible to practitioners. Through this instantiation it has become a phenomenally destructive hegemonic force, a philosophy of social control and domination that is sold as honest inquiry in the public service.

From the 'inside' philosophical critique is effete, the quibbles and musings of armchair theorists who fail to grasp the essential issues being addressed. From the outside this alleged rigor rests atop a bundle of absurd propositions and developed apologetics for an existing social order. As social apologetics, 'explanations' in support of an existing order, where is the accountability for this order, for iterative reconstitution of its dubious social philosophy in the institutions of Western political economy?

This patina of logical and methodological rigor rests atop a set of propositions so absurd that they are rarely put forward in public debate of economic issues. How do we know economic actors are 'rational?' It is only rational that they would be rational. What is the nature of the self-determination of these Western 'selves?' Who else would determine the self but the self? What is the practice of economics? It is rational selves using rational methods to 'prove' that rational selves using rational methods would act as economic models say they will. Why is rationality important? It is the only rational way to tie economic theories to their theorized outcomes.

'Who' is the object of Western economics? 'Economic man' is the object. Who is 'economic man?' S/he is a methodological construct—both no one and everyone. How can someone be both no one and everyone? S/he is the aspect of this no one in everyone. Is s/he the preponderance or a residual? Necessarily, s/he is the preponderance else there is no reason to believe s/he would act 'economically.'

Stated out loud, these propositions would likely find few takers. Placed within the formal logic of partial differential equations and dynamic stochastic general equilibrium (DSGE) models the appearance of rigor effectively renders the absurdity of these propositions opaque. Was it not for the reconstitution of this capitalist economics in the institutions of Western political economy and their impact on millions of people there would be little need for comment.

The Western idea of inquiry is presented as oppositional—'free' or 'not free,' when the more fundamental question is: why inquire? The analytical frame offers insight: the base metaphysical proposition is of an 'inside,' the inquirer, looking 'out' onto 'the world.' The premise is of a 'separation' of the Western 'self' from 'the world' it inquires about. The goal of Western economics is to reach 'out' into 'the world' to bring back its 'truth.'

This 'truth' is 'about' the world without being 'of' it, it is a psychic 'marker' indicating 'possession' of something 'of value,' 'knowledge.' Outside of geographical metaphor, where precisely does this knowledge reside if not in 'the world?' The general proposition finds analog in the capitalist goal of reaching out into the world to bring back 'wealth,' the 'product' of competent interaction with 'the world.'

The Western economist's 'product' is 'economics' and the capitalist's product is 'wealth'—capitalist production is to circumscribe the social value in theory produced, not to possess the 'products' produced themselves. This 'wealth' is a psychic marker as social artifact, its 'possession' a metaphor for a social 'claim' on its 'representations.' The Western social convention of intellectual 'property' is the formal reconstitution of these psychic markers as 'possession.' Western 'inquiry' is the accumulation of these 'possessions.'

The idea of 'freedom' at work in 'free inquiry' is as unimpeded by 'political' restrictions, the act of self-determined individuals to ascertain 'true' truth through agreed upon modes of proof as social demonstration. In Western economics 'freedom' of inquiry is within agreed upon constraints, from within an agreed upon set of existing 'truths,' using agreed upon methods.

As long as the premises are of 'rational,' 'self-determined' individuals using an operational mode of 'rationality' to interact with a world they are not a part of, anything goes. The 'practice' of economics is as a bounded realm of inquiry—how else can 'it' 'be' economics? Its overwhelming preponderance occurs securely within the political economy it purports to describe; from the circular concept of the 'self' of 'self-determination' that is also the 'object' of its inquiry.

'Objectivity' is the relation of this 'self' to 'truth' that 'can't be helped,' the proof from 'the world' that stands outside of human interests and social relations. 'Objectivity' keeps the economist clearly on 'the inside,' as observer of the 'truth' of 'the world,' without risking contamination as actor in / on 'it.' Western economists 'have views' through deference to 'objectivity.' Through 'the data' they speak on behalf of 'the world.' 'Free inquiry' is thus also bounded by 'the world,' by its facts as they are 'brought back' through competent method to the economist.

The quest of capitalist economics follows the Cartesian 'will to truth' where, despite enthusiastic disagreement amongst practitioners over many of the particulars, the idea of timeless and universal truth 'discovered' through 'rational' methods is its primary motive. Despite two centuries of economic 'discovery' recurrent economic catastrophes have forced a façade of humility, a public posture amongst economists that public service is their ultimate goal.

'We' still have 'a lot of work to do' is the eternal refrain. The economic truths of the world are difficult 'to uncover.' 'We' are 'only at the beginning' of 'this line of inquiry.' The rhetorical strategy is to be the 'true' arbiter of what the circular 'we' 'know,' the hard facts of the world that confronts 'us.' But the imperial language and reach of Western economics illustrates its totalizing hubris.

This economic 'truth,' 'market' economics, is being used to restructure global political economy in 'its' image with no such humility in evidence. The capitalist motive—'profits,' is metaphor for truth as evidence of competence in traversing the distance between the metaphysical ether and 'the world.' Profit is 'proof' of the bundle of premises of capitalist economics through backward induction—profit wouldn't exist if the capitalist alchemy didn't produce more than the sum of its parts. However, profit as metaphor faces the challenge of circularity. Like the gambler who loses one million dollars to 'win' ten thousand, only the theorized costs of capitalism enter the calculus, not the actual costs.

The 'freedom to' economic inquiry is fundamentally reactive, it is 'freedom from' politically imposed restrictions under a narrow view of politics. It proceeds from the premise that the 'freedom to' is unimpeded by material want, that the capacity for inquiry is determined by the social utility of the inquiry rather than from the closed set of economic interests that fund it.

The mythology is of patent clerks and tax collectors discovering important scientific truths in their 'spare' time when its fact is of developed bureaucracies working in the service of existing political economy to produce strategies of legitimation for prevailing social relations. Economic inquiry is posed as oppositional within its circumscribed realm; its 'truth' is the product of rule-based contests between inquirers without regard to its worldly reciprocal, the realm of that not inquired 'into.'

This point is more material than effete; the social value of economic inquiry is presupposed through the filter of existing bureaucracy in the service of prevailing political economy. How is it known which inquiries will yield 'results' before they are undertaken and who determines the value of the prospective results? 'Free inquiry' in its Western incarnation is a rhetorical device of the 'will to truth,' the posture of allowing the secular god of science to answer questions so carefully framed that they leave only the desired answers among those to be 'discovered.'

The economics that are brought to the fore—that 'inform' public perceptions of scientifically 'correct' modes of social organization, are those that support prevailing economic relations. Following the Great Depression Keynesian economics prevailed because the economic prescriptions derived from it 'saved' capitalism without questioning its fundamental premises.

Within Western institutions of political economy 'oppositional' economics are tightly circumscribed—Keynes 'saved' capitalism by explaining its tendency toward catastrophe as 'paradox' rather than as destabilizing contradiction. The 'free market' economics that followed Keynes prevailed in large measure because the political-economic rupture that the Great Depression threatened had been resolved by the time it was recovered.

With the ascendance of Keynesian economics organized opposition to the pre-Keynesian worldview had been effectively diminished, scattered and re-directed. In its 'time' Keynesian economics was considered 'true,' as was the economics that preceded and followed it. This 'truth' is held together through the rhetorical device of 'progress.' The idea of progress was used to frame these theoretical breaks and ruptures as innovations, to frame post-Keynesian economics as 'correcting' mistakes and enhancing 'truths' when its preponderance is a return to the antique totalizing logic that preceded Keynes.

Method is the Western economist's mechanism / technology for seeing the world 'as it really is' and those who are competent with it—intelligent in the sense of possessing a specific form of operational rationality, can do 'the work' to see the world and therefore to 'possess' its truth. Method ties to capitalist theory in that it is the fundamental capacity of economic man. Western economists are 'economic wo/men' acting in the capacity of 'economists.'

'Rational' extension through method is the way economic man as economist studies 'himself' to gain 'true knowledge' of the world. 'The economy' of the economist is the profession of economics and its remainder as actor in political economy. The economic 'models' of Western economists represent the 'method' of rational extension—of Cartesian metaphysics, and therefore the implied 'method' of economic man acting economically.

Economic method—deductive logic expressed as mathematics and 'proved' with statistics, is the economists' toolbox and general analog for the method of competent capitalists. Business schools teach the technologies of rational extension, of capitalist economic method, through applications—through 'rational' business management, accounting, finance and human relations. It is not accidental that most Western economists are employed in business—in capitalist enterprise.

Disagreement over possession of economic 'truth' is disagreement over competence with method, not disagreement over the 'truth' existing to be 'discovered.' This 'truth' is true knowledge of 'the world'—timeless, universal and standing outside of human interests. It is social currency, a possession that accrues social power to its possessor.

The tendency of the truths that best support prevailing political economy to be brought to the fore adds institutional context, and with it 'support,' to the truth 'discovery' process. Economic 'truth' that stands in contrast faces a 'factual' counter-factual, the mode of social organization that 'works' until it doesn't, as evidence 'to the contrary.'

Keynesian economics worked until it didn't. 'Free-market' economics worked until it didn't. Sequential replacement of one timeless and universal truth, or set of truths, with another does nothing to diminish the 'truth' standing of this truth while it is true. 'Proof' is the arbiter that stands outside of social life, the artifact from 'the world' that closes off argument over true possession.

This 'proof' finds its truth in prevailing political economy—who can argue with 'the facts?' The 'data' supports the 'truth' it is drawn from. Its possession is demonstration of competent relation to 'the world' that yields its object, 'truth,' as social capital. Capitalist economics has similar structure—profits are demonstration of 'true' understanding of 'the world' and of response to its truths in ways that demonstrate this competence. Profit is truth reconstituted as social currency.

In Western academic economics the capitalist metaphysical construct is 'decomposed' into the 'microeconomics' of the rational, self-determined actors of capitalist theory and 'macroeconomics' that concerns itself with economic 'system' as it is theorized to exist / function.

Microeconomic actors choose between consumer products and 'labor / not labor'—existents that precede them in time-space. Labor is to participate in an existing 'job' and 'not labor' is to not participate—'leisure.' 'Job' is reaction to explicit and implied instructions within pre-existing circumstance as part of a metaphysical 'production function.'

Likewise, macroeconomics presupposes economic 'system,' the aggregation of microeconomic actors with frictions and paradox standing between 'system' and straight aggregation. Micro and macro economic actors react to a pre-existing world by degree of 'rational' relation to it. Economic 'satisfaction' as psychic / social artifact is acquired through degree of rational competence in relating to 'the world.'

This satisfaction as social artifact is currency, the 'payoff' for a job well done to be used to purchase goods and services. As psychic artifact it is the reward for competent expenditure of social currency, for making the 'correct' choice between a loaf of bread and a gallon of milk. Capitalism as it is posed in Western economics is a satisfaction generating system with the distance between its 'promise' and simple aggregation of individual satisfactions expressed as macroeconomic 'performance.'

The inability of capitalist economics to explain historical development—to explain how its base objects of 'markets' and 'economic system' came into being, is a function of the temporal / atemporal divide of Cartesian metaphysics. The Cartesian construct is of dual realms, the realm of the world and the realm of truths 'about' the world that stand outside of time and space.

As atemporal thought 'objects' these truths were as 'true' in the age of the dinosaurs as they will be ten thousand years hence. Because these eternal and invariant truths are theorized to be about 'the world,' the world that they are about must also be eternal and invariant.

The antique political economists John Locke and Adam Smith attempted to bridge this temporal / atemporal divide by positing implausible histories—anti-histories really, of an amorphous 'earlier period' that led to a 'starting point' for economic truths after which they were invariant.

In their favor, both Locke and Smith at least attempted to address the problem of geographical metaphor—the existence of atemporal 'truth' that nonetheless exists temporally. Back in 'the world,' if people create history and its 'objects'—markets and the economy, the 'timeless and universal' truths of capitalist economics are temporal, they didn't exist before they were socially created and won't exist with some other configuration of political economy.

The question of the genesis of markets is fundamental in terms of both their nature and preponderance. If markets 'self-generated' as artifact of 'nature' as Western economics have it there is the question of why they did so where and when they did rather than across the whole of history? The 'self-evidence' of market exchange requires overlooking other modes of political economy—the overwhelming preponderance of economic production throughout history, that doesn't fit within the narrative of either markets or exchange.

Framed differently, the 'markets' of capitalist theory are metaphysical imposition, thought 'objects' overlaid on the breadth of temporal social relations as 'essential' characteristic. 'Markets' are a central object of capitalist theory because they are assumed to be, not because they have outsized relation in political economy.

The relevance is that in capitalist theory economic production is reactive—capitalists produce goods to sell in markets that are theorized to already exist. But how did the markets in their capitalist incarnation already exist without products to be traded in them? History provides an answer, largely from the role of agricultural 'surplus,' the excess of what was grown, fished or farmed over what was needed by the farmer that was traded in markets created for this purpose. However, the question is not whether or not markets exist, but rather how they came to exist within the wholly reactive worldview of capitalist economics?

The theorized purpose of capitalist production—to produce what rational, self-determined people want and will pay for in 'self-generated' markets, faces challenges in each of these dimensions. Cartesian 'rationality' is both characteristic and method—deductive logic premised on 'first principles.' This rationality in capitalist economics has particular structure—it is 'operational,' meaning logically 'mechanical,' 'demonstrated' through logical deduction.

The 'choice' between buying a loaf of bread or a container of milk weighs relative psychic 'satisfactions' against prices and a 'rational' calculus results in a decision of which to buy. These satisfactions exist in the metaphysical ether, demonstrated only by solving for missing values in the economic algebra. Again, genesis is an issue—the two 'goods' are assumed to already exist.

In capitalist economies the people who buy goods and services also largely produce goods and services. However, capitalist economics poses the 'choice' on both ends as reactive. The producers of goods are divided between 'labor' which reacts to 'choice' of jobs and capitalists who react to markets with 'choices' of products.

Labor also reacts to this choice of goods as 'consumers.' Inside of this construct historical development, the social creation of factual political economy in history, can't be explained and outside of it labor both produces and consumes goods—the role of the capitalist is administrative, responding with supply to market 'demand' in markets already assumed to exist.

Labor is presented as reactive—it 'chooses' between jobs already existing in the labor market. The true genesis of this market is historical—tied to two centuries of imperial strategies to 'free' labor from indigenous economic production so that 'it' would have no choice but to participate in capitalist production.

The absence of history in Western economics 'mystifies' this historical development, but it does so from the Cartesian ether, not from some brilliant conspiracy to hide history. Left unaccounted for in the capitalist calculus is the value of the indigenous economies destroyed. Within this economic logic capitalists hire labor as 'input' into the production 'process'—labor doesn't produce goods, capitalists, or rather the 'system' of capitalism, does.

The question then is: where did these capitalists with the capital to hire labor in anticipation of markets for their goods self-generating into existence come from? Infinite regress is the logical strategy in the Cartesian frame when the questions are historical. History as lived existence begs the question of the geographical location of this 'view from nowhere' that is capitalist metaphysics? Without some accounting of history Western economics devolves into simple assertion under the insistence that it is something more.

The temporal / atemporal game of 'deduced' history goes far in explaining the capitalist conceit that nothing existed before capitalism. Inferred in this theory is that people were rolling around in the dirt unable to feed themselves before capitalism 'rescued' them from starvation. This view of history and the role of capitalism is part of the neo-liberal canon and motivation for its true believers.

In this economics 'labor' exists as 'leisure'—dim lay-abouts swilling beer and watching endless re-runs on television, without a job 'supplied' by capitalist enterprise. Psychic 'satisfactions' again come into play with the 'choice' of work or 'leisure' theorized to be a function of the price of labor. When the psychic satisfaction of 'leisure' is outweighed by compensation for labor people get up off of the couch and go to work. When the price is too low labor returns to the couch. The question of what supports this 'natural' state of human existence, the rent, beer and the television set, without a paycheck is left unasked and most certainly unanswered.

Once 'labor' is assumed to be reactive—to act rationally based on our 'selves' reaching out from the ether to deduce the true state of the world, an opposition, a 'choice', is required—'labor' or 'not labor.' The Cartesian frame cannot accommodate physicality because physicality requires breaching the ether—allowing 'in' a tie between 'the world' and the metaphysical 'self' that is not the result of rational method.

Endless debate has been had by Western economists around the relative importance of 'needs' such as food, shelter, education, health care and social life versus the psychic 'wants' put forward as the choice between existing goods and services. The problem again is that needs are of 'the world' while the process of 'rational extension' proceeds from the metaphysical ether—hunger, cold and ill health are 'felt' rather than deduced.

The Western 'philosophy of science' poses the problem as induction versus deduction; 'evidence' based 'rational' inquiry versus deduction from first principles. But induction assumes / requires the same metaphysical divide as deduction, a distance between the inquirer and the inquired into. It also requires a realm for 'storing' information brought back from the world. The realm occupies 'economic' space as what 'we,' the no one in everyone, 'know.'

Both are put forward as methods to 'true' truth as social currency. Rene Descartes' deductive 'proof' of his own existence—'he thinks, therefore he is[78]' could in theory have been, 'he eats a peanut butter sandwich, therefore he is' with his 'proof' being the act of eating the sandwich, but there is no method to 'true' truth there—no analytical 'system' of separating 'truth' from the mundane musings of those who never thought to question their own existence.

The metaphysical frame assures that 'needs' will never seriously challenge the psychic 'wants' of capitalist economics—any such effort quickly devolves to competing 'truth' claims without resolving the broader understanding of material being that renders the Cartesian analytical construct reductive to the point of irrelevance.

Within the frame of capitalist economics 'needs' may be evidence of broader being but they 'occur' in the mind as psychic objects—how else could they be 'known?' As psychic objects there is no 'objective' basis to privilege needs over wants—the rich man 'wants' a thirteenth television set and the poor man 'wants' a meal and shelter from the weather. In the broader capitalist frame both have 'reacted' to the choice between 'labor' and 'not labor' at prices relative to their 'endowments.'

Endowments result from both innate ability and from self-determined actors choosing to forgo 'leisure' to 'earn' them. The 'price' of labor is a function of endowments 'earned' and / or 'naturally' occurring. And paying labor more than 'its' value is to redistribute the capitalist system's resources away from productive uses to unproductive uses—everyone loses because 'the system' suffers.

In this context fulfilling needs outside of the economic distribution of markets 'rewards' market failure. The 'system' is an efficient allocation device. If everyone 'plays by the rules' 'it' will produce the most that can be produced. To divert resources to 'needs' makes all of us poorer.

Within this frame history is nowhere to be found—the genesis of Western 'property' in genocide against indigenous peoples, race 'relations' from the chattel property of slavery to the prison industrial complex and the tendency of capitalists to favor strategies of social repression and immiseration that keep labor poor, hungry and desperate, have no place in 'economics.' And again, 'markets' here are metaphysical imposition, the simple assumption that they 'are' their own objects.

Capital plays its role as social currency outside of history because in capitalist economics there is no history to explain how it evolved. Without history it is the result of rational acts in a rational system—the 'product' of the efficient allocation of capital that itself was the 'product' of the efficient allocation of capital—a 'deduced' history of infinite regress that relates the 'fact' of capital to the rational reaction of the capitalist to market 'demand.'

Just as 'self-determined' individuals avoid the clutter of iterative—historical, relation with 'the world' that threatens to breach the metaphysical divide, capital 'accumulation' is always kept in the 'current' period to avoid the iterative arithmetic of exponential accumulation and its historical genesis.

The market 'competition' theorized to prevent aggregated accumulation exists through deduction—if market 'opportunities' arise market competition will arise in response. How do we know this?—it is the 'rational' response of rational capitalists to market opportunities. There exist complicating factors—barriers to entry, frictions and institutional restrictions, but these are natural / social factors, not evidence of the implausibility of capitalist theory or of the inconvenience that history poses to them.

Capitalists are the 'heroes' of Western economics even though in their own theories they didn't create capitalism—it developed from the infinite regress of capital allocation and not from people 'creating' anything, ever. Alternatively, once 'capital' entered the capitalist 'system' its genesis in history was washed clean and it now exists between the metaphysical ether and its virtuous application on / in the world.

This cleansing effect is evidenced in the capitalist West by the social prestige and power accorded those who 'possess' wealth regardless of its provenance. Here backward induction is at work as well—in an economic system that allocates resources based on the social 'utility' produced; wealth is irrefutable evidence of social virtue.

Even in the moral netherworlds of child pornography and methamphetamine production there would be no 'market' if there weren't 'demand.' 'Superior' profits accrue to the entrepreneurs who service these markets because of the legal risk incurred.

This isn't a gratuitous assertion—risk-taking entrepreneurs will respond to this market demand or others will—this is the fundamental 'logic' of capitalism. The manufacture of cluster bombs, chemical weapons and 'suicide' seeds finds no sanction in 'the West;' its agents stay in five star hotels and eat at expensive restaurants without any relation made or assumed about the source of the money used to pay for them.

Conversely 'leisure,' as in the inability to feed oneself and live indoors, is the alternative to reacting to market demand. As with 'real estate' in North Carolina or California and investment banks started with proceeds from the slave trade, 'capital' is cleansed through the Western economists' sleight of hand that history began when capitalists willed markets into existence. And regardless of historical provenance it exists 'today' in the eternal 'current period' as social virtue, as the source of social wealth that renders labor and capitalist alike mere functionaries in 'system.'

'Self-determination' as the metaphysical 'core' of Western 'self' is likewise reactive, the 'agent' of capitalism who responds to 'its' imperatives. As 'capitalist' this agent reacts to market demand with supply, as 'labor' s/he reacts to market price with 'labor' or 'not labor' and as 'consumer' s/he reacts to the choice of goods and services put in front of her. As with the capitalist, 'labor' and 'consumer' always exist in the 'current period' that nevertheless stands outside of time and space.

Iterative relation of these selves and world—acting in and responding to 'the world,' compromises the fundamental raison d'etre of capitalism, that the 'wants' it fills derive from these metaphysical 'selves' and are therefore 'real.' 'Creative' labor, the labor of agency, challenges the role of capitalist 'system' in creation.

The problem of agency, of creating 'the world' capitalist theory reacts to, is to take the theory without its historical facts. Through trade agreements and control of the social institutions of Western governments capitalists are actively creating 'the world' capitalist economics put forward as purely reactive.

Imposition of trade agreements that override civil governance and breaking labor organization are to 'remove barriers' to the 'proper functioning' of markets are posed as reactive. 'Free' markets are posed as an absence of social imposition when imperial history tells the more probable story. The theoretical-analytical problem comes from the forced amnesia—the forgetting of having previously acted historically, that always reacting in the 'current period' requires.

The 'big question' in capitalist 'macroeconomics' is: does supply respond (react) to demand or does demand respond to supply? This is broadly the basis of the Western 'left / right,' 'Keynesian / market fundamentalist' divide that is put forward as oppositional but that jointly proceeds from the ahistorical 'current period.'

If demand responds to supply then business 'incentives'—tax cuts and government subsidies, are the way to get the economy growing. If supply responds to demand then government programs to spur demand—unemployment benefits and government 'transfer' payments are the way to get it growing.

These theories are only oppositional within the frame of capitalist economics—they jointly presuppose that capitalist political economy is virtuous, that it is a 'system' motivated by 'rational' reaction to economic 'opportunities' and that historical development has no bearing on outcomes.

The question itself is logical—there is no interest in whether supply 'originally' responded to demand or vice versa. Supply and demand is wholly metaphysical, they are circular reference to reactive response—the 'bounty' of 'the world' and economic production more broadly considered are nowhere to be found.

This is an economics of metaphysical imposition, political economy that has no idea where it came from. By posing only metaphysical oppositions the internal logic of capitalism is never questioned.

As argued below, capitalism is a 'totalizing' ideology, a circle of beliefs that is 'argued' from within 'its' internal logic or not at all. In capitalist mythology capitalists are heroes, the brave 'creators' whose intelligence and hard work are responsible for Western 'prosperity.' In capitalist economics these same capitalists are mere functionaries and the 'system' is the hero.

But both mythology and theory stand outside of history—they proceed from the premise that the capitalist 'system' being described is a self-contained totality, all that needs to be 'known.' Therein lays the power and the danger of the metaphysical construct 'behind' Western science. The paradox of creating a world theorized to be reacted to finds its 'logic' by remaining wholly within the metaphysical ether.

The 'selves' creating ever more intrusive and repressive social controls—'free' trade agreements, technologies of coercion, domination, subversion and forced participation in capitalist production, see themselves as reacting to 'imperfections' in 'the world' that interfere with the proper working of 'system.' This formulation forces history 'back up' to the metaphysical ether, but only from within metaphysical understanding of 'the world.'

And from within this logic all of the catastrophes that capitalism produces—recurrent economic crises and environmental and social calamities, result from 'impure' execution—there is no other 'internal' explanation available. Creating ever '-purer' capitalist political economy is reaction to the unseen threat of real breach—political and economic rupture, within capitalism's internal logic.

But here paradox illustrates the role of history in the determination of the capitalist 'self.' The 'impurities' of execution in the capitalist 'system' are better explained as the residual of history, as the factual outside of capitalist theory that is the preponderance of political economy and being. The capitalist 'self' is delimited by history, culture and ideology—and as with ever more stringent prayer to one god or another in response to crisis, the increasing intrusion of capitalism in response to the 'external' threats its crises pose are evidence of this delimitation.

'Self-determination' as it is conceived in Western political economy is wholly driven by this internal logic. Capitalists can 'act' in history, but only within a frame of understanding that poses action as reaction. This in no way diminishes the material impact this action has—its impact on 'the world' broadly considered. But it poses capitalism's growing environmental and social catastrophes as unwanted entrants from the 'outside' to which capitalism can only respond with ever 'purer' capitalism.

This isn't 'conscious' evasion of responsibility per se, but rather the only response possible within this internal logic. The realm of self-determination within this logic is the choice of 'labor' or 'not labor,' of a loaf of bread or a gallon of milk. This stands in fundamental contrast the historical-iterative idea of the 'socially-constructed' self in that the ether from whence it arises is irresolvable because it is resolutely atemporal—there is no entry point from 'outside' of its 'inside.'

To invert this point, and by setting the capitalist metaphysical construct to the side, what would be the material conditions—the conditions of political economy, which would facilitate the Western idea of self-determination? The capitalist premise of 'labor,' 'not labor' assumes the material viability of 'not labor' even as the capitalist institutional infrastructure asserts that everything not being bought is already owned.

For people with material needs, a/k/a 'people,' 'not labor' is not an option—the choice as presented is fraudulent. The institutional backdrop of 'property' with 'rights' is presented as the 'natural' state of 'the world.'

But existing 'property' with 'rights' is the institutional impediment to meeting the material requirements of existing outside of 'labor.'

Property and property rights are part and parcel of the capitalist institutional order, not accidents of history with which capitalism is forced to contend. To the point made by Karl Marx in discussing 'the Americas' before the genocide against indigenous peoples had evolved into total re-allocation of lands as 'property,' people who weren't directly forced to labor in capitalist enterprise were remarkably reluctant to do so.

And colonial and neo-colonial strategies—hut taxes, property taxes levied on indigenous lands, tenant farming and forced conscription into 'private' service, were designed to force people from the 'self-determination' of indigenous economies—'leisure,' into the service of capitalist enterprise.

The anti—history of Western economics recontextualizes the 'self-determination' of working in capitalist enterprise or starving as the choice between lengthy tours of Europe in 'leisure' or 'contributing to society' by cooking French Fries and hamburgers for minimum wage. From copper mined in Chile to fast food served in Detroit, all evidence of the circumstances of production has been 'disappeared' in the anti-history of catastrophe-nomics.

An Economist Explains Work to a Dead Hare

THE LIMITED ABILITY OF CAPITALIST THEORY TO ACCOUNT FOR ACTUAL economic life is well illustrated in the way that Western economics treats 'work,' the everyday acts of economic production that are reduced in this economics to 'labor.' 'Work' is a loaded term in the Western psyche—the 'self-determined' mission, a fundamental relation between self and world and ultimately the socially given measure of one's life.

The collision between this theorized self-determination and the expected reactive nature to labor 'markets' where labor avails itself of 'opportunities' that are premised on a division between work and labor is rendered fact by wages and their ethereal calibration. That capitalist economics can only 'recognize' paid labor means the residual difference between work and labor—household labor, unpaid social labor and the life-effort given to paid labor that remains uncompensated is 'uncounted.' And in the capitalist calculus it is 'worthless.'

Like 'profit,' in capitalist theory wages are the circular relation of the producer to the produced, the measure of metaphysical conversion through induction. Labor is hired out of leisure to do a job of known quantity, to sit or stand and do what it is told to do. 'Mental' labor is the application of rational methods to the 'job at hand' in known quantity. How do we know? The wage paid necessarily equals the quantity of work produced; else it wouldn't be either supplied or demanded.

Markets 'signal' demand to the capitalist and the capitalist sets in motion the human machine of organized production. Managers are the conversion mechanism of capitalist imperative through the rational structure of organized production, the technocrats of bureaucracy, and the arrangers of the factors of production.

Managers manage 'human capital' and 'physical capital' in varying quantities to produce the most output at lowest cost. In the aggregate everyone is paid what he or she is 'worth' because labor markets are infinitely fungible. The wholly circular nature of this 'logic' is a closed universe within which everything has a place and outside of which nothing from the inside does.

The relation of 'mental' to 'physical' labor is rendered indeterminate within capitalist theory. Mental labor may require 'more' thought and physical labor less but all labor proceeds from 'inside' of thought and its objects reach 'out' into the world to act on it. The favor of mathematical and scientific skills is as 'superior' methods of acting on the world because they 'rationally' relate thought to action.

This rational relation is 'knowledge' work, the application of operational knowledge to the 'task at hand.' The task at hand is in all cases given because it is reacted to, the 'job well done' that relates task to outcome. Skill in operational reasoning comes from natural endowments and education. Education that increases operational skills is 'the key' to getting a 'good job.'

The number of available jobs that require this education bears no relation to the value of the education because labor markets assure that everyone is paid 'what they are worth'—if you increase your 'worth' you will in overwhelming preponderance be paid for it. This mythology can be found in the oft repeated contention that unemployment and underemployment can be 'solved' through education.

'Worth' is its own price by definition. The ability to reach out into the world and act on / in it is the source of economic production, economic production is compensated according to its product, therefore superior ability—skill through education, is compensated, even when it isn't.

Paradoxically, reaction to market 'opportunities' to work brings information from 'the world' 'inside' as the realm of possible labor being 'demanded.' To 'work for oneself' is as individual capitalist, a reaction to market 'demand' for a good or service that is channeled through the organization of the 'self.'

Management of this self is as capitalist production, the rational allocation of physical and human capital to produce that that markets 'demand.' The inability of capitalist economics to account for the genesis of work, the millennia of labor that took place outside of labor markets, wages and capitalist production, is a function of the atemporal metaphysical 'inside' theorized to do the reacting.

Without the fluid, the thing-act, of 'money' there is no commensurability in capitalist theory between the act of production and the produced, no 'metric' of equivalence. Because most economic production in history was undertaken without either need or knowledge of this 'equivalence' the act of production was the measure of its product as indicated by its fact. Alternatively, the millennia of economic production that was 'creatively' undertaken in the sense that it took place outside of the capitalist frame points to the radical implausibility of the frame.

The 'innovation' of capitalist labor theory is that it reduces work to operational relation of producer to produced. Antique capitalist theoretician Adam Smith's 'division of labor' was the proposition that productive efficiency could be had through specialization in the application of labor. Left out of modern economic explanation is the genesis of even this constrained idea. The act of moving from ad hoc to 'specialized' production was creative, not reactive—'nature' didn't send down blue-prints for how to get from here to there.

This tendency finds its modern expression in the occasional recognition that many of the best ideas come from the 'shop floor.' Conversely, as much as capitalists and their academic apologists wish it to be the case, the exchange of work for wages doesn't settle the issue. Capitalist work is temporal act 'compensated' with atemporal measure—money, the two are not commensurate because they exist is different theorized realms.

As temporal act of producing temporal product work persists embedded in its product whereas the act of the exchange of wages for it is atemporal stopping point. One illustration of this point can be found in the art of Vincent Van Gogh who received a few hundred dollars for paintings he created without any predictable 'market' value to 'react' to. The paintings sell today for tens or hundreds of millions of dollars. Exchange has done nothing to 'improve' the paintings nor has it added 'value' to Van Gogh's act of production—they are what they always have been.

The problem for labor theories of 'value,' the argument that the quantity of labor that goes into producing goods and services determines their value in market exchange, is that capitalist exchange is the theorized conversion between metaphysical realms where labor's 'fact' makes it incommensurable. The claimed capitalist 'innovation' that value is a function of psychic quantum—'utility,' as it is expressed in the act of exchange, is a strategy to keep the entire process in the metaphysical ether.

With the case of Van Gogh's paintings, the Western economist's explanation combines 'scarcity' with increased psychic 'satisfaction' from owning them. However, Van Gogh's paintings are no scarcer today than they were when they were painted. Additionally, 1974 Yugo hatchbacks are scarce but hardly valuable. Any increase in psychic satisfaction from owning the paintings requires a material basis to be realized.

The phenomenal concentration of wealth in recent decades found expression in the 'commodification' of art, real estate, fine wines etc. 'Art' has been commodified-monetized as 'store of value' by an international plutocracy that has a limited number of 'liquid' places to stash 'its' wealth.

The market value of Van Gogh's paintings is socially embedded— without the means the 'will' is irrelevant as explanation. And once the fact of social embedding is considered 'psychic' explanations of economic value are relegated to the 1-800 numbers and urban storefronts where they belong. (See Dying of Thirst While Sitting atop a Mountain of Diamonds below for further explanation).

The need to 'explain' exchange in metaphysical terms comes from the internal logic of capitalism—supply and demand are 'psychic' responses to theorized market imperatives. The relation is tautological—people respond to these imperatives 'freely', unaffected by material conditions, or else they wouldn't take place.

Labor 'freely' chooses to work for a wage and once it is provided and the wage is paid the transaction is 'complete.' Alternatively, if this exchange doesn't complete the transaction then the circumstance of labor's product is rendered indeterminate in exchange. Labor theories of value don't 'fit' into capitalist theories of exchange because they require a plausible conversion process from temporal to atemporal realms to fit into the atemporal character of capitalist economics.

To be clear, the capitalist critique has no bearing on the coherence of labor theories of value. The problem within this economics is that capitalist metaphysics can only answer its own questions. The implausibility of the genesis of political economy as reaction to capitalist imperative renders capitalist 'value' theory a quaint irrelevance, the 'plug' that makes capitalist accounting 'work' as a fairy tale for gullible academics.

The contention that wages don't end the relation of labor to what labor produces finds confirmation from the unlikeliest of places, from the titans of capitalist enterprise who 'negotiate' give-backs, reduced or wholly looted pensions and reduced benefits for which labor has already been provided. Investment bankers and corporate executives regularly use strategies of coercion and extortion against labor in order to 'monetize' this embedded labor value.

Was the 'value' Wall Street's leveraged buyouts are claimed to 'unlock' ethereal in the sense of capitalist value theory it would already be fungible wholly outside of labor's share. To be clear, these practices are different from 're-negotiating' future labor; they are to monetize labor that has already been 'supplied.' If exchange truly affected metaphysical conversion there would be nothing left for investment bankers to take. Capitalist value theory is in this way a rhetorical device, its 'frame' designed to admit only one answer and its 'fact' designed to persist from a position of social power.

The historical genesis of labor in the U.S. is through slavery and genocide, forced labor from kidnapped Africans and genocide against indigenous peoples to impose Western property relations for those doing the imposing. Slavery is political economy where social power is used to take the product of labor from its producers—there often was market price for this extracted product but it went entirely to the slave 'owners.'

In the case of slavery the act of exchange conferred none of 'its' product back to the producer. In fact, through the institution of slavery slave 'owners' were considered to be producers through their 'investment' in slaves and through managing the 'factors of production,' the 'human' and 'physical' capital, that were combined to produce as much as could be produced at the lowest cost.

The 'cost' of slaves was between slaver and slave 'master,' not as one-time payment from 'master' to slave. This relation has been used to claim that slavery in the U.S. wasn't 'capitalist' because slaves were 'owned' and not hired into capitalist enterprise. However, the concept of 'property' under which slaves were considered 'chattel' property derives from the early theorists of capitalism including John Locke.

As grotesque as these analogies are, as chattel property slaves were as farm animals or factory machinery inasmuch as their 'economic' roles were as 'factors of production' in capitalist production. Conversely, the idea of 'free' labor as the exchange of labor for wages requires overlooking the entirety of Western political economy dedicated to coercing labor through controlling alternative capacities to fill material needs and through the social mechanics of engineered dependencies.

And while the political rationale of designating slaves three-fifths of a 'person' in the U.S. Constitution was to accrue additional social power to slave 'owners,' its analog has long history in Western imperial strategies of coercing labor. Slavery was / is as 'capitalist' as any social institution could be.

These modes of social control have persisted since slavery was nominally ended following the Civil War. In the U.S. slaves were 'freed' to 'compete' as 'free' labor in labor markets as Reconstruction and post-Reconstruction modes of social control were configured for purposes of continuing the economic extraction of slavery. Without property or possessions the question of the 'freedom' to forgo work offered at any price was left unanswered?

'Vagrancy' and minimal possession laws were passed with express understanding that they applied to 'freed' slaves. 'Convict' leasing programs and work camps reconstituted slavery under the cover of 'the law.' This had the effect of forcing 'freed' slaves and their descendents to take any work they could get to avoid being incarcerated or otherwise to be incarcerated in which case their labor was directly expropriated.

Even within the oblivious frame of Western economics coerced and stolen labor has the effect of taking a significant proportion of the labor 'market' with it. Economic production from expropriated and / or coerced labor depresses wages across like labor markets by leaving less to be produced in 'functioning' markets.

The conceit that 'outsourcing' Western jobs at less than Western wages is 'efficient' 'flattens' imperial history. It is hardly an accident that victim-states of imperial aggression—El Salvador, Haiti, Bangladesh, China, Vietnam and India today produce low-cost 'goods' for the West as Western capitalists 'find' sudden fortunes reminiscent of the imperial fortunes of Venice or London in their possession.

Once 'imperial extraction' replaces 'efficiency' in the economist's vocabulary the relation of the rich being rich to the poor being poor recovers its social expression. This is a central reason why capitalist economists are forced to claim that all labor is 'freely' provided at a 'market' rate—once it is granted that the wage 'rate' is a function of asymmetrical social power broader labor markets become 'distorted.'

The claim that former imperial relations left behind functioning labor markets finds its analog in the plight of property-less and penniless slaves 'freed' to compete with the propertied and socially connected in labor markets. And today those on the wrong side of asymmetrical social power 'compete' for wages with the formerly employed in these newly reconstituted empires.

Once history is 'taken out of the picture' Western social hierarchy is its own proof—how else could those in positions of power have gotten there? Indicated by this place and its 'proof' is that those who occupy it are most competent at deciding how to 'rationally' allocate economic production between new empire and old.

The anti-history of Western economics famously argues that income distribution is 'market' driven through this same circular logic—markets allocate wages according to individual contribution; therefore wage differentials are 'proof' of individual contribution.

Conversely, because those at the top of capitalist hierarchy, like all labor, 'react' to the choice between labor and leisure in 'competitive' labor markets; executive pay is necessarily the minimum amount necessary to induce executives to 'choose' labor over 'leisure.'

Taken in its totality, Western economists assume a perfectly ordered universe where 'everything' is as it should be, always. How is this proven? Capitalism is the 'system' of political economy that most efficiently 'allocates' economic resources, Western political economy is capitalist, and therefore within this 'system' the existing order is everywhere and always the result of efficient allocation.

This circle of fabricated and wholly implausible conceits is nowhere as vicious as with unemployment in the U.S. Every bout of mass unemployment elicits theories that the 'wages' of 'leisure'—unemployment, are too high and that the way to reduce unemployment is to reduce these 'wages.'

These 'wages,' unemployment insurance and occasional food assistance, were in fact developed to serve the capitalist 'system,' and not its victims, under the Keynesian theory that in certain circumstances capitalism can enter a death spiral unless government spending comes to the rescue.

From the end of WWII to the start of now regularly recurring finance-related depressions in 1990 the length of unemployment insurance approximated that of the engineered recessions of Western political economy. (The recessions were engineered by the Federal Reserve to protect the value of the debt owed to banks from 'inflation').

The implausibility of unemployment insurance leading to preference for 'leisure' over labor lies in its inadequacy—in modern debt-based capitalist political economy all but the very rich live paycheck to paycheck and the costs of extended periods with incomes below the wages of labor quickly result in personal economic 'death spirals.'

Conversely, the number of unemployed can be measured against the number of jobs that are available[80]. As recently as 2009 there were seven unemployed for every available job. Were every available job to have been filled this would have left six of the original seven unemployed with zero jobs available. Perhaps the capitalist economists working with the 'higher' mathematics should revisit their elementary school texts for refreshers on addition and subtraction and ratios (Again, 7-1 = 6).

The opposition of 'leisure' to 'labor' is evidence of the implausibility of capitalist labor theory. Historically, working outside of capitalist enterprise was an attractive alternative when feasible. But working outside of capitalist enterprise isn't 'leisure.' Within the terminology itself the implied trade-off is between sailing the Mediterranean on one's yacht and doing data entry for Citibank.

The material backdrop the overwhelming majority in the West face is of highly structured social circumstances—existing property relations that turn 'self-sufficiency' into crimes of trespass and unlawful taking as well as the aforementioned 'vagrancy' and minimum possession laws designed to force people into labor 'markets.'

Western economists pose the opposition for methodological reasons— the choice must be between relative psychic satisfactions because the idea of 'free' choice central to legitimating capitalism, to locating the market price of labor that makes 'everyone' happy, becomes muddied when material circumstances impinge on this theorized freedom.

But through this highly constructed opposition the posture of the question is made evident—labor either labors in capitalist enterprise or it does nothing in social circumstances where doing nothing is not a reasonable choice for most people. The choice is posed as fact of 'nature' when its fact is two centuries of capitalist ideology reconstituted in the social institutions of the West.

The facts of unemployment have no bearing within capitalist metaphysics—again, the structure is reactive. The ratio of the unemployed to jobs is in 'the world' and has no way to reach into the ether to force its 'facts' onto capitalist theory. In the circular logic of the metaphysical construct the theories of capitalism are its 'facts.'

Within the theorized choice of 'labor' or 'leisure' there is only choice—no material need or context from 'the world' enters the construct. This is why during the Great Depression, when the industrial unemployment rate reached twenty-five percent suddenly, violently, and within the context of one of the worst economic catastrophes in human history, the conventional view within capitalist economics was that twenty-five percent of the industrial labor force suddenly decided to 'choose' leisure over continuing to work.

At the time there were few 'wages' of leisure—the weak social guarantees that emerged from the Great Depression weren't present at its onset. Economist John Maynard Keynes developed theories to explain the implausibility of the conventional view of unemployment within the capitalist frame. But even he drew a tight circle around its circumstance—in 'extraordinary' times the 'system' of capitalism could fail to create enough jobs but during 'normal' times the 'choice' remained between 'leisure' and 'labor' at wages determined through market 'competition.'

Both the reactive 'nature' of labor to the labor 'market' and the separation of work from 'labor' in capitalist economics contributes to the relative indifference of Western economists to unemployment. Historically, working with others toward a common goal creates social bonds—community. In social terms unemployment is exile from one's community.

To the extent the capitalist imperative is internalized, assumed as the mode of determination of 'self-determination,' unemployment is self-exile, separation of one's 'work' from one's 'self.' In the capitalist economic frame economic man is the core 'self' to be realized. But that is all that this theory 'chooses' to see, not all that there is to see. However, with their reactive, generic frame for 'labor' what is 'seen' is everything but economic life.

Dying of Thirst While Sitting Atop a Mountain of Diamonds

FOR THOSE WITHOUT A FORMAL EDUCATION IN WESTERN ECONOMICS ITS 'great controversies' are likely perceived as technical quibbles, arcane differences that would better be solved by looking at 'the evidence.' As laid out above and below, 'the evidence' tends to settle very little. This has basis in social power relations—the West today is ruled by a small plutocracy that uses its economic power to determine public policies. But it also has basis in the implausible theoretical frame from whence economic questions emerge.

One textbook definition of this economics is: economics is the study of the allocation of scarce resources. One quick look at the breadth and bounty of 'the world' suggests that this 'scarcity' is more a state of mind than factual description of a state of affairs. The frame itself establishes a contest for limited supply—resources are scarce and therefore the means by which they are distributed, their allocation, makes this economics a relevant realm of study. Additionally, 'scarcity' is put forward as an artifact of nature, as a limitation imposed by the natural world.

Within this frame one of the great 'mysteries' in Western economics is the 'diamond-water paradox,' the low price of water so important to human existence relative to the high price of diamonds that are of relatively little importance. The 'solution' Western economists came up with is that water exists in relative abundance whereas diamonds are scarce and therefore that scarcity—the supply of something relative to that of other things, determines its value relative to them.

Conspicuously missing from this 'solution' is the historical role of diamonds as 'treasure,' as quasi-money like gold that is found in jewelry and industrial applications but that also has long history as a 'store of value.' Alternatively, as mentioned above, 1974 Yugo hatchbacks are also 'scarce' but have little to no implied or actual economic 'value.' In fact, capitalism is in the process of producing one of the greatest die-offs of 'scarce' endangered species in world history and responsible capitalists place little to no value on this 'scarcity.'

Moreover the idea of scarcity at work is as a dearth of metaphysical objects—the commodities that exist in the ether of capitalist economics—both 'water' and 'diamonds,' are unified in the formulation of the puzzle as psychic objects as they exist in the ether, not in a particular container of water or a particular diamond.

Framed differently, want of 'diamonds' is pornographic in the sense that it is decontextualized, it is for the 'shared' qualities of diamonds as social objects and not for a particular diamond except as it relates to these qualities. Money is the conversion device that bridges the metaphysical divide between these things in their thing-ness—the metaphysical objects of water and diamonds, to form equivalence.

In addition to relative scarcity what is needed to render this theory coherent is that diamonds are socially valued which reduces to the tautology that diamonds are valued because they are valued—hardly the 'solution' economists were looking for. However, the reason why the puzzle had to be formulated the way it was is that value must be intrinsic to its objects or the broader logic of capitalism is rendered circular.

If what people 'value' is what 'society' values the 'natural' basis of capitalist democracy—the fulfillment of self-determined political and economic wants, enters the death spiral of iterative relation between the 'self' and 'the world.' What is the role of personal choice if it is better explained as instantiated social choice? Alternatively, who is this 'society' that wants what it wants because it wants it? In the puzzle both water and diamonds have intrinsic value—value in and of themselves that stands outside of space, time and human interests.

'Scarcity' likewise exists in the ether as a characteristic of 'the world' that is independent of time and space. But in the temporal world 'everything' exists in its particularity and 'scarcity' makes no thematic sense—without being united with one another in the ether of psychic 'objects' there is no metaphysical 'thingness' to 'possess.' This is to say that scarcity pertains to a particular type of 'object,' that which is wanted. Water is needed, it is necessary to physical well being, also making it 'wanted.' Outside of industrial use value diamonds are only 'wanted' so it is necessary to understand the basis of this want.

Conversely, in this realm of want detached from need infinite iterations of 'thingness' are possible and none are 'in and of themselves' plausible as other than generalized social objects, as commodities. 'Intrinsic' value is extrinsic to actual water and actual diamonds and extrinsic to metaphysical 'objects' as well in as much as they only 'exist' in the theorized ether. The realm of the 'scarce' is everything, everywhere, always in its 'extrinsic' sense and nothing, anywhere, ever in its intrinsic sense.

The 'scarcity' of this paradox is generic want, the want of something in particular for the qualities it 'shares' with others of its 'type.' But this type is metaphysical imposition and its 'shared' characteristics are as social currency—there is no plausible reason why 'individually' 'self-determined' wants would aggregate around something like diamonds and not 1974 Yugo hatchbacks other than their value as social currency. In other words, without self-determined collective 'want,' 'demand,' has no aggregation mechanism. This want is for the wanted, not from it. 'Demand' has social basis as demonstrated through the aggregation of what is 'demanded.'

The 'great' and not-so-great bubbles and busts of history—tulip bulbs, junk bonds, technology stocks and Beanie Babies make this point evident. They are social phenomena, not the sudden realization determined by unrelated persons that their individual psychic satisfaction requires that they own a Beanie Baby no matter what the cost. Additionally, the capacity to buy these suddenly 'scarce' objects is a function of material conditions, not of nebulous detached wants.

The 'value' of diamonds as fungible 'stores of value' depends on particular form of political economy where the idea of fungibility through commensurability—metaphysical 'understanding,' is developed. This idea of 'savings' being fungible, as opposed to food and water that require no metaphysical 'conversion,' derives from capitalist metaphysics, not 'nature.'

There is nothing 'wrong' with this social quality that gives value to diamonds, but it is socially given, not individually determined—the locus of 'value' is between persons, not 'inside' them. The challenge falls back onto capitalist theory that posits that market value is a function of the aggregation of individually determined 'wants' when the reason 'individuals' 'want' diamonds is for their social characteristics. Every diamond is 'scarce' in that it is the only diamond that it 'is.' So is every blade of grass and every breath of air. The confusion comes through conflating metaphysical with 'material' objects.

By placing economic scarcity back into the social realm the 'natural' basis of capitalism as satisfying self-determined wants is called into question. The remarkable convergence of what the peoples of the West 'want' is only related to the idea of self-determination through tautology. It is its own 'proof' that what is is what is wanted. But the totalizing frame of capitalist theory, illustrated here in the tautological relation of want to wanted, is remarkably resilient precisely because it is totalizing.

The Day René Descartes Lost His Mind

AT THE TURN OF THE TWENTIETH CENTURY A PHILOSOPHICAL MOVE-
ment named 'logical positivism' developed a following under the pro-
scription that 'only statements that can be proven to be true' would be
considered by it. It took only a decade or so and a few thousand 'man
hours' for it to dawn on the movement's proponents that its base premise
that 'only statements that can be proven to be true' is rank assertion, not a
'proven' statement. The mathematically inclined might see general analog
to Godel's Theorem in this revelation.

Left unaddressed by the logical positivists and mathematical logicians
like Godel is the radically different line of inquiry that 'Continental' philosophers in Germany had taken with 'phenomenology.' By the late nineteenth century challenges to Cartesian 'metaphysics' had raised serious
questions about the philosophical 'foundations' of Western science. The
base issues are laid out below. But from this inquiry a schism developed
that led to development of two broad schools of philosophical inquiry
around issues of 'science.' Following from early phenomenological inquiries the Continental school was unable to recover the philosophical foundations that make Western science plausible on its own terms.

The Anglo-American school plowed ahead as if the 'crisis of metaphysics' didn't exist—it didn't attempt to address the issues raised in Europe
except inasmuch as they found their way piecemeal into the questions
asked within the Western, essentially Cartesian, frame. In the U.S. in particular this led to bitter resistance to challenges to the metaphysical frame
by scientists and philosophers of science who displayed little to no understanding of the bases of the critique. In Europe the critique was taken as
given and an effete word poetry using the terminology of science without
its content became known as 'post-modernism.'

Of relevance here are the original phenomenological critiques of metaphysics. Capitalism is 'scientific' economic production in the sense that
particular types of 'evidence,' including its product, guide its organization.
Rene Descartes developed this broad frame of the relation of 'observer' to
'observed' that is both historically locatable and the background 'position'

of the Western 'individuals' of capitalism. To Western scientists and philosophers of science this conceit is conceived as 'self-evident,' 'universal.' Western scientific methods derive from it. Capitalist democracy is both conceived and 'legitimated' through this same conceit.

It is important not to overstate the case here. Through a number of intellectual back-and-forths the Anglo-American philosophers of science came to positions of relative humility toward the idea of philosophical foundations not that far from where the Continental 'crisis of metaphysics' left them. The central difference is that the Anglo-American effort left the Cartesian metaphysical frame, and with it the 'mind-body' dualism, intact.

The argument made here is that this dualism has political content—the 'inside / outside' dualistic model of Western 'individuals' poses a separation of Western 'selves' from each other and the world that is neither plausible nor socially workable. Through irresolution of the crisis of metaphysics the Continental approach largely abandoned Cartesian dualism. Setting aside the philosophy of science for the moment, from where does this dualism emerge once its basis in Cartesian metaphysics is abandoned?

Coming out of the Anglo-American frame is the conception of economics and politics that are choices made by self-determined individuals. The conception echoes the flawed conceit of the logical positivists—it depends on 'unprovable' assertions about who 'we' are and the nature of 'the world.' The idea of 'evidence' in logic and science is deference to a 'god's eye view' or 'view from nowhere' premised not just on disinterest in the sense of 'fact,' but on the capacity to step 'outside' of oneself to ascertain it.

The relationship of the thoughts and methods of Rene Descartes to Western economics is reasonably well-traveled territory. The relationship to 'capitalism' is less well traveled. But other writers have visited it a few times in recent decades. The latter relationship is straightforward—capitalism is all that Western economics has. Western economics is capitalist economics. Some economists will no doubt take issue with this claim, largely from the perspective of not having thought about it very much.

This is true of practicing scientists to a large extent as well. Economics and science are substantial industries and are deeply embedded in capitalist enterprise. The philosophical quandaries raised over the last century have had very little impact on either discipline, which is in some fair

measure 'the point.' Asserting that these practices have no philosophical 'foundations' while leaving Cartesian dualism intact, as the Anglo-
American schools largely have, is false humility when economics and
science are crucial components of capitalist political economy.

Once the relation is made there is little left but to address the ideology
behind it. What hasn't tended to be related is Descartes' 'metaphysics,'
'Cartesian' metaphysics, to the broader Western worldview that supports
capitalist democracy as political economy. It is this broader worldview
that has evolved to give capitalism and democracy, capitalist democracy,
their hegemonic character that has instantiated them so deeply into the
political economy of the West.

The lure of scientific truth is easy to understand as 'facts' about the
world that come from it, not from 'mere' opinions and rhetorical ability.
And the role of 'evidence' in discourse has intuitive appeal—if someone
says that the oak tree in the front yard has a lot of leaves on it, it either
does or it doesn't. But science proceeds from premises that by the rules
of science have not been 'demonstrated.' And the history of science is of
discovered truths that are no longer considered true. One can claim that
the truth eventually won out, but that is always made after the fact, after
'true' truth has been asserted.

This latter point is tied to the idea of progress, as in incremental addition to the store of 'human knowledge.' But this 'knowledge' resides with
particular humans, not with 'humanity.' And rather than incremental
addition the tendency has been toward break, rupture and replacement
of one theory, or set of theories, with another. Thomas Kuhn made use of
this point in 'The Structure of Scientific Revolutions'[82] a half century ago.
But this isn't the heart of the criticism here. Science is an approach to the
world shared by a relatively small group of theorists and practitioners that
is put forward as the embodiment of true knowledge. Science claims the
privilege of ending 'the discussion' that it hasn't earned.

The idea of 'evidence' is legalistic; it derives from a technical concept
of human relations. Its truths that are admitted serve particular arrangement of social circumstance. Nuclear weapons demonstrate scientific
truth in the sense that they do what they were created to do—a sequence
of mechanical operations causes a gigantic explosion. Their threat, caused
by their mere existence, is state terrorism, a widespread dread that they
might actually be used. The knowledge of how to create these weapons,

the physics, metallurgy and engineering that make them 'operational,' is true truth within the scientific frame while the dread that they cause is the 'mere opinion' unless relegated to the 'soft' sciences for evidence collection and interpretation.

Global warming and dead and dying oceans are every bit as much a product of 'scientific' economic production—the application of evidence based methods to the machinery of this production, as are the products on display in stores. In the realm of economic production science is the mode of economic exploitation, of producing 'the intended' with little to no regard for the unintended. So the charge made here isn't that science doesn't 'work.'

The charge is that it is an ideology that is only capable of seeing what it is already looking for. Without irony this can be found in Edmund Husserl's theory of 'intentionality' that correspondingly is the philosophical premise behind the 'variables' of modern probability theory. The shift from deterministic to probabilistic 'modeling' in the sciences is broad metaphor for the step down of truth claims that the late nineteenth century crisis in metaphysics caused. Edmund Husserl's 'bracketing,' part of his attempt to recover a 'scientific' basis for science, is the fundamental device used by statisticians to create the 'variables' of scientific inquiry. (See The Parable of Family Income).

The operational approach to the world that is science derives from Cartesian rationalism, from the premises embedded in Rene Descartes' philosophy and his methods of 'proof.' There are many other paths / contributors in the genesis of scientific reasoning. But Descartes is at the heart of the development of the Western 'self' of capitalism as well as science. This isn't to suggest that he was a capitalist or that he had had any interest in political economy—these ideas had no place in his time. He was the cloistered 'individual' who acts through a narrowly considered rationality and to whom the social currency of 'proof' accrues.

Descartes' philosophical question of Western renown: how does he know that he really exists? —is considered one of the fundamental philosophical inquiries of the Anglo-American branch of philosophy as it diverged from 'Continental' philosophy. His answer, that he knew he existed by way of the internal dialogue of his 'mind'—he 'thinks,' as he determined it using deductive logic, launched thousands of 'brain in a vat' philosophical speculations of life in a world separated from physical existence.

'Internal' dialogue as 'proof' of existence implies an 'individual' who exists in 'thought' and as such is 'self-determined.' Once Descartes erected the walls of fortress 'self' all acts on / in 'the world' proceeded from inside of it. This conception of 'self-determined' 'individual' constitutes the fundamental social unit of capitalist democracy. And the idea of 'proof' is of 'truth' gotten to through method. Capitalism is the social philosophy of self-determined individuals who relate to 'the world' through rational method. This is likewise the base premise of Western economics.

The genesis of Descartes' 'insights' descended from the philosopher Plato's ontology, his theories of the nature of 'the world' and how it 'holds together.' Plato's ontology as he outlined it in 'Allegory of the Cave[83]' was of relatedness in 'essences,' the 'central' truths of the particular existents of 'the world' as they exist in 'knowledge.' The distinction between existing 'in knowledge' and 'in the world' is fundamental to the Cartesian worldview.

An apple as particular existent in 'the world' is united in 'knowledge' to all apples through its 'apple-ness,' through its 'essence' as apple that is shared with all other apples. In Plato's allegory knowledge is by degree—most people only see the shadows of things 'as they really are.' But these worldly existents are unified in 'true' knowledge as Plato had it, in their 'essences' that unites them with their 'kind.'

'Wise' wo/men see these knowledge-objects as they 'really are' but the 'ultimate' truths aren't reducible to essences as Plato had it. Of current relevance is the idea of 'essence' as the central 'truth' of existents that unites them in 'knowledge' and the notion of a hierarchy of knowledge that through the combination of work and wisdom can lead to 'possession' of 'true' truth, to true knowledge of 'the world' 'as it really is.'

These Platonic 'essences' that exist in thought are atemporal—once the abstraction is made that an apple has essence in its 'apple-ness,' time, space and temporal being disappear. 'Apple' is the thought-object that 'unites' apples from before the time of the dinosaurs into an infinite future. Actual apples exist temporally, they exist and then they don't. This is where Descartes' distinction between existing 'in thought' and 'in the world' ties to the thesis of his radical alienation—where does this thought reside if not in the world?

Within the metaphysical frame this atemporality makes metaphysical 'knowledge,' knowledge of the unifying characteristics of existents, 'superior' in the sense that they are 'timeless and universal' while temporal existents are fleeting. Descartes' 'proof' in thought brought these metaphysical 'objects' 'inside' as personal possession. If his 'proof' of his existence was 'self-determined' then the 'objects' of thought were contained 'inside' of him. Implied are dual realms of the temporal and the timeless and universal.

Through his method of 'proof,' deductive logic, Descartes could 'prove' that his 'knowledge' was true truth as possession of timeless and universal thought objects. 'Proof' through method, deduced premises run through the hypothesis testing of science in modern terms, related the timeless and universal 'rules' and 'laws' of nature to 'true' knowledge in thought and the logical circle was closed.

This otherworldly realm is 'metaphysical' in the sense of being the substance and structure of 'the world' that exists 'above' the temporal world that is 'its' order—'its' rules and relationships that remain hidden until 'discovered' through philosophical / scientific inquiry. 'Nature' as conceived as 'timeless and universal' 'laws,' 'rules, and 'order' of the 'natural' world is a contemporary analog.

Particular existents may come and go but the 'laws' that 'govern' them, scientific 'truth,' are theorized to exist across time. And through this atemporality of 'truth' the objects of truth, representations of particular objects—'atoms,' 'rocks,' and 'sunsets,' are theorized to 'exist' as metaphysical 'objects.' Subsequent distinctions have been made between content and 'structure.' But this is straightforwardly analogous to the Cartesian distinction between rational 'method' and 'its' 'objects.'

From existing in thought Descartes faced the problem of transcendence, of traversing the realms of the worldly and the otherworldly—of 'the world' and the metaphysical 'ether,' to establish the 'true' truths of 'the world.' Through the 'methods' of deductive logic—the formal logic of mathematics, inquiry could be made into 'the world' and 'its' 'true' truths could be 'discovered' and rigorously 'proved.'

As in Plato's allegory, 'true' knowledge in the modern scientific sense is the product of method and endowment, of work and wisdom. It is 'truer' than the 'uninformed' opinions of those who have either not done the work to 'discover' it and / or those who lack wisdom as a capacity.

Following from Plato, Cartesian metaphysics established a hierarchy of truth with its 'possession' a social currency.

Through this philosophical frame evolved the idea of the Western 'self' existing in the 'life of the mind' that became the basis for 'individuals' as the fundamental actors of Western political economy. 'Self determination' as the base act / purpose of capitalist democracy requires a metaphysical 'self' existing simultaneously 'in' 'the world' and as 'individually' circumscribed.

'Self-determination' comes through this circumscription, the theorized creation of this 'self' from 'inside' the life of 'the mind' to act in 'the world.' Conversely, embedded, non-metaphysical 'selves' lack the confidence / arrogance of metaphysical circumscription and the idea of 'determination' gets muddied when one acts 'on' 'the world' while existing 'in' it. The alienation of this self-determined self is as radical as it is implausible—it is fundamentally theological in its otherworldliness.

Descartes could have 'proved' he existed through any of a number of explicitly temporal acts that are part of everyday life or he could foregone the exercise entirely while nevertheless reassuring himself that he existed by asking his friends and family to confirm it? But his was an 'individual' act of 'self-determination' in the most fundamental sense, the act of 'individually' 'determining' himself to exist.

That he felt the need to 'prove' his existence to himself or to anyone else is evidence of a fundamental and profound alienation from 'the world,' a radical 'homelessness,' that was / is nevertheless put forward as the supreme act of the Western self of 'self-determination.' Paradoxically, a truly self-determined self would have no need of 'proof.' Descartes' 'self-determination' was in the legalistic sense of social currency, a 'proof' meant to convince anyone who inquired.

Through this metaphysics the idea of discoverable 'timeless and universal' truths about 'the world' became the raison d'etre of Western science. To be clear, all scientific 'truths' are metaphysical, put forward as standing outside of time, space and human interests. They occupy Western social space legitimated by the circular logic that 'true' truth is timeless and universal, that science is the method to 'true' truth, and therefore that truth 'discovered' through the methods of science is timeless and universal.

The conspicuous temporality of this atemporality—the eternal truths whose half-lives are measured in years, months and sometimes days, is evidence of their social genesis, of the fickleness of several billion tightly circumscribed nation-states of the 'self' in their 'individual' acts of 'self-determination.' 'Gravity' may be 'true' within these 'rules' but the rules themselves are social artifacts dependent on a wide array of assumptions that are no more 'provable,' or even relevant under the internal logic of science, than is the existence of god.

Conversely, these 'timeless and universal' truths live and die with actual people. The conceit that they are part of the 'knowledge of man' is wholly metaphysical—where is this 'man' in whose interest this 'knowledge' is being accumulated outside of actual people? The lives 'spent' in the pursuit of these 'truths' are as temporal existents, as monks living lives of penance for some theorized transgression or as Renaissance artists painting the glories of a theorized god.

The very idea of 'proof' is an exclusionary tactic designed to silence competing concepts, the legalism that finds expression in Western courtroom proceedings as 'that which can be proved' regardless of how irrelevant to 'the facts' of 'the case' such proof might be. With courtroom as metaphor, the social nature of this 'proof' is brought forward in the goal of convincing a jury of one's case through careful arrangement of 'the facts.'

If the facts could 'speak for themselves' there would be no need for social institutions dedicated to speaking for 'them.' If their arrangement were self-evident there would be no need for lawyers and juries. Through this idea of a hierarchy of 'truth' a social hierarchy was created from its possessors 'down' to those who don't possess 'true knowledge,' always as vague allusion to those on the other side of imperial social relations, and a political economy of truth 'creation' was brought into being.

This mythology of 'method' to 'true' truth led to 'math and science' curriculums gaining currency as a core function of Western education. The Cartesian worldview is so deeply instantiated into Western understanding that a long history of robust challenges remains little known. And any challenges to the coherence of the metaphysical 'self' of capitalist democracy is perceived as an attempt to annihilate that which is only implausibly theorized to exist in the first place, the historical artifact confused with the base fact of existence. Western metaphysics could be seen as an historical wrong-turn, a rectifiable mistake, were it not for the impermeability of its internal logic as it has been reconstituted in Western institutions and social relations.

Cracks in the Cartesian worldview began in earnest with the publication of philosopher Edmund Husserl's 'The Crisis of the European Sciences and Transcendental Phenomenology[85]' in the late nineteenth century. Mr. Husserl developed challenges to classical metaphysics through 'phenomenological'—experiential, exploration of temporality. An essential goal of Mr. Husserl's work was to recover a basis for Western science in the face of growing critiques of its foundational premises in metaphysics—his goal was to save science, not to destroy it.

'Thought' occurs temporally, as part of broader embeddedness in 'the world.' Neither 'thought' nor the atemporal objects of metaphysics are 'detachable' from this temporal realm forcing the question of geographical metaphor—if they do exist in an atemporal realm then where is it and how does it relate to temporality? Without plausible answers to the question of the location of the thought 'objects' of metaphysics they are returned to the realm of actual persons.

Alternatively, Western science as a 'god's' or 'nature's' eye view of the world places scientists in the role of 'interpreters' of 'truth,' not the 'determiners' of truth that Cartesian metaphysics leaves open to possibility. Mr. Husserl attempted to recover a 'scientific' basis for circumscribing the objects of science, of placing their implausible metaphysical relatedness into the realm of the externally circumscribed.

The strategy was of 'bracketing' temporal 'objects' to in effect 'define' essences rather than to presuppose them as objects of 'nature.' 'Nature' might no longer hand 'its' timeless and universal objects over to science due to the implausibility of the metaphysical construct, but Mr. Husserl believed they could be reconstructed through thoughtful circumscription as 'plausible' objects that nevertheless led to the indubitable truths of science.

Separately in the realms of linguistics and cultural anthropology the questions were asked: if metaphysical 'essences' are artifacts of the substance and structure of Western languages as they evolved historically then in what sense are they timeless and universal, 'true' truth? Language is other than its 'objects.' The word 'amoeba' is not an amoeba. And again, deference to structure finds analogy in Cartesian 'method.' To whom would structure / method be relevant? The answer: to the type of being to who structure / method is relevant.

Western metaphysics is premised on this confusion. Some languages may by their nature provide the 'sense' that they are. But this sense exists only as long as the languages and the people who share them do. In the tightly circumscribed 'individual' of the Cartesian 'self' the very question of 'language' arises? Descartes' internal dialogue as he expressed it publicly was in a shared language, the language he learned through social interaction. Language is a social act with shared vocabulary and structure.

Metaphysics is a 'taking inside' of language, an internalization that makes particular claims about the nature of what it is. As social-discursive object-act language exists 'between' people, not inside the Cartesian 'individual' who, despite several centuries of speculation to the contrary, exists socially. For linguists who may be reading, capacity for language isn't language, it is capacity. If this capacity could be individually 'determined' this would support Cartesian 'self-determination.' But language, particularly as it relates to metaphysics, is socially and culturally circumscribed—no social relations, no language.

Was the Cartesian 'self' plausible there would be no language because every 'self' would have his or her own language? There do exist theories of 'natural' language—of intrinsic structure to be filled with social-cultural 'content' put forward by brilliant and lovely people. But Descartes 'thought, therefore he was,' in a shared language. His 'proof,' his 'self-determination,' was in a language that he learned as he existed socially, its 'facts' were socially given, not internally 'generated.'

Likewise, Western science is social practice, a mode of inquiry with place and purpose in historically and culturally locatable political economy. The mythology of lone 'individuals' 'discovering' the eternal truths of 'the world' is rather as socially circumscribed 'individuals,' people engaging in social acts in which multitudinous others engage with generally analogous results. And the truths 'discovered' are of particular type, the type that knows how to build a nuclear weapon without regard to its social consequences.

Western science is 'truth' creation within socially circumscribed rules and practices. Conversely, were Cartesian 'individuals' engaging in lone acts of science there would be no reason to share findings, no shared language to facilitate communication of them, no context within which to make sense of them, no political economy to make them socially possible and no set of social practices within which they are identifiable as 'science.'

The 'timeless and universal' truths of science are social truths, acts of social negotiation within historically and culturally locatable political economy. Rene Descartes could have stubbed his toe or eaten a sandwich to 'prove' his existence and kept the entire project to himself.

His 'self-determination' was a social act that only has meaning in the social realm, else 'we' never would have heard of it. Likewise 'proof' is an act of social negotiation—there is no need or purpose to proving anything to oneself unless the ultimate purpose is to convince others of what is to be 'proved.' And modes of proof not deemed socially acceptable don't 'prove' anything even if they are 'internally' coherent.

Science is in theory a method of relating premises to conclusions. To maintain a patina of rigor the premises of scientific inquiry must be as rigorously circumscribed as the findings they facilitate. Vague or implausible premises may be related to conclusions, but only without the pretense of scientific 'rigor.' This was the motivation for Edmund Husserl's investigations, to isolate and identify the premises that would support the idea of scientific rigor.

Through his investigation Mr. Husserl concluded that classical metaphysics was implausible and tried to reconstruct the 'objects' of science from 'the world' up to the necessary categories that could be the basis of scientific inquiry. However, if there are no 'things in themselves' that exist 'above' temporal existents then scientific 'truth' is bound to the temporal realm. And in fact for the preponderance of history the 'self-evident' truths of science as both its method and it 'facts' were unknown, unconsidered and irrelevant to the lives lived.

With varying degrees of theoretical clarity Western economists and statisticians regularly draw circles around—construct, objects of interest to be used in their 'scientific' inquiries. The economic 'variables' of 'Gross Domestic Product,' the 'Unemployment Rate,' and 'Household Income' are examples of this practice. However, in contrast to the premise of metaphysics, these objects are constructed, not given—any 'scientific' results derived from them can be called into question by re-defining them.

This process of defining is a social act in the sense that if its 'objects' aren't 'convincing' they disappear. And the question of to whom they need be convincing is of relevance? While there are ways of methodically constructing these 'objects,' there is no way to 'scientifically' construct them without using unprovable assertions. Edmund Husserl's solution to the 'problem' of metaphysics was to draw a circle around the objects of science as a process of social agreement and to proceed with the scientific 'project' as if the problem was solved.

One of Mr. Husserl's students, the German philosopher Martin Heidegger, took a more critical look into classical ontology, first in 'History of the Concept of Time[87]' and later in greater detail in 'Being and Time[89]'. Following from Husserl Mr. Heidegger developed a deeper phenomeno-logical critique of Cartesian ontology to raise in detail the question of the simultaneous existence of temporality and the hypothesized metaphysical realm? Epistemic relativism, the boogeyman of science proponents, can find Mr. Heidegger's location of epistemology in the realm of improbable metaphysics in both books.

But as Mr. Heidegger exposited it, temporality as experienced 'being' is irreducible and both classical metaphysics and Edmund Husserl's 'bracketing' are reductions, the assumption-imposition of 'essential' char-acteristics not of 'the world,' and in so being not 'about' the world in the metaphysical and scientific senses. Existents 'exist' as irreducibly embed-ded in 'the world.' The theorized atemporal 'relatedness' of metaphysics is imposed from the linguistic-discursive dimension. Any 'truth' found in metaphysics is a truth 'about' metaphysics, not about its alleged 'objects.'

In scientific practice either the 'objects' of science are given or scientif-ic results are a function of 'subjective' circumscription of the 'objects' of interest. From the obverse, within the theoretical frame of science there are an infinite number of 'truths' to be 'discovered' depending on the questions asked and how they are 'framed.' A given question with different frames will yield different results and different questions within a given frame will yield different results.

Once the 'given-ness' of the objects of science is in question its ques-tions take on different meaning. Science can and does produce social results and science and engineering are deeply embedded in Western political economy. But without the indubitable premises of metaphysics its results become roughly analogous to 'scientifically' written insurance policies or methodically conceived dust-lint rollers, operationally 'useful' within particular political economy but hardly capital 'T' 'Truth.'

Edmund Husserl's 'bracketing' of the objects of science was asser-tion that its objects are not given in the sense that Descartes put them forward. And Martin Heidegger's phenomenological exposition detailed the radical implausibility of the metaphysical worldview and found no redemption in the 'soft' metaphysics of Husserlian bracketing. As rough metaphor 'the sciences' shifted from deterministic to probabilistic scientific 'models' without foregoing the implied 'truth' claims of 'science.'

Rene Descartes could have eaten lunch or taken a walk to prove his existence if doing so were for his own 'benefit.' His broader project—the real purpose of his 'question,' was a philosophical 'will to truth' that is now a foundational precept of Western political economy. Descartes' 'truth' was and is social artifact, the act of encasing the Western 'self' behind a wall of dubious 'truth' under the rhetorical guise of 'self' 'determination.'

As 'will to truth' the self—subscribed burden of 'proof' of the metaphysical realm falls to Mr. Descartes and his adherents in Anglo-American philosophy and the Western sciences. Given the claims of intellectual and methodological rigor made from 'inside' the Cartesian frame, it is mere superstition to speculate on the existence of an atemporal sphere where truths that stand outside of time, space and human interests reside.

To be clear, this is fundamentally different from saying that Western science and technology have no effect on political economy, that they 'do' nothing. But their social currency is a function this deep embedding, not from the power of abstract truth claims. Once this is taken away science and technology become a social choice, not the expression of the will of a secular god as Descartes and his descendants had / have it. And to be clear, nuclear weapons and global warming is as much 'its' product as are antibiotics and computers.

As mentioned at the start of this chapter, critics of the critique laid out here are plenty and include people who I respect without reservation. And at the end of this book I launch a very brief, but what I believe to be more insightful and better informed, critique of the anti-politics, or more pointedly, the social apologetics for capitalist revival political economy, that is philosophical post-modernism. Technology as scientific economic production is quickly making the planet unlivable. I spend much of this book arguing this case.

In his essay 'The Ends of Man[91]' French philosopher Jacques Derrida argues, correctly in my view, that Martin Heidegger left behind an implied metaphysics with the unified view of his 'fundamental ontology.' Taken from this by followers of Mr. Derrida was the 'radical subjectivity' believed to be the final goodbye by post-modernism to metaphysical reasoning.

The question then is: what is the fundamental unit of this subjectivity—who is it that is subjective?

As dismal irony had it these radical subjectives turned out to be the 'consumers' and 'voters' of capitalist revival and Western triumphalism of the last forty years, the 'free' individuals of capitalist democracy who are the objects of this theorized subjectivity. The alleged fall of 'meta-narratives' was followed by the 'micro-narratives' of capitalist 'choice' and the phony 'choices' of Western Party politics.

Through the implicit and / or explicit 'unit' of subjectivity being 'the individual' what post-modernism supported were the base premises of capitalist democracy. The political context put forward is that by writing that all views are equally 'valid', with science being one view among many that this would make it so. This is the same assuming away of social power that underlies the theories of the self as the fundamental unit of social organization in Western economic theory—capitalism, and in the political theories that support Western democracy.

The theory of the Western self of capitalist democracy is the most effectively hegemonic meta-narrative in modern history because it is put forward as micro-narratives in the support of subjective 'free-choosers.' But to be clear, none of this has bearing on the critique of metaphysics presented here. If language is between people, social object-act, rather than the personal possession of metaphysics, the tight circumscription of Western 'individuals' is placed in social history, not in the atemporal determination of science. I expand on this in the final chapters of this book.

The Method to the Madness

One of the great mystifying factors of Western economics is the arcane terminology used by its practitioners. The actual ideas behind the terminology generally aren't all that complicated. In fact, when economists are forced to put them into plain speak they are often only convincing when they appeal to successfully instantiated ideology as with the idea of 'scarcity' addressed above or in the Western conceit that people are naturally acquisitive.

While development of technical languages has long been a strategy of circumscribing those on the 'inside' of a discipline or practice, in economics much of the terminology serves a functional purpose. Western economics is a hybrid of ideology and methodology through its basis in Cartesian metaphysics. The terminology was in many cases developed to fit capitalist ideology into methods 'borrowed' from other disciplines. As profoundly uninteresting as these methods might be to non-economists, they need to be understood because they illuminate the structure of capitalist ideology, they give it form.

Modern graduate economics programs treat method as accoutrement, as 'tools' that allow economists to conduct 'legitimate' research. However, the methods of Western economics are the content and vice versa. Was it not for their social consequences critique could be aimed quite specifically at the engineers and math majors increasingly in demand in these programs. It is not incidental that engineering and mathematics are methods in search of applications; the 'how' whose 'why' is external to the methods employed.

The tendency of 'economics' in recent decades has been to create increasingly arcane technical languages in proportion to degree of specialization and the need to maintain control of outcomes. In contrast, Western economists understand their methods—the formal logic of mathematical models and the empirical methods of statistical analysis, to be ideologically neutral tools that give logical rigor and scientific credibility to the enterprise of economics. The problem is that this method suffers from the noun-verb confusion of metaphysics—it is 'act' and actor, the set of beliefs that is its 'own' belief.

Capitalist economics evolved from the Cartesian metaphysical frame that in theory relates atemporal—timeless and universal, mental objects to 'the world' through 'rational extension'—through logical methods of which mathematics and statistical analysis are types. Statistics is used to associate the probability of 'objects' theorized to exist in the world with the metaphysically circumscribed mental 'objects' of formal mathematics.

The atemporal nature of these 'objects' is essential in that they are theorized to exist 'above' existents in 'the world' as its rules, laws and unifying tendencies. Taken from the same basic frame as Western science, the goal of 'economics' is to discover these rules and laws to obtain 'true' knowledge of the 'the economy.'

From the Cartesian tradition this economics is largely deductive, e.g. if people are 'rational' and their economic 'aspect' can be represented by homo economicus, economic man, then conclusions can be drawn about how s/he will act in economic circumstances. The mathematical models economists use are a type of formal logic and they are used to 'rigorously' deduce economic 'truths'—the formal content of Western economics. This process of rigorous deduction is both the base humanism of 'economic man,' the 'actor' of Western economics, and 'his' mode of engaging with 'the world,' his 'act.' The premises delineate the realm of possible conclusions.

The logical 'objects' of mathematical models are wholly metaphysical—they are 'atemporal' by design. The theoretical frame is posed as: if the economic premise—'rational' economic man, is correct and the logical objects of the model are 'representative' of static—timeless and universal, things / relationships in the world, then their manipulation through the formal logic of mathematics should provide essential 'truths' about the world that are themselves timeless and universal—that stand outside of 'the world' and human interests.

The models are theorized to 'represent' these characteristics with the irrelevancies peeled away. For instance, as a possible object of inquiry a running horse shares both 'running' and 'horse' with other running horses but it is also irreducible in its temporal 'fact'—there is no 'factual' equivalence to match this theorized metaphysical equivalence. One running horse is only related to other running horses through the interest of the inquirer—there is no 'disinterested' perspective making the relation.

A philosophical challenge to the process of metaphysical reduction is that the distinction between the 'essential' and the 'irrelevant' is arbitrary within the logic of the analysis—the choice of running horse as 'object' of method is either to choose metaphysical 'object' or to have nothing to say within the chosen method. 'Running' could just as reasonably be associated with persons or dogs as another horse and 'horse' could just as reasonably belong to the realms of brown things, 'meat' or things that stand. These objects of inquiry can be related, but the relation is an imposition, it isn't the choice of a disinterested 'nature.'

And the 'irrelevancies' that are peeled away are only irrelevant within an arbitrary frame—they are assumed to be irrelevant without having an internally coherent basis for the assumption because the 'starting' premise is metaphysical. And theories of 'atemporality,' of timeless and universal 'objects,' beg the question of where they reside? Put differently, how can inquirers claim to stand outside of themselves as observers when the fact of their inquiry places them firmly in their own skins?

'Rigorous' analysis that depends on arbitrary assumptions about dubious existents is its own opposite—the terms of 'rigor' are internal to the Cartesian project, not imposed from without. The latter point is important because the 'truth' claims of Western economics, and sciences more broadly, are assigned social value as 'true' truth that stands 'above' other ways of seeing the world. If this project fails on 'its' own terms there is no other 'legitimating' frame for it to fall back on.

Mathematics is a central part of the economists 'toolbox' because in theory it confirms the rational premises of capitalist humanism. Rational method points back toward its object, rational man, as restatement of its base premise. Irrational man using rational methods would only accidentally produce rational conclusions. Rational man using irrational methods would only accidentally produce rational conclusions.

The hegemonic role of the metaphysics 'behind' mathematics is so deeply embedded in the Western psyche that challenges tend to meet enthusiastic resistance. This point is illustrated through the Western scientific conceit that mathematics is the 'universal' language shared by 'intelligent' beings across an infinite universe of time and space.

That mathematics is claimed to be timeless and universal, knowable to 'intelligent' beings in times past and future and on planets in galaxies far away, but is unknown to the overwhelming majority of people on Earth right now points to both the imperialist tendency of the conceit and to its utter implausibility. The 'universality' of mathematics is its own logical circle, the 'confusion' of method with content. It is theorized to be timeless and universal because its 'objects' are theorized to be timeless and universal. And if this were true why wouldn't it be the only language?

It isn't that Western economists are entirely unaware of these challenges—there is a long history of enthusiastic debate around them. But they are treated as methodological issues when their premises lie at the heart of capitalist ideology. As formal logic, mathematics is tied to the 'will to truth' of Cartesian metaphysics. 'Economic man' is theorized to be rational in the same operational sense as mathematics, to embody 'rationality' as an essential characteristic and to act on / in the world rationally.

Rationality in its economistic sense as 'essential' characteristic is arbitrary within its own terms. Its 'proof' is wholly circular—people are 'rationally' rational, the answer is presupposed in the question. Likewise, method and content are united in the 'will to truth.' To reiterate, rational' methods used by 'irrational man' could hardly be either a 'rational' point of departure or endpoint because 'irrational man' couldn't traverse the metaphysical divide, even using 'rational' methods, to 'competently' interact with 'the world' in the ways theorized to make capitalism a 'rational' system of political economy.

'Irrational man' would render the models of Western economists indeterminate—who knows what 'he' would do? Without the premise of rationality of particular type there is no 'actor' for Western economists to speculate over. These economists reify their own metaphysical humanism—they make themselves the object they claim to study. With little apparent sense of irony empirical studies of 'rationality' by Western economists have tended to be 'rationally' conducted, to presuppose the answer in the question. With this premise of rationality every failure of capitalism is put back as the failure of people to act according to the economists' models. The 'free-trade' agreements eternally being negotiated are to impose this capitalist rationality ever more aggressively on the world.

Western 'intelligence' is the quantum of rational competence, its 'multiplier' in the discovery of Cartesian truth and in earning capitalist profits.

'Logic' and logical 'rigor' are its objects as the methods used to determine economic 'truth,' 'intelligence' in the realm of the economic, which is also its subject. 'Intelligent' economists use the methods of intelligence—logic, mathematics and statistics to 'discover' the truths that are themselves 'intelligent' objects, 'higher' knowledge of 'the world.'

This same intelligence is the Western economist's explanation for relative economic 'success.' 'Successful' capitalists are 'intelligent,' as demonstrated by their 'success,' and they use the methods of intelligence to both gain and demonstrate 'superior' intelligence in the realm of capitalist enterprise. Successful capitalists 'best' their 'competitors' in games of wit, they 'invent the better mouse trap,' they 'rationalize' 'their' businesses and they possess superior 'human capital.' Wall Street hires 'rocket scientists' to help earn outsized 'profits.'

Education 'is the key to economic success.' 'Re-education' 'is the key to solving unemployment.' There exists a 'marketplace of ideas' where those ideas that withstand the rigors of market 'competition' 'rise to the top.' Conversely, as a theory of political and economic 'freedom,' the highly constrained idea of 'rational man' as it is reconstituted in political economy is an imposed identity, the 'freedom' to exist in social circumstance designed to facilitate only one narrow conception of existence. And economic 'method' lies at the heart of this conception.

There is a saying amongst Western economists—'if you're so smart, why aren't you rich?' that is telling in several dimensions. The premise that relates material wealth to intelligence is wholly Cartesian. Intelligence is the capacity that 'legitimates' capitalist economic distribution—who can better apply 'society's' resources to the betterment of us all, the 'smart' wo/man or the 'stupid?'

The history and methods of wealth accumulation in the capitalist West—genocide against indigenous peoples to 'convert' land into 'property,' kidnapping Africans and forcibly expropriating their labor through slavery, war profiteering by bankers and munitions manufacturers and the use of state power to install totalitarian governments for the purpose of securing access to cheap 'natural' resources, suggest that thuggish brutality is 'wealth's' more prevalent explanation.

In the current epic the suicide finance Wall Street is kept alive with transfers and guarantees from the 'public,' from the targets of its financial gamesmanship, at the point of a metaphorical gun—'give us your money or we will destroy the global economy.' The high technology 'tech' entre-preneurs of legend made minor innovations to technologies developed in government labs at public expense and they use the residual of empire to underpay 'low cost' labor to 'earn' 'their' fortunes.

The historical genesis of the mathematical models of modern Western economics is through those built and later discarded by physicists in the late nineteenth century. The models were 're-purposed' by capitalist econ-omists under the twin conceits that economic 'rules' and 'laws' are anal-ogous to physical rules and laws—that they share 'structural' similarities, and that they are expressible through the formal logic of mathematics.

For the economists these conceits were a century or more old before the physical models were co-opted. The 'innovation' was the metaphysical 'structure' the models provided. As irony has it, Western economists con-fused the metaphysical reasoning and 'content' of physics with temporal 'knowledge' of 'the world' and proceeded under the premise that 'physical' models provide a 'material' ground for their economics.

The conspicuous implausibility of much modern economics—e.g. that unemployment is 'leisure' and that people are economistically 'rational,' evolved from efforts to fit capitalist theory into these models developed for other purposes. Despite the 'complexification' achieved through the use of 'higher-order' mathematics, the basic content of these models is economic man rationally 'acting' on the world in near infinite iterations.

The use of complex models to express mundane, largely implausible, ideas 'elegantly' illustrates the nexus of method and content—the models were the 'structure' through which the ideas were 'motivated.' The 'struc-ture' was the ideas as they were arranged; the organization of thought objects by the 'laws' believed to govern them. Left ambiguous, if not fatally confused, is that this economics was / is imposition, not 'discovery.' This relates back to the question of why mathematics isn't the universal lan-guage if, as Western practitioners assert, it is the 'universal' language? And if it isn't then the insistence that it is is imposition, not 'discovery.'

There has also been a history of pushback from within Western eco-nomics against primitive capitalist ideology expressed / obfuscated with complex mathematics. This pushback has come in its most articulate form from those raised in the Keynesian tradition. Keynes forced the issue of logical 'paradox' onto the 'elegance' of classical / neo-classical economics and with it onto the deterministic mathematical models being used by

Western economists. If paradox renders 'logic' indeterminate then the application / manipulation of paradoxical ideas through the formal logic of mathematics likewise renders outcomes indeterminate.

And this may seem off point to practitioners in the Keynesian tradition because paradox has been 'operationalized' in mathematical models, left unasked and / or unarticulated is where paradox left capitalism more broadly considered—for who is capitalist political economy the 'appropriate' form once paradox renders economic man indeterminate?

Capitalist democracy is 'legitimated' as the form of political economy that best facilitates rational self-determination. If paradox renders this rationality indeterminate—'its' acts have ambiguous, or even perverse, effect on 'the world,' then capitalist democracy does not follow from the premises. Psychology adds depth to this idea of paradox—the subconscious / unconscious renders self-determination 'rationally' unpredictable by adding hidden-ness to this 'self.'

'Rationality' as capacity and method requires both to form 'rational' predictions for economic competence to result. If a sub-conscious 'subverts' the capacity to act rationally, then rational method is extrapolation of this subverted 'rationality.' The problem for capitalist economists is that either a wholly implausible set of premises about 'human' being is taken at face value or there are no 'legitimating' premises for the broader project of capitalism. Efforts to make capitalist economics more plausible by chipping around the edges misses the point—capitalist theory is a 'take it or leave it' proposition as theology based in antique metaphysics.

As evolved from Keynes, the capitalist economists who tend to be most critical of the crude humanistic premises of 'economic man' work with 'big picture' macroeconomics, the economics of national and international economic relations. However, working with 'second-order' premises based on implausible first-order premises doesn't really 'buy' macroeconomists anything. Ideas like 'comparative advantage,' the antique theory that through specialization and endowments nations can mutually benefit from international trade, proceed from the 'self-evidence' of what constitutes a 'benefit.'

Under what set of premises is 'more' always 'better,' the unstated premise of comparative advantage? Without the premises that surround the metaphysical humanism of 'economic man' there is nowhere to go with capitalist economics—there is no set of virtues on which to serve as premise for capitalist political economy. Always left out of consideration is the residual of these economic virtues in the world. They are purposely delimited to fit within the discipline of 'economics.' But what gives confidence that what is delimited is virtuous, even within the realm of economic virtue, when the residual—that not considered, is the outcome?

Given these implicit and explicit 'virtues,' in what way are Western macroeconomic policies not the imposition of capitalist ideology by the very same economists who dismiss the conceit of 'economic man' as a caricature? What, precisely, is the goal of macroeconomics if not to impose the virtues that cruder capitalist ideologues attribute to the metaphysical humanism of their own economics? And the ever more intrusive 'trade' agreements being 'negotiated' away from the visibility and consent of those who will be affected by them is testament to the imperial nature of this macroeconomic 'project.'

It is hardly an accident that the neo-capitalist theory that emerged in the West since the 1970s was 'proved' by its proponents with pre-Keynesian deductive logic run through superficially 'sophisticated' mathematical models. When antique capitalist theory is run through antique capitalist economic models antique capitalist economics emerge. The premises do indeed 'prove' the results. Should this read as unduly harsh; the 'rational expectations' movement that took over academic economics in the 1970s is precisely this.

The central conceit of the movement was / is that people are rational in a specific operational sense—straightforward capitalist ideology if I haven't already made that clear. If 'rational' people believe what 'rational' economists believe about 'the economy' they will act as the rational economists say they will goes the theory. To get a sense of how implausible this is, how will your economic behavior change if food stamp expenditures are cut in half? How about if the corporate tax rate is raised by ten percent? What economic model will you base your decisions on?

The methods of Western economics derive from the rationalist premises of Cartesian metaphysics. While put forward, and generally perceived, as being evidence based, this economics derives from assumptions about what it is to be human, what we value and how the world is structured that are unproven within the self-imposed constraint of evidence. The 'rational' methods of mathematics and statistics are inextricably tied to this same web of assumptions. Capitalism itself is premised on this same set of assumptions. With this the circle is complete—economic methodology is capitalist ideology reconstituted as act, as the method of economic man acting economically.

Of sociological interest is the broad social buy-in that this epic found. The combination of arrogance and implausibility—the arrogance that people believe what economists believe about 'the world' and the implausibility that they are the cartoon automatons who act in the ways put forward in economic theories, renders the economics of this era testament to the hegemonic character of capitalism at work.

Finally, the relation of Cartesian rationalism to capitalism made here doesn't follow a traditional left / right divide. Many on the political left are dogmatic rationalists and firm proponents of science and mathematics as objective methods to determine objective truth. I personally spent twenty years using scientific methods to conduct empirical research in economics and finance using / developing mathematical and statistical models. From that experience and continued reading of philosophical texts around the issues I was working with I found the Western economic 'project' to be poorly considered ideology. If it weren't for the deep embedding of this ideology in political economy it wouldn't be worthy of comment.

From this experience I assert these propositions: 90%+ of the empirical results that I've investigated produced different, if not contradictory, conclusions with only slight shifts in the premises. The more rigorous the analyses in terms of strict adherence the 'structural' premises of mathematics and statistics the less plausible the results were when considered in broader context.

Of the fraction of empirical results that 'held up' in the sense of being plausible and well considered, they were all local—they were relevant to temporary and particular circumstances, not timeless and universal truths. The base issue is that people act in the world, not 'on' it. The Cartesian frame can't account for this embedding and as such poses it as a failing, as subjectivity in need of the corrective of 'objects.' Left largely unconsidered is that you are it, your own 'object' and everyone else's, within the frame.

The Parable of Family Income

WESTERN ECONOMICS IS PREMISED ON THE 'SELF-EVIDENCE' OF ITS objects in a specific operational sense. The 'method' of economics, deductive logic from first principles that is 'extended' to the world through the formal logic of mathematics and 'tested' using statistical analysis, 'proves' economic truths by manipulating metaphysical objects put forward as of 'the world.'

Most economists who have considered the matter tend to profess humility toward their 'toolbox,' the methods of Western economics. But the inference from this humility, particularly as it is expressed in 'informal' adjustments to methods that undermine their 'own' basic premises, suggests more a paradoxical relationship than humility. If the 'structural' premises are 'correct' then the methods need no adjustment and if they aren't then the project isn't what it purports to be.

This is particularly true with the statistical methods of 'empirical' research and analysis where adjustments tend to be used after the methods derived from formal statistical theory have failed to yield their desired results. To be clear, even when method follows theory empirical research remains wholly metaphysical—the realm of possible 'answers' follows from how the questions are asked, not on the 'intended' objects.

A saying among statisticians who think about these things, economic and otherwise, is that any statistical result can be undone by redefining the terms (variables) of interest. This ties to the idea of metaphysical 'self-evidence' in that were statistical 'objects' self-evident they would be invariant, they would be what they 'show themselves' to be. What statistical methods count is metaphysical 'objects'—there is nothing else to be counted.

As metaphysical objects they must be self-evident in the sense of being invariant, the 'in and of themselves' of the metaphysical ether—an apple is an apple is an apple, that leaves debate over their 'truth' to method, to competence with the methods of 'rational extension.' Alternatively, if the metaphysical objects of interest are variant the question of commensurability arises—in what ways are they equivalent and in what ways not?

The premise of counting, of statistics, is that a base equivalence exists—the idea of statistical 'distribution' from which statistical results are derived assumes groupings of like objects—the average of a tree, a car and your uncle Fred has no meaning. The weaker standard of 'agreement among reasonable wo/men,' Husserlian in a metaphorical sense, that objects are 'alike' typically used by economists is tacit inference that the broad project of capitalist economics is suspect.

A practical example of these methodological challenges can be found in the statistical object of 'family income.' Intuitively, with full deference to the deeply instantiated ideology behind this intuition, if family income rises families are better off and this portion of 'the economy' is performing well.

However, intuitive understanding of the 'family' and 'income' of 'family income' offers no help in rendering it statistically 'operational'—the requirement of Western economic methods, not of 'nature.' To render it operational is to establish metaphysical equivalence as like 'objects' to be counted.

Without doing so there is no way to 'measure' economic outcomes, the mode of demonstration chosen by Western economists, and there is therefore no reason to believe that rising family income is a 'good' thing. The 'arbitrary' character of rendering economic 'objects' operational is their residual, the ontological 'context' deemed irrelevant to the questions being asked as inferred by 'its' exclusion.

This dissociation has no basis in the internal logic of Western economic methods—it can be done but doing so 'settles' nothing because there are infinite iterations as equally demonstrable. To be clear, this relates to the 'construction' of the inquiry, to what is used as evidence and what isn't. A realm of concern guides this construction and selection of 'its' 'objects,' the objects don't choose themselves. This is to state that the realm of possible outcomes is a function of the premises at work, of the 'objects' chosen.

For instance, depending on the structure of 'an economy,' the proportion of paid to total economic production could be quite low. This is the case with many 'developing' countries. In this case, and depending on how it's counted, a rise in family income could indicate a drop in economic production—e.g. the forced foregoing of a successful garden that feeds a family to be paid below subsistence wages in an underwear factory.

NAFTA (North American Free Trade Agreement) and subsequent 'free-trade' agreements are responsible for exactly these types of outcomes. What is put forward as economic progress in capitalist theory, as an increase in economic growth attributable to 'structural reforms' based on this theory, is derived by not counting what was destroyed—the residual of this operational logic.

There is a long history of Western corporations using state power to implement strategies such as hut taxes, land taxes or industrial agricultural 'dumping' to destroy functioning indigenous economies that force people to labor for cash wages. Family income can increase while the economic well being of the family declines substantially. This is a central reason why agricultural 'reforms' in trade agreements have been politically sensitive.

Through economic 'measurement' the success of these strategies can be 'proven' when its opposite is true. And ironically, rendering the terms of Western economics operational is 'empirically' equivalent to the endless debate held in earlier centuries by 'schoolmen' around how many angels fit on the head of a pin—there are just as many ways of making a term operational and none of them derive from the methods proclaimed to provide logical 'rigor.'

So, what is the 'family' of family income? Is it a married couple? With children? Any couple living together? With children? Any married couple regardless of whether or not they live together? With young children? With adult children? Grandparents aunts, uncles and cousins? Adults who live together but aren't in a relationship? Single adults who live alone and who aren't planning to marry? Multiple 'families' living together in a single household? Children who split their time between divorced parents? Between re-married parents who also have their own children? What about foster children?

If there were any 'method' to resolve the question it would be found in 'self-evidence,' the 'object' of family that shows itself as its timeless and universal self. So, which from the list above is showing itself as the self-evident 'family?' Again, economists can agree on a definition much as they can agree on how many angels fit on the head of a pin, but in what way does doing so relate to the project of empirical research to determine economic truths? To be clear, the tedious legalisms of defining 'family' operationally are a function of Western economic methods alone. An 'informal' understanding functions as effective discursive object outside the realm of Cartesian truth claims.

One strategy attempted to resolve the problem of 'family income' was to count 'household income' instead—all of the income received by 'households' regardless of the relationships of their inhabitants? In the U.S. 'household income' increased as women entered the workforce in the 1970s because more people in a given household were working for wages. Women weren't working for 'wages' before they entered the wage economy, but does this mean they did 'nothing,' the Western economist's alternative to labor, 'leisure?' The answer is no. Women were an integral part of household 'production.'

No matter how much nuance is put into producing operational objects, into defining them, they are the result of a 'subjective' inclusion / exclusion process, not from the 'givenness' of the resulting 'objects.' Philosopher Edmund Husserl wrote an entire book, 'Crisis in the European Sciences,' to develop a way of defining these objects and wasn't able to recover a plausible basis for doing so. And once the broader context of an inquiry is considered what becomes apparent is that narrow 'truths' can easily be their opposite. The much lauded 'evidence' of Western economics (and science) can hide and obscure as much or more than it renders visible.

Would putting young children to work for wages to raise household income make households better off? And most fundamentally for Western economists, what is the 'rational' basis for any of these definitions when within the internal logic there is no 'method' that favors one over another? Conversely, to let statistical results 'speak for themselves' begs the question of the 'objects' from which results were derived? Unless they also 'speak for themselves' there is no 'there' there to support results.

So, what is the 'income' of family income? Is it all monetary receipts within a given period? For work done? Outside of the house? What about uncompensated labor that yields an economic result like a raising a vegetable garden that feeds the family? Inheritance? Capital gains? Unrealized gains from investing? Deferred compensation? The write-down of debt owed? A travel allowance? Discounts on products and services purchased? An income tax rebate? Gambling losses deducted from a tax liability? Gambling winnings? Gifts?

As tedious as these 'questions' are, they wouldn't be questions at all if the metaphysical construct of capitalist economics were either plausible or coherent. The method of 'economic man' acting economically requires an atemporal 'self' on the 'inside' for whom these questions are already answered. Again, 'answers' here refers to the objects of inquiry, the 'family' and 'income' of 'family income as self-evident and indubitable existents.

If economic man must reach out into 'the world' to answer them then the world informs the atemporal self and thereby renders it truths temporal. In other words, if both the questions—what is family, what is income, and the answers are from 'the world' the methods of Western economics are rank pretense as anything other than particularly tedious discourse. This isn't to argue that this discourse shouldn't take place amongst those for whom it has meaning. But the claim-assertion that it should take precedence over other related discourse is a power grab, not 'science.'

Assume for a moment that 'family' is defined to be a married couple with children under the age of eighteen. From the list of possibilities presented above, defining the term narrowly excludes more than it includes and it does so arbitrarily within the logic of the metaphysical construct.

By putting 'family,' 'household,' or 'income' forward as statistical objects a totalizing claim is made—without carefully considering what is both 'inside' and 'outside' of their definitions any economic 'results' that are associated with them simultaneously represent and misrepresent any conceivable relationship.

Why would either 'family' or 'household' be self-evident and / or relevant as unit of social organization? And by putting them forward as economic 'objects' they become impositions. 'Family' and 'household' are what they are defined to be—the act of circumscription is imperial assertion. Again, without broad knowledge of 'all' sides of this circumscription any results are necessarily indeterminate—is a rise in household income 'good' or not?

Asserting that it is 'good' is to impose a 'virtue,' to force a broad set of premises about political economy under the guise that it is politically 'neutral' 'information.' This isn't to argue against social judgments as discourse outside of the social power to force one's will onto the matter. It is to argue that Western economic methodology is ideology with imperialist tendencies. Capitalism is a broad package of 'virtues' based upon questionable premises and Western economic methodology is the mode of delivering them.

On the Inside Looking Out

The metaphysical worldview is premised on the separation of the Western 'self' from 'the world.' This separation is fundamental—it is separation of the self from society, from 'the world' and in so being, of the self from the self. The frame of capitalist economics is of self-contained, self-circumscribed 'individuals' reaching out from a metaphysical 'inside' to act on 'the world.'

The paradox of existing in 'the world' while reaching out from the realm of the 'self' to act on it separates existence from being. To act 'on' oneself as the 'self' 'inside' reaching out to act is radical alienation, the view of the self of 'the world' as an alien presence.

It is through this homelessness that the environmental and social catastrophes of capitalism find logic as acts on alien presence, a competition for 'its' resources among the self-circumscribed nation-states of Western 'individuals' as distant from ourselves as we are from each other.

The implied premise is that capitalism can exist without 'the world' and 'we' can as well, the 'brains in a vat' of Western philosophical speculation, only without the physical constraint of actually needing brains. With the scope and scale of capitalism's catastrophes on upward trajectory this premise may one day be put to the test.

The metaphysics expressed in capitalist political economy is of worlds bounded only by 'the imagination.' Through it 'resources,' the bounty of 'the world,' are but psychic artifacts, a tree psychically transmogrified into 'paper,' building material' or 'armchair,' while keeping its 'tree-ness' as economized commodity in psychic being.

As mental object 'tree' is just like every other tree and simultaneously like 'ocean,' 'sky' and 'person,' the 'something' that is nothing. If one tree is 'destroyed' it is of no consequence because it is 'just like' every other. If one ocean is 'destroyed' it is of no consequence because it is 'just like' every other. In the realm of the imagination all that need be done in the face of catastrophe is to imagine another world.

'Competition' for 'resources' is a game between metaphysical equivalents, the 'reaching out' into the world to claim for ourselves 'its' bounty that becomes through social claims 'our' bounty as the royal 'we' in the isolated nation-state of the individual. The 'want' that is a fundamental premise of capitalism presupposes separation from its object.

'Possession' is to make a social transfer from outside of one's social realm to inside of it—it doesn't 'breach' the metaphysical ether to meet its corresponding 'want' because they are 'determined' to exist in different realms, on different planes.

Capitalist production is this 'self' reaching out to act on 'the world' through method. 'Method' is both the transfer mechanism of this reaching out and the measure of competence inferred back on it through efficacy, its metric of social competence in the society of oneself.

Capitalist democracy is the aggregation of self-contained individuals who nevertheless share language, culture, history and who entered 'the world' with 'its' particular arrangement of social circumstance. The 'outward' directionality of capitalist metaphysics has these brave individuals building the hospitals in which they were born, educating the doctors who birthed them and building the schools in which they were educated.

This can be found in the capitalist premise that circumstance is a function of competent interaction with the world—doing your job 'well' or building a business that 'succeeds.' As system of 'natural' distribution capitalism in theory distributes according to contribution. Prior distribution, the temporal facts as they exist historically, have no bearing on metaphysical 'self' determination.

The 'problem' of prior distribution is that it is 'unearned.' If capitalism distributes according to contribution but some are born with far more than others then capitalism is only one distribution system among many. The necessary conceit then is that Western selves built the world that they enter when born. This is particularly pertinent when considering the distribution of 'capital.' If it is inherited it isn't 'earned' and therefore it only serves as the basis for one theory of 'natural' distribution—hereditary.

Following from this equality of 'opportunity' is the logical 'starting point' for metaphysically equivalent selves because reaching out to 'the world' begins with us. History has no bearing on 'the present' or 'the future' because it has no persistence—it is stories about a world there for the taking.

Material circumstance likewise has no bearing because 'we' are necessarily prior to it as actors with equal capacity to choose among its objects.

Metaphysical equivalence and the directionality of atemporal 'time' render all social distribution subsequent and therefore 'just.' Put differently, that which is inherited is necessarily part of an infinite chain of 'earned' wealth else it is a corrupt basis for its future application as 'capital.' But even if it was 'earned' its fact is corrupt because it is 'unearned' by the inheritor.

'We' 'deserve' the circumstances of 'our' temporal existence because it is but the social allocation of atemporal existents, the social circumscription in capitalist democracy of that competently 'gained' through a fair game amongst equals. Every wo/man is an island. And a world that begins with 'us' only need persist as long as 'we' do.

Social organization premised on theories of the aggregation of unrelated individuals, as capitalist theory is, is fundamentally incoherent in 'its' own terms. Were the self-determined 'individuals' of capitalist democracy plausible the theoretically coherent mode of social organization would be to dump babies at birth in an open field so that they could determine themselves unimpeded by 'society.'

And if theories of human development enter the picture then so does history: if 'we' are 'in' 'the world' as children until the age of eighteen or twenty-one then we are 'of' 'the world' thereafter—the 'self-determination' of capitalist theory proceeds from 'selves' who existed socially before they didn't. Karl Marx made a related point when he referenced the 'Robinsonade[93]' pretensions of capitalist theory, the contention that its production occurs as if by thousands of Robinson Crusoes on their individual desert islands toiling alone rather than in social production.

The capitalist theories of 'system' of Adam Smith and David Ricardo are fundamentally incoherent for this same reason. Without the self-determined 'individuals' of capitalist theory there is no reason why capitalist democracy is any more 'legitimate' than any other 'system' of political economy. And with 'them' there is no coherent theory of social organization. If every person is 'self-made,' is 'responsible' for what they have and what they are, then what conceivable need could they have of others, in particular the 'system' that makes it possible?

This creates the paradox that Smith's and Ricardo's 'systems' are necessary for the self-determination of capitalist individuals. And if the 'system' is necessary, the 'system' of capitalism, then how is it that individuals are self-determined? Once a context is granted, a 'system,' then people are only self-determined within it.

However, the type of system that facilitates self-determination is necessarily premised on the type of being whose self-determination is facilitated by that system. The paradox of self-determination comes full circle. The 'freedom to choose' is as a particular type of being within a 'system' that takes the type of being it facilitates as given. The endpoint is that 'self-determination' can only take place when the self is already fully determined. Otherwise there is no necessary relation between these 'selves' and system.

The paradox is a function of Cartesian metaphysical dualism found in the relation of the Cartesian self to 'the world.' In the scientific view 'the world' is a system or group of systems. Scientists 'reach out' to gather evidence and then bring it 'back inside' (think about it) to draw conclusions. The relation of knower to known is of the type of being who 'knows' to a world that can be 'known.' What is known is a function of the world to be known. These are mutually dependent premises, not 'facts.'

Art, music and literature are ways of 'knowing' that don't take as their type the scientific worldview. Within the scientific worldview these necessarily take place 'in' the same world from whence the type of knowledge of science is 'taken.' However, they make no necessary premises about the type of world they are knowledge of. Music might be explained in terms of acoustics or composition but it isn't reducible to them. Scientific knowledge is reducible to its 'facts.'

Capitalism is also reducible to its facts. Like science these facts derive from premises about the world and the premises about the world derive from 'its' facts. Capitalism is the system of Western self-determination because self-determination is the base premise of capitalism. 'Choice' is that which is chosen, its fact. How is this known? Because it was chosen. The 'proof' of self-determination is through what is chosen, the type of 'object' chosen.

The Marxian idea of alienation as the abstraction of producer from product in capitalist exchange presents a collision of worldviews, an attempt to reconcile economic production as 'praxis[95],' the fully engaged, and therefore non-metaphysical, 'act' of production with the metaphysical idea of thought reaching 'out' into 'the world' to act on it.

Within the capitalist frame the 'act' of economic production leaves 'its' product in the world—there is no way to 'bring' it 'into' the atemporal realm of the self. Capitalist product isn't alienated because it never existed in the same realm as the producer. Because praxis, or some related engaged idea of 'act', occurs entirely in the temporal realm there is no theorized distance between producers and produced, no 'view from nowhere' from which to see it as anything other than what it is.

The idea of equivalence in exchange is incoherent in this material view—exchange remains fully plausible as social act but it is exchange of this for that, a loaf of bread for a basket of peaches, not of 'equivalents' through metaphysical conversion. And the loaf of bread didn't bake itself and the peaches didn't pick themselves.

Western economists consider this process of metaphysical conversion through the thing-act of money to be a great innovation, the 'fluid' that facilitates modern economic production. But to the Marxian point, when the metaphysical 'construct' behind this idea of conversion between realms is carefully considered —first in the act of production and then in the act of exchange, it is wholly implausible—where precisely does the realm of atemporal equivalence reside?

It could be, and is, argued that capitalist 'equivalence' in exchange is a useful social convention. But that leaves its 'facts' in the realm of the temporal. Unless there is a separate realm of metaphysical objects the very idea of equivalence is incoherent and it leaves the Marxian charge of alienation both intact and more plausible than the capitalist account.

Without this metaphysical equivalence the broad frame of Western 'market' economics falls apart. The capitalist conceit is that no trade would take place without either implicit or explicit equivalence—what would be the motivation? 'Price' plays the role of metric of equivalence in exchange. But asserting capitalist metaphysics ever more fervently hardly makes it any more plausible.

'Praxis' as fully engaged 'act' of economic production can be explained entirely within temporal being, there is no need for rank speculation about a netherworld that exists somewhere—no one knows exactly where, from which 'labor' reaches out into the world to act on it as alien presence in an alien realm.

Yet this is exactly how labor is framed in Western economics—'it' reacts to market 'opportunities' to perform work not of its creation because it is determined by market demand, structured through capitalist organization and compensated through wages that sever producer from produced. To be clear, the Marxian explanation of the relation of producer to produced need not be, and isn't, competing metaphysics as the capitalist critique generally asserts.

This latter point is relevant inasmuch as capitalist economists have long argued that labor theories of value such as Marx's are incoherent within the mainstream economic frame. The divide can be seen in the competing ideas of the determinant of value. The mainstream view is that the psychic quantum of 'utility' determines value—people buy and sell goods and services at the point where the psychic satisfactions of doing so are 'equalized' through price.

This is reiteration of the base metaphysical frame of self-determined individuals acting on 'the world' from 'inside.' The Western economist's 'utility' is the quantum of want, rational calculation is the method of its determination and exchange is the interaction of these individuals in 'the world.' Because economic production through praxis poses no metaphysical divide, no division between the 'self' doing the producing and 'the world,' there is no quantum determined on the 'inside' to be equilibrated through market price in 'the world.'

The capitalist critique of labor theories of value is in this way an insistence on the metaphysical worldview, not a critique from within the terms as they have been put forward. Forcing a non-metaphysical conception of economic production into a metaphysical frame is to pose a division that didn't previously exist. The charge of alienation, of an imposed separation of producer from product, is wholly coherent outside of capitalist metaphysics. In this way capitalist economics can be seen as the imposed ideology it is.

In historical terms the preponderance of economic production has taken place outside of Western economists' explanations of it. The burden that this poses is that capitalist explanations are imposed on this totality, not simply on capitalist production. This can be seen through motivation. Either the psychic quantum of utility explains all economic production or it explains none of it because it is either a fundamental characteristic of 'man' or it is an imposition.

Here Marxian alienation can be seen as both fact and metaphor—fact as the imposition of market relations on non-market economic production and metaphor as insistence on the divide between self and world posed by the metaphysical frame when theories from outside of it demonstrate its limited power as explanation. And this imposition becomes its fact through capitalist imperialism expressed through trade agreements, monopoly strategies to destroy 'competition' and military adventures to secure economic resources, particularly 'malleable' labor, such as the U.S. has carried out in Central America for much of the last century.

The premise of capitalist exchange equilibrated through money must take the entire metaphysical worldview with it for coherence. If price is the metric of equivalence, as Western economic theory has it, then what is it equivalence of? Within this Western frame if price doesn't represent the entire social costs of production—the adverse social and environmental consequences that are 'profit' to the capitalist when forced onto others, then exchange as equivalence is a 'taking' by both capitalist and consumer.

To be clear, capitalist profit is the reconstitution of these social harms as metaphysical equivalents—the contention that social 'costs' are vague and uncountable finds their precise count in profit within the capitalist frame. Outside of this frame the temporal 'costs' of production are its material facts, not its exchange value. And the capitalist distinction between 'profits' and economic 'rents' assumes complete knowledge of the residual of economic production, the costs as they exist in fact outside of self-serving capitalist calculus.

To the extent capitalist 'profit' derives from imperial history and relations, wars for economic resources, global warming and regional and local social and environmental catastrophes, these measure the in-equivalence of capitalist exchange, the quantum of mis-measure that renders its metaphysical 'objects' propaganda for its dystopian facts.

It is little wonder that capitalists and Western economists want for 'exchange' to put the matter to rest, to cut off further relation lest the difference between market and material-social costs be seen in the 'uncompensated' residual.

'Alienation' is in this way both metaphysical 'product' and analog, the premise of separation reconstituted in capitalist exchange as its fact, the misdirection needed to allow dissociated beings to reconstitute their metaphor as facts of political economy.

The Day That 'Free' Became 'Natural'

QUITE SPECTACULARLY, ACTUAL CAPITALISTS APPEAR TO PUT VERY little stock in capitalist theories of 'the self.' It took a century of increasingly expensive and intrusive advertising based on principles of Freudian psychology to create modern 'consumers' and 'consumer culture.' When Karl Marx wrote of 'commodity fetishism[97]' in the mid nineteenth century it was as minor artifact of then emergent capitalism, not as 'consumer culture' as it exists in the present.

Backward inference that the world was 'always this way,' that modern consumer culture reflects timeless and universal 'facts' of human existence, is an attempt to place it in 'nature' rather than in historical development. Capitalist economists are forced to frame advertising as the conveyance of 'information' as psychic 'objects' because theories of psychology challenge the notion of 'self-determination' that serves as the 'natural' basis for capitalist democracy.

Determination of the Western 'self' through social means such as advertising reframes capitalism as a 'system' of social control rather than one of economic 'freedom' it is put forward as. Modes of social coercion reverse the directionality of the metaphysical construct to posit 'the world' reaching into the ether to 'determine' its 'self-determined' 'individuals.' The paradox for capitalist theory is that unless material wants are 'internally' determined they don't represent, and thereby 'serve,' the atemporal core of economic man, the metaphysical 'self.'

The political-theoretical frame of capitalist democracy is that it provides the 'freedom' for 'self-determined' individuals to act on their wants and desires. Psychology as it is used in advertising is everywhere 'political' in the sense it contradicts the very idea of 'self-determination.'

Western economists are forced into framing advertising as the comparison of product characteristics because allowing for complex psychologies, the fundamental premise of advertising, renders the 'rationality' of capitalist theory indeterminate—conclusions no longer follow from economic premises without accounting for this psychology.

The 'structural' political frame is of coercers and the coerced. Those doing the coercing, advertisers in the service of capitalist enterprise, also have psychologies within the frame put forward—there is no 'view from nowhere' or basis in 'nature' from which 'they' can deduce modes of economic coercion that don't contradict the premise of self-determination.

Political economy that uses coercive methods to create the wants and desires it is then purported to fulfill is totalizing—it is a social-logical circle from which there is no escape outside of total repudiation. The problem for capitalist theory is that the issue is binary because of the metaphysical frame at work. Psychology is assertion that capitalism isn't reducible to its facts.

Psychology is a buried type of knowledge. Like art, music and literature, there is no necessary 'external' referent, no 'fact,' to which is 'corresponds.' Psychologists have psychologies. There is no posited 'view from nowhere' such as science rooted in Cartesian metaphysics claims. This poses a fundamental issue for capitalist theory not just because it 'complicates' the 'inside' of self-determination but also because it challenges the Cartesian division of 'inside,' the 'life of the mind,' from the world.

Cartesian rationalism is taxonomy of the mind unencumbered by ambiguity and paradox. The 'want' of goods and services of capitalist theory is only self-determined when it is 'siloed,' the product of rational calculation 'unencumbered' by the buried knowledge that is psychology. The use of psychology in advertising is emotive, as opposed to strictly informational; advertising is direct appeal to this hiddenness. There is no rational 'component' to how advertising makes us 'feel.'

The idea of economic 'freedom' that supports capitalist theory is as 'free from coercion.' The theory of coercion that supports it is 'external' such as a gun put to our heads to force us to do something. The 'internal' coercion of advertising appeals to hiddenness, away from the front-and-center of rational calculation. And in so being it is deeply 'totalitarian' within the Western frame of political coercion.

The history of Western advertising agencies hiring psychologists and basing their advertising campaigns on developed psychological theories suggests that actual capitalist practice bears little relation to the theories of 'freedom' used to legitimate capitalist democracy.

The psychology of advertising is dimensional with hidden-ness of / in the 'sub-conscious' a fundamental characteristic. As advertising was founded and developed by Sigmund Freud's nephew, Edward Bernays, it is the appeal to this hidden-ness that capitalist theory necessarily insists doesn't exist. The alleged difference between advertising and political propaganda[99] arose only after the latter found ill repute as an articulated tool of Nazi social control in the Second World War.

'Psy-ops[101],' or psychological operations, is every day practice of the U.S. military using psychology, including against U.S. citizens, to achieve political goals. Psychology as it is used in Western advertising is the 'science' of the irrational. It is hardly an accident that today young children are its prime targets. Capitalist theory depends not just on the separation of the 'inside' of the 'self' from the 'outside' of 'the world;' a very specific type of 'inside' is needed, one that resides in metaphysical 'flatness.'

Neither Freud nor Bernays need have been 'correct' with their respective theories of 'the mind' to pose a fundamental challenge to the Western conception of the self—the creation of advertising is enough. The wholesale buy-in of Western capitalists goes far to suggest that they believe it 'works.' Again, this doesn't mean it needs to 'work' to point to intent. It is 'ironic' that advertising is used against the very selves capitalism is conceived to serve.

Within the 'rational' analytical frame there is hardly a social philosophy cum hegemonic 'identity' more conducive to 'external' manipulation and control than this Western self that believes itself both indubitable and impenetrable. The effect on Western economics is that 'externally' instantiated wants take the whole façade of capitalism to the ground—if market 'demand' is created through advertising then capitalist economics is circular reconstitution of the wants capitalists create—its 'objects' are wholly temporal.

Framed askew, if advertising can create wants it can also 'resolve' them wholly outside of capitalist production. And even within this economics the scale and growth of advertising as capitalist enterprise either represents the 'efficient allocation of capital' or the broad capacity of capitalism to do so is brought into question.

A rough analogy would be Western businesses spending a trillion dollars a year to build theme parks on the moon—a project that would make the most ideologically motivated caricatures of 'central planning' models of economic 'efficiency' by comparison.

And if the production and purchase of advertising is an efficient allocation of capital the system of capitalist democracy it purports to support has no 'legitimate' basis within 'its' internal logic. It becomes the political economy of 'soft' coercion that depends on and facilitates its theorized nemesis, the externally determined 'self.'

The absence of perfect correlation of advertising 'intent' to outcomes, 'failed' advertising that doesn't lead people to buy more of a good or service, has no bearing here. The capacity of any advertising to influence people requires breeching the metaphysical ether by reaching 'inside' from the 'outside.' And any broad look at modern advertising demonstrates this precise intent of creating 'externally' conceived selves.

This Machine Likes Fascists

THE OFT CALLED 'KNOWLEDGE' ECONOMY BROUGHT INTO BEING IN THE 'developed' West in the 1940s but brought to full flower in the 1990s is composed of several industries that are broadly related but also quite specific unto themselves—artificial intelligence, telecommunications, finance, information technology and digital commerce—the Internet. More broadly, these can be divided into 'finance'—Wall Street, insurance and real estate; and 'technology', modes and methods of operational interaction with the world.

One branch of these technologies in particular, the algorithmic 'intelligent' technology of computing tied together through global telecommunications infrastructure, is often put forward by Western economists as a second 'industrial age', a group of innovations that revolutionized the way the world 'works.' The development and growth of these industries was coincident with the revival of the political economy of neo-liberalism and the return of finance capitalism in its most intrusive and destructive form. And finance—Wall Street, played a prominent role in inserting these new technologies into global political economy by financing them.

Finance and information technology are 'Cartesian' capitalism reconstituted in its purest form, the form, function and facilitation of the 'rational' interaction of 'economic man' with 'the world' of capitalist theory. Finance is the 'fluid' of capitalism, the Aristotelian ether that unites commerce and suspends it in a body of metaphysical equivalence, the 'this equals that' that facilitates the aggregation of claims on 'the world.'

The 'intelligence' of 'intelligent' machines is algorithmic, the product of instructions written in mathematical languages to be operationally efficient, the reconstitution of 'time is money' into machine action. Not coincidentally, finance and technology are the twin 'explanations' offered by capitalist economists for the stupendous fortunes suddenly found in the pockets and bank accounts of a group of actual persons so small it could barely fill a large meeting room.

The typical frame of 'technology' in Western economics is as method / mode of economic 'efficiency' in capitalist production. Opponents of technology are 'Luddites,[103]' labor displaced by technology whose blame is 'misplaced' because making more from less—economic efficiency, makes 'the world' better off. The 'tradeoff' offered is that this displaced labor can now buy lower priced goods made possible through 'technology.'

And if the new found absence of a paycheck hinders those directly displaced from reaping economic benefit then the economic 'system' is argued to benefit. Finance, 'money,' is the fluid and metric of equivalence here, the object of 'system' that renders irrelevant whose pocket it ends up in. The fact of displacement is its own proof, the backward induction that technology found the right target.

This theoretical sleight of hand is wholly circular—economic efficiency made possible through technology benefits the economic system, labor displaced by technology is part of this economic system and therefore displaced labor benefits from being displaced. However, 'technology' as method, mode and machine never displaced anyone—it is a tool of Western political economy, not its actor.

Like science and mathematics, technology is claimed to be ideologically 'neutral,' the tool / act that builds the toaster oven more efficiently and makes it 'work' for Libertarians and Communists alike. As it evolved from Cartesian metaphysics, the Anglo-American philosophical tradition places the use of technology (tools) as a central characteristic that 'separates' humans from animals.

Why such a separation is needed gets to the heart of the metaphysical construct—so profound is her alienation that technology is the only link economic man has to 'the world' s/he needs for sustenance. This operational mode of relating makes technology essential to the internal logic of capitalism as 'rational' reconstitution of economic man's 'imperative' in 'the world.'

The circular relation of technology to 'profit' is through economic 'efficiency' as the theorized metric of competent interaction with 'the world.' The efficiency of firing ten million workers employed in manufacturing in the West and hiring ten million workers to do the same work at lower wages in other countries is measured by the profit 'earned' from doing so.

Technology as 'ways of doing things' is a strategy of social circumscription, the circular 'proof' that social wealth finds 'its' way into the 'right' pockets. And Western technology is so deeply instantiated into modern political economy that imagining different ways of relating to 'the world' faces the hurdle of establishing 'practical' alternatives.

As with capitalism broadly considered, the challenge for technologists is the indissociable relation of technology to both wanted and unwanted outcomes—the 'efficiency' of technology depends on counting only 'its' 'intended' consequences.

This is in part why the Cartesian fluid of 'profit' is so frequently put forward as 'its' own proof of economic 'efficiency'—any look at the broader results of capitalist production quickly renders narrow 'proofs' implausible. The technologies of the 'tech revolution' were by and large developed with public resources in government laboratories or with government funds and then sold to 'private' interests.

The great 'tech' fortunes were built with the expropriated labor of imperial consequence, the 'states of nature' that evolved from three centuries of imperial dysfunction imposed from without on 'developing' economies for the purpose of economic extraction. Technology as it is conceived in capitalist theory is the fact / act of economic imperialism—'its' object is 'the world' and its perspective is 'efficient' exploitation.

The knowledge of the 'knowledge' economy is operational, the uniting of thought 'objects' with operational technologies to accomplish specific tasks. 'Knowledge' workers are technocrats of capitalist enterprise, the 'inputs' that are also 'outputs' in the sense that the 'objects' and modes of their knowledge are 'externally' given, the creators whose realm of creation is the task at hand.

These technocrats—e.g. financial 'engineers', computer programmers or investment bankers, are no more likely to 'know' carpentry, how to make 'fine art', or the history of Slovakia than anyone else. 'Knowledge' in this sense is as technology in particular mode of capitalist production, the 'creation' that is its own product.

The 'machines' of this technology are both inputs and outputs, the 'useful tools' that require that 'users' become tools in return, that we learn 'their' rules and methods before they become 'useful' to us. Strategies of monopoly are everywhere in evidence in the gadgets that are both 'essential' and that each require the commitment of learning their particular operational rules and 'languages.'

The 'knowledge' of knowledge work is the competent learning of these rules, the development of operational competence within given realms of economic production. Like 'labor' and 'capital' in Western economic theory, this 'knowledge' reacts as / through technology to market imperative as created creation in the service of externally given task.

The reactive nature of this knowledge and 'its' technologies are a function of capitalist metaphysics—technology as both method and objectified method are premised on 'operation' as the transmogrification of thought through method into action 'on / in' the world. The premise is that input 'operated' on through technology is its total output.

This again is how / why 'profit' is so logical / useful a 'cleanser' as metric of technological 'efficiency.' Technology is both ways of doing things and the reconstitution of method in concrete form—a toaster 'toasts,' a computer 'computes' and insurance 'insures.'

Back in 'the world' manufacturing toasters and computers produces 'unintended' toxic waste, the energy used to transport and operate them contributes to global warming, their production and use have social consequences and the 'product' of insurance requires negotiation based in asymmetrical social power to be brought into being—for claims to be paid.

A primary conceit of Western economics is that the automation of 'routine' functions with algorithmic machines is 'efficient,' that it 'frees' labor to do more 'meaningful' work—'knowledge' work. Left unstated is that these routine tasks were made routine by this 'knowledge' applied through technology, 'rationalization,' and that the externally circumscribed 'choice' of this 'system' is between different types of rationalized production, between machines and rationalized labor.

This newly 'freed' 'routine' labor is placed in competition with other 'routine' labor in the present and with knowledge workers whose work has been made routine in 'the future.' 'Knowledge' work is the temporary 'privilege' of rationalization, the routine of making production routine. The implied 'goal' of technology as capitalist enterprise is total rationalization—to either make 'labor' 'like' machines or to make 'it' just go away.

In considering the social conditions of production the capacity to make labor 'predictable,' willing and able to 'be' technology, comprises the basis of this 'equivalence.' 'Multi-tasking,' the analog of algorithmic 'efficiency' applied to labor, is technology as backward induction, the thoughtless thought of the 'intelligent' machine.

That multi-tasking doesn't 'work' in the sense of making people more 'productive' is evidence of the nature of both the 'task at hand' and of algorithmic 'intelligence.' The task at hand is machine application and algorithmic intelligence is machine 'efficiency.' Knowledge work is the reconstitution of capitalist imperative as 'self' realization. It is the act of producing the social conditions of un-knowledge, the de-thinking of economic production.

This critique is not 'fear' that machines and machine 'thought' will overtake 'us,' that 'they' might really be 'smarter' than we are. 'Intelligent' machines were / are insipid delusion from the get-go, Cartesian 'brain in a vat' hallucinations premised on the circular conceit that 'intelligence' is rational interaction with the world, that machines can be built to rationally interact with the world and therefore that 'rational' machines are intelligent.

The logical 'position' of this 'intelligence' acting 'on' 'the world' is of paradox, the objectification of the 'selves' doing the objectifying. The metaphysical frame of 'economic man' has its 'selves' acting on the very same world that they exist in, acting 'on' themselves as objects of exploitation.

'Intelligent' machines are the objectification of this objectification, the automation of the technologies of exploitation from the perspective of radical alienation. They are 'useful' by forcing a particular conformity—conformity with the requirements of 'rationalized' economic production, by training 'us' to fully participate in our own exploitation.

The work of 'knowledge' workers is ultimately to reduce 'their' jobs to their machine analog as routine function and then 'rationally,' as 'objective' observers, choose between their continued employment and replacing themselves with 'intelligent' machines. The only 'intelligent' conclusion of knowledge work is to cut 'its' own pay or to fire itself.

It is hardly an accident that the single largest use the Internet has been put to is the distribution of pornography. The Internet is 'information' as metaphysical thought objects dissociated from 'the world' and put forward as new forms of completeness, the reconstitution of the Cartesian netherworld in machine 'space.'

Pornography is the decontextualization of the social relations of 'being' together in 'the world' to reframe them as 'commodity' complete with the metaphysical categories needed to sell the invariance of 'product.' The exponential increase in the quantity and availability of pornography is coincident with the re-emergence of rabidly ideological capitalism and it broadly reflects the social relations of capitalist production.

Specific social relations are obliterated in favor of theories of eternal interchangeability in metaphysical equivalence, the mothers, fathers, sisters, brothers, friends and neighbors recontextualized as 'sex' 'objects' in categories of dissociated body parts and 'acts.' As with toaster ovens and lint rollers, there is no information about the social production of pornography provided in its 'product.' And as with these 'products,' the exchange of money promises absolution, the contrived ignorance of the circumstances of production that serves dual purpose as 'self' knowledge.

The ongoing devolution of the Internet into tool of the corporate surveillance state comes straight from the internal logic from which it was conceived. Technology has long been used to 'leverage' state power through weapons production, surveillance, 'logistics,' communications and the manufacture of prosthetics—artificial 'limbs' to replace those lost in wars.

The nations and alliances with the 'best' weapons wield state power as imperial object, as both threat and fact of 'external' domination and control of political economy. Through the re-emergence of high capitalism and its consequence in the concentration of wealth and power it is only 'logical' that this imperial reach would look 'inward.'

Those allegedly being 'protected' from terrorist threats through surveillance face actual threats on weekly, daily and hourly bases by those who now put themselves forward as 'protectors.' The trajectory and existing facts of economic immiseration in the West has behind it those doing the immiserating, the technologists and financiers whose fortunes depend on the technologies of economic extraction and wealth protection.

The factual threat from 'terrorism' is infinitesimally small whereas the threats of environmental catastrophe, diminished incomes, inadequate health care, 'outsourced' employment, 'commercialized' education and diminished recourse through the institutions of capitalist 'democracy' are realized every day.

As with the distribution of political and economic power in the West, the 'unity' of the 'protected' is as royal subjects to the Lords and Ladies of the manor, as those whose 'freedom' is to act in the interests of a social order that places them on the 'losing' end of the power being 'protected.'

Through this implausible 'unity' surveillance is sold as a benefit, as the application of knowledge work to machine power in the service of the public weal. Left unspoken is that surveillance in the service of state power is only the slightest variation on its use in the 'commercial' technologies of economic coercion, subversion and extraction in the service of capitalist enterprise.

Without irony the same 'unity' that claims labor displaced by technology 'benefits' from its displacement has the surveiled 'benefiting' from corporate-state surveillance and technologies of coercion. The surveiled have 'nothing to hide' because they have internalized the corporate-state imperative as loyal subjects of a social order that sees only contingent 'value' in their continued existence.

Electronic surveillance is the 'passive' eye that keeps the 'freedom' to be surveiled, coerced and immiserated free. The required suspension of disbelief is found in the careful parsing of the public-private divides; the same tools in the service of maintaining public 'order' in the hands of the state are used for active economic coercion in the service of capitalist enterprise.

The social divisions of Western history are reframed through imperial prerogative as police matters, the maintenance of a unified social order by decree. The overwhelming prevalence of these technologies leaves 'nothing to hide' with 'nowhere to run.' The logic of technologies of social control is to ever more efficiently achieve the ends of its architects.

By the early 1980s Wall Street had found confluence with emerging 'intelligent' technologies to produce the 'fluid' of transactable equivalence needed to radically alter existing relations of economic production. A central challenge was that plausible alternatives needed to be created from 'nothing' as a place to send the employment to be outsourced. And finance was the means to this end.

Whereas in 'the world' 'labor' exists in the embedded context of time, space, social relations, history and culture, money 'liquefies' the capitalist 'production function' to provide the illusion of metaphysical equivalence across these dimensions.

Through this illusion labor in the U.S. was placed in implausible 'competition' with labor embedded in other political economy—in Mexico, India and China, where the barriers to factual competition include geography, national boundaries, language and existing social relations.

Through the creation of metaphysical equivalence the money of finance reduced these factual barriers to 'price.' It is 'efficient' to fire highly paid manufacturing workers in the West and hire low paid workers to do the same work ten thousand miles away because the only metric used to determine this efficiency is 'profit.'

And profit is a simple accounting exercise—if costs 'fall' while revenues hold steady then profits increase. Profit is the central metric visible to capitalist economists because it is the one denominated in the 'currency' of metaphysical equivalence. Rococo theories of capitalist fantasy are put forward in theoretical debate when what is missing from the economic accounting is a full, or even partial, social accounting.

When Money Hits the Lottery

THE EXPONENTIAL GROWTH OF FINANCE OF RECENT DECADES, AND WITH it financial gamesmanship and increasingly intrusive financial cum economic catastrophes, has precedence in the run-up to the Great Depression of the 1930s. The looting of the Savings & Loans in the 1980s[105] and related recession in the early 1990s, the 'dot-com' stock market bubble[107] and crash of the 1990s and early 2000s and the housing bubble and bust of the mid-late 2000s[109], all resulted from the return of 'finance capitalism' after its forced hiatus following that earlier catastrophe.

This growth was directly related to the broad restructuring of Western political economy including the creation of 'intelligent' technologies now deeply instantiated into capitalist production, diminution of the lot of most working people through contrived 'competition' against the wreckage of former and current imperial relations and the rapid consolidation of wealth made possible through the 'fluid' of finance.

Western economists treat these as largely unrelated events while in fact they all had basis in the bank money system where banks and bankers given the social 'right' to create money did so to enrich themselves and other connected insiders. The shared 'effect' was the creation of speculative bubbles based in finance and political economy broadly reordered to serve the already wealthy.

The S&L 'crisis' was accompanied by a rapid rise in commercial and residential real estate prices in areas where insiders did their looting. The dot-com stock market bubble saw stock prices 'leveraged' to twice the level that preceded the stock market crash of 1929. And the housing bubble and bust of the 2000s saw housing prices driven to twice their 'inflation-adjusted' value nationally. In each of these cases prices that had been driven higher through financial gamesmanship subsequently crashed leaving behind those who had little to do with the looting as victims.

Mainstream economists in the West have largely been at a loss to recognize these financial calamities in the making, to relate them one to the others through this current epic of finance capitalism, or to come up with meaningful 'solutions' to their recurring nature other than to react to the economic catastrophes they cause.

Some liberal-left economists have gone so far as to develop theories of 'self-generating' financial bubbles[111] that place banks and bankers as help-less rubes who had the misfortune to occupy their chairs as bubbles arose around them. In fact, each of these bubbles had large degrees of insider fraud associated with them.

This isn't to dismiss the 'systemic' nature of these bubbles and busts—the 'system' of banking developed historically and it is a socially created 'system'. And the financial looting that occurred is related to the broader imperial tendencies of resurgent capitalism. It is hardly an accident that 'outsourcing' economic production to regions of imperial wreckage was deeply related to 'financialization' of Western political economy.

Bank insiders created these bubbles as means to loot 'their' banks and each other—the bubbles didn't 'self-generate.' In the S&L fiasco over one thousand bankers went to prison, in the dot-com bust a few bankers were forced out of the industry and in the housing bust culpable banks and bankers were provided with up to twenty-five trillion dollars in contin-gent bailout funds and they received trillions, and possibly tens of tril-lions, in direct and indirect bailouts, guarantees and assumptions of bank liabilities by the Federal government.

These events have been well-chronicled elsewhere and it is their broader tendencies and facts that are of interest here. Money is the eco-nomic alchemists' tool, the thing-act that transforms decades of econom-ic production into 'collateral,' the financial pledge that renders economic production convertible into money as debt.

Money is the thing-act that makes a car equal a horse in exchange. The 'natural' evolution of capitalist democracy toward concentrated economic and political power exists within a sea of this 'money,' the fluid of wealth and commerce. Its value, to the extent it has any, is socially determined, a placeholder of value that in its fluid sense reconstitutes metaphysical equivalence in the world, the social converter that says this equals that in trade.

Through this reconstitution money serves to 'naturalize' capitalist metaphysics, to 'move' the facts of 'the world' into the ether where it joins other 'commodities' in physic equivalence.

One dollar buys three apples or two pencils rendering three apples 'equal' to two pencils. 'Apples' and 'pencils' had already been commodified as metaphysical existents and money renders them equivalent both amongst and between themselves in 'the world' of capitalist exchange. Money is the quantum of conversion, a 'thing' in itself and the social contrivance that 'proves' the metaphysical ether by rendering existents 'equal' by their factor of conversion—their 'price.'

Money is the physical reconstitution of the price of 'everything,' the insistence that capitalist metaphysics 'covers' the totality of 'the world' as it is visible. While most of 'the world' is resistant to commodification—conspicuously lacking the static thing-ness that is the realm of commodity, money is the 'fact' of political economy that 'pushes' the world in the direction of commodity.

Money is the philosophy of the commodity, the insistence of a base equivalence that can be counted and 'traded' within its realm. Given the 'right' price the family farm is a sailboat, Picasso's painting 'Guernica' is wallpaper for a bank lobby and children are a luxury that only 'the rich' can afford. As fluid-equivalence possession of money is the measure of the division of everything, 'the world' divided into pieces by its quantity.

As social claim money is imperial power asserted onto the portion of 'the world' that accepts it 'in kind' and / or that is acted on 'through' it. The capacity to create money is the capacity to create social claims, the 'right' of claim that both fashions price and 'pays' it.

As 'act' money is social fact, the expression of the will of 'its' creator-spender as it is applied-imposed. A billionaire stranded alone on a desert island with her or his billions has only the product of their own labor because without exchange as social act money is worthless. Creating money outside of social order-convention is either to create its convincing replica or to create failed money, the thing-act that fails as act.

Finance is the business of money from its creation in the banking system to its allocation by Wall Street and the broader banking system. As such, understanding the 'nature' of money is essential to understanding its role as its own 'proof,' as the social object that most resembles Cartesian psychic object.

Money is also one of the great mysteries of Western economics—what it is and where it comes from are mystified to an extent that hardly seems accidental. This isn't to suggest its analysis isn't part of a typical education in 'economics', but the way its explanation is framed—as 'store of value', 'medium of exchange' and 'means of payment', 'naturalize' it by assigning intrinsic characteristics that are socially given, 'extrinsic' to money itself.

And even when these characteristics are explained as extrinsic the metaphysical noun-verb confusion confounds clear understanding. The source of this money, the fount from which it emerges, is overwhelmingly 'private', created by banks through the process of making loans. It is the act that unites money with debt plus a rate of interest that must be repaid by borrowers.

Without debt there would be no money as the Western money 'system' has developed historically. And there is nothing either 'natural' or necessary in the relation of money to debt. It is an historical contingency resulting from the social power of banks and bankers over Western political economy as it has developed. A money 'system' unrelated to debt is not only possible, but there are good reasons for considering such a system.

These 'uses' of money as explained in economic textbooks are metaphysical—they are presented as existing outside of history and culture. And they allude in an unintended way to the noun-verb confusion of metaphysical reasoning. They come into being through the act of use—storing, exchanging and paying are acts, not characteristics 'stored' in the ether for recovery when needed.

Money is the measure of the capacity of capitalist enterprise to 'act.' Wall Street produces nothing but contingently 'owns' everything through this relation of money to debt. Through credit creation 'private' money is brought into being as money and debt.

Money doesn't exist and then it does against contingent ownership of what 'it' produces—capitalist production financed with debt. And debt carries with it the institutional leverage of capitalism, the set of contingencies that 'externalize' the most destructive aspects of capitalist political economy through rules of repayment that 'structure' resolution regardless of the 'costs' of related outcomes.

The terms of money as debt have deep social implications as the 'enforcement' mechanism of capitalist extraction. Repayment terms force adherence to a particular form of organization—'products' must be produced and sold on a 'rationalized' schedule determined by principal and interest payments.

Debt based money is put forward as a form of market 'discipline' that in fact assumes that factors entirely outside the purview of the terms considered when establishing the loan—general economic conditions, extraordinary circumstances like wars and weather related catastrophes etc., may compel the transfer of technologies of economic production to the lender to be dealt with under their own economic imperatives to assure debt repayment.

This characteristic is behind the economically destructive predations of investment banking and much of the 'externality' generation of capitalist enterprise. In pirate capitalism debt is incurred to force the liquidation of economically viable production for the benefit of investors—debt is used as a weapon. And money as quantum of equivalence asserts perfect symmetry between production and this destruction.

The capitalist premise that 'profit' is its own justification, its 'proof' that more was created than was required to produce it, is premised on the metaphysical quality of money as equivalence no matter how it is gotten. Creating money through lending is to create the power to force circumstances in one direction or another—it isn't socially neutral. In this way money as debt is a tool of economic domination and control and in the West the power to create money as debt has been granted to capitalist bankers.

Western economists remain insistently ignorant of money in some measure because of the metaphysical noun-verb confusion. It is a 'thing' in the sense of existing to the extent it does. But it is brought into and out of being through 'act,' through a loan being made or repaid. The central confusion is between the state's 'authority' to create money and the fact that most money is created though the system of 'private' credit—money as debt.

In capitalist theory bankers are 'expert' in the allocation of credit because they are motivated by the 'rational' desire for profits—to maximize the rate of interest charged given the likelihood of the loan being repaid. In theory this probability is realized by lending to viable capitalist enterprises as demonstrated by their existing profitability and accumulated wealth or by their potential to 'earn' these. Here again profits and wealth are their own 'proof.'

Within the capitalist frame the state is motivated by political concerns, not profits, and it will allocate money as debt 'sub-optimally.' The 'market' mechanism works more 'efficiently' because it is driven to economically 'rational' action by the profit motive. And within this theory the quantity of money—both public and 'private', is 'naturally' bounded by the amount of debt that can be absorbed by debt 'markets.'

'Private' money is created against debt, which is used to buy the debt created against private money. In this theory public borrowing reduces the amount of this money available to capitalist enterprise—it 'crowds out' 'efficient' uses. This web of social contingencies is 'naturalized' in Western economics as 'facts' of nature, as the will of a secular god applied to 'human' relations. Money is 'neutral' in Western economics because its social genesis is mystified and not because it is socially-economically neutral.

Because there is no 'natural' relation between money and debt—in its modern incarnation it is social convention in favor of capitalist institutional practice as it has developed historically, there is no 'natural' bond between public and private debt. The conflation of the two is a function of the psychic equivalence of the money that results from debt issuance and willful misdirection for political gain.

Western 'economics' of money and finance is pure capitalist ideology reconstituted in social institutions as means of rendering capitalist political economy concrete. Federal taxes are a public policy tool, a means of allocating and re-allocating resources to serve public policy needs—largely the programs of 'free market' welfare that sustain 'private' enterprise under the illusion it is self-sustaining.

The Federal budget 'deficit' is the perennial canard used by capitalist ideologues to argue that cuts to social programs are necessary. Their argument depends on the mystification of money—on conflating public with private debt to argue that a wholly invented public accounts 'crisis' —a budget deficit, exists as a 'natural' limit on the government's ability to fund spending.

There may exist factual limits but they are broadly contextual and bear little relation to these public policy debates and none whatsoever to capitalist theory. The premise that tax receipts place a 'natural' bound on public expenditures ties to capitalist ideology through its reconstitution in Western institutions.

In practice all money—public and private, could be created 'out of thin air' with no relation to debt being either made or necessary. The reason this might be desirable is to cut capitalist extraction of economic resources out of the money system. Of the 'uses' of money—store of value and medium of exchange would be unaffected by 'pure' fiat creation of money.

And 'means of repayment' references the debt-based money system that would be irrelevant with the issue of pure fiat currency—there is no need for repayment if there is no debt to repay. Economic production could be 'financed' through the creation and allocation of money in the public interest.

What debt-based money does establish is a set of social relations around money, of lenders to borrowers and of existing money as 'wealth' and 'capital' to money created through new bank loans to finance economic production and consumption.

As they exist these social relations are hierarchical and extractive—lenders and creditors have rights 'over' borrowers including in many cases the right to dictate the terms of use of monies lent and the right to seize the means of economic production against outstanding debt.

The capitalist assertion that the profit motive assures that money is 'efficiently' allocated depends on the wholly circular idea of capitalist efficiency—that profitable enterprise is efficient because it is profitable. This leaves enterprises with the greatest capacities for economic extraction through the use of asymmetrical social power—through monopoly pricing and the ability to force the costs of their economic production onto others, as the most 'creditworthy' in the 'private' debt based money system.

And all of this assumes that the capitalist metaphysics of 'money' is and of itself socially beneficial. The metaphysical equivalence that money reifies is factual inequivalence—a week's work isn't a flat screen television and a horse isn't a motorcycle. As capitalist 'object' money renders this inequivalence invisible, the partition theorized to render the social facts of economic production 'settled' by imperial fiat.

Banks, and more particularly Wall Street, function as the ultimate capitalist enterprises because they act 'rationally' in the economistic sense of lending / securing money to be used to act on 'the world' with the goal of achieving the secular 'truth' of profits.

The 'products' that Wall Street banks create are wholly of the ether—stocks, bonds and derivatives that are intrinsically metaphysical, they 'represent' financial interests in economic production but they aren't economic production and they only 'facilitate' it through the socially contingent debt-money system.

The monies Wall Street creates / allocates come from the 'private' right to perform the public function of issuing money and Wall Street exists through public assurance of 'its' business via direct guarantees, transfers, recurrent 'bailouts' and through a global institutional infrastructure, the IMF (International Monetary Fund) and World Bank, dedicated to assuring 'external' debt repayment.

In theory Wall Street is self-determined and rational while in fact 'it' owes its very existence to the historical role of banks using state power to create the public institutions that support it. This latter point gets to the very heart of the imperial role that debt-based money plays in social relations—Western banks bear next to no relation to their theorized forms and roles in capitalist economics. They are agents of state power in the service of capitalist imperialism.

Wall Street relies on public guarantees of 'its' business and it 'profits' through the application of this social power. The IMF has effectively reconstituted global political economy in the interests of Western social relations—it has 'restructured' the political economies of former colonies in the interests of Western bankers and it has installed puppet governments under the contrived illusion that capitalist extraction has no bearing on the realm of the 'political.' In this context 'private' money is the 'fluid' of capitalist imperialism.

Wall Street 'profits' serve as circular 'proof' of its social value because they derive from its acts of reconstituting capitalist ideology in social institutions. Banks allocate money to capitalist enterprises based on their theorized ability to 'succeed' in capitalist terms—profits play the same role in capitalist metaphysics as 'truth' plays in Cartesian metaphysics, as social currency derived from the virtues they are theorized to demonstrate.

But profits only demonstrate what they are theorized to demonstrate—they function as proof through the internal logic of capitalism, not through what Wall Street and capitalist enterprise actually produces. Companies that are best at using 'public' resources through retained social power, at wielding monopoly power to control 'market' outcomes and at shoving 'their' costs of production onto others also tend to be the most profitable. And as such they are Wall Street's favored 'customers.'

Alternatively, the relation of debt to money could be ended along with all public support, both implicit and explicit, of Wall Street and it would cease to exist in anything resembling its current incarnation in a relatively short period of time.

In theory corporate monopoly power, control over state policies and institutions and the capacity to shift the costs of production could be greatly limited through state controls and little to nothing would be left of the 'economy' Wall Street exists to support. The 'profits' that Wall Street sustains result from social relations as they have developed historically and not from the factual efficacy of capitalist metaphysics reconstituted in political economy.

As such they demonstrate the opposite of the social 'virtue' they are theorized to demonstrate in capitalist economics. Why the existing role of Wall Street won't be 'voluntarily' ended is that the existing order in the West is dependent on the imperial role that it plays. This includes the hegemonic role money is given as imperial 'object' in the service of imperial interests.

Wall Street's system of reconstituting existing social power through its financing function and the reactive nature of capitalist metaphysics assures that the catastrophes it creates are irresolvable within the circular logic of capitalism.

The 'power of money' over public policy is seen as external to it when corporate profits derive from public policy—from the debt-money system and from the deep institutional embedding of the 'public' mechanisms—government spending, development, contracts, infrastructure and standing armies, that are the basis of 'private' profits.

The rationale for capitalism is as a system of 'virtuous' allocation via the 'laws' of nature. 'Profit' itself is metaphysical, the theorized result of the competent interaction of the capitalist with 'the world' through method—through capitalist enterprise. The capitalist mantra of 'privatizing' public institutions ignores both the role they already play in producing 'private' profits and that these profits only accrue by drawing a tight enough circle around capitalist production's total product.

Money is the great mystery to Western economists because the debt-money system can only be theorized to react within the circular logic of capitalist metaphysics. It is conceived as the metaphorical equivalent of hydraulic fluid that when pushed through 'system' has determinable outcome.

This focus on the 'thing' character of money—on its metaphysical 'thingness' as reified in paper currency, metal coins and digital entries, is near perfect misdirection. This can be seen in the social fact of 'monetary' policy in the West that has recently restored the fortunes of the already wealthy and no one else. Were money 'neutral' this particularity with where it lands would be inexplicable, the flip of a fair coin that lands heads up fourteen thousand flips in a row.

In fact this debt-money system is no more 'capitalist' than are public schools and unemployment insurance. The internal logic of capitalism—its mode of 'proof' through profits, assures that capitalist enterprise is perceived to be central to capitalist political economy when it is but a result of social relations expressed through 'public' policies. What this money system demonstrates is that public policies and institutions are more central to the functioning of capitalism than capitalist enterprise is to economic production.

Interest paid on debt is a form of economic extraction. The internal logic of this interest is as 'payment' for the economic use-value of borrowed money. Again, the ability to 'create' this money is socially and historically contingent—banks are given the 'right' because of their historical role as moneylenders and for their perceived place in capitalist economic allocation.

This role in the allocation of money as credit is theorized to be socially beneficial wholly within capitalist economics. There is no theoretically coherent basis for this 'right' of banks outside of this economics. The internal theoretical constraint that economic production be funded through banks either directly or through 'capital markets' asserts that capitalist production—that which 'earns' a profit, be the only socially beneficial production undertaken.

In neo-liberal revival theory economic production outside of capitalism—public schools, public healthcare, infrastructure etc., is 'inefficient' because it lacks the profit motive. As implausible as this premise is, it is a base conceit behind the capitalist drive for 'privatization' of economic production in the 'public' interest. As counter-factual, the 'private' healthcare system in the U.S. provides far less healthcare than other 'developed' systems at about twice their price per person.

This outcome in health care is broadly attributable to cartel-monopoly pricing power that health insurers and healthcare providers have arranged for themselves and their 'profit' driven tendency of only providing health-care that is 'profitable.' This system is metaphor for broader capitalist production where the idea of 'efficiency' is local but its effects are 'global.'

It is economically 'efficient' for health insurers and health care provid-ers to use cartel-monopoly power to 'overprice' healthcare and to deliver less of it than is needed because doing so maximizes 'profits.' This is the capitalism that debt-based money is intended to serve—cartel-monopoly pricing power and providing only 'profitable' healthcare increase the like-lihood of repayment of debt.

Likewise Wall Street does everything in its power to secure monopoly position for itself through its dubious stream of financial products and the 'public' institutions that support its economic extraction. Through this system Wall Street is the 'magnifier' of asymmetrical social relations—economic production that lacks the ability to 'squeeze' its 'customers' is less likely to get funded and pays higher rates of interest providing a 'natural' tendency toward capitalist consolidation in order to exert market 'power.'

Finance—Wall Street and 'private' banks, provides the structural imperative that those who borrow money behave as businesses and earn a 'profit,' either actual or metaphorical, because doing so determines the cost and availability of borrowed money. A high level formula for this profit is R − C = P (revenues minus costs equals profit). Profits rise when either revenues rise (and costs remain the same) or costs are reduced (while revenues remain the same).

The point was made above that this leads (prudent) lenders to favor borrowers who have monopoly power in their respective businesses because it raises the likelihood that loans will be repaid. But this monopo-ly power also exists on the cost side—Wal-Mart is an example of monop-oly power being used to squeeze suppliers. Using monopoly power to squeeze suppliers (and labor) lowers costs, but one firm's costs are anoth-er's revenues.

Through debt-based money the Wall Street imperative is made the economic imperative of wholly unrelated types of economic production. An organic farming collective that borrows bank money to get started is ruled by the same economic imperative that large corporations are. The difference is that large corporations generally have and use multiple forms of monopoly power to reduce costs. And the monopoly component isn't 'competition'—monopoly power is anti-competitive.

The farming collective has to 'rationalize' its 'business' in the general frame of R − C = P in order to get a bank loan. This makes sense within the logic of the capitalist frame. However, the idea of starting a collective is precisely contrary to that of capitalist enterprise. A collective isn't hierarchical, it isn't an 'efficient' form of economic organization within the capitalist frame and as such, its primary motive isn't to earn the most profit possible.

A bank may 'give' the collective a loan but the imperative that revenues meet costs to make scheduled repayment of principal plus interest becomes the governing imperative of the collective else the bank takes over and makes it the governing imperative. Bank money is in this way of governing ideology of economic organization. And this same ideology has so permeated political economy of the West that all public functions that can be privatized are being privatized.

Finance is reified capitalist ideology that has been given the economic privilege of creating bank money through making loans. Were it capitalist enterprise Wall Street would have gone out of business en masse in 2008. The broad rationale given for saving it is that it provides the 'fluid' of capitalism, money through bank loans, which makes the rest of the economy possible. The truth is that it makes particular political economy, reified capitalist ideology, possible.

Therein lies the paradox—the ideology that Wall Street forces over the breadth of Western political economy through its control of money has made it immune to the consequences of this very ideology. Within the constraint of prudent lending Wall Street wouldn't lend money to itself. Creating the illusion that it would are the too-big-to-fail government guarantees and Federal Reserve efforts to flood the financial 'system' with money following Wall Street's self-immolation in 2008.

Meet Your Meat

IN 2006 THE U.S. CONGRESS PASSED THE AETA (ANIMAL ENTERPRISE Terrorism Act) in an attempt to criminalize public expression of horror and disapprobation[113] toward the factory farm system as well as toward particular 'farms.' For the uninitiated, the dictates of capitalist 'competition' have so reduced the circumstances of the animals within this system that the central economic danger to it is making its horrors public.

The Federal government's (and individual state's) conflation of disclosure of these horrors with 'terrorism' frames the relation of the factory farm system as capitalist enterprise to its protection and enforcement mechanisms in government. It also offers insight into the actual rationale for the anti-terrorism industry as public-private 'partnership' to maintain the existing social order at all costs.

From the perspective of capitalist economics the state has an interest in protecting 'private property' but none whatsoever in protecting 'producers' from disclosure of the broad circumstances of 'their' production. 'Complete information' is one of the central conceits of modern capitalist economics.

That the full force of state sanction is being brought to bear through 'terrorism' prosecutions provides some indication of exactly how horrible the secrets of factory farms are. And the state's interest in protecting 'economic value' by preventing disclosure that threatens economic harm puts a lie to the market / state frame of capitalist theory.

In the broader sense there is no necessary reason why people should eat animals—nutritionally complete and far less toxic meals can be made without animal 'products.' Eating meat is a choice. And for all of the claims of capitalist 'efficiency,' the costs of producing meat in terms of the 'feed' that could be eaten directly rather than fed to animals; the energy used in raising, butchering, distributing and refrigerating 'meat,' the environmental destruction from animal waste and the broad circumstances of 'meat' production, Western diets heavy in animal 'products' are among the least efficient ways of feeding people.

Here again capitalist production that is economically efficient in tightly circumscribed theory is socially inefficient when considered more broadly. Factory farms are 'rationalized' capitalist production premised on the social virtue of 'profit' to the exclusion of all others. For those who do choose to eat meat there is no reason why animals need to be put through this 'system.' There are other modes of living with animals that are premised on different virtues or that stand outside the capitalist idea of economic virtue entirely.

The high concentration of animals forced to live in close proximity to one another, the forced feeding of foods to which they aren't biologically adapted, the use of breeding and hormones to promote faster growth and the associated use of antibiotics to suppress infections and sickness from all of these combine to form the science of reducing living beings to the imperatives of capitalist production.

As 'rationalized' production the same processes that posit living animals as 'meat' are applied to persons by degree. Factory farm animals both 'are' and produce 'their' product—their living selves are killed and cut up into types of 'meat' and they are bred and 'raised' as 'product,' 'prospective product' and as producers whose product is the 'property' of the factory farm.

Grotesque analogs can be found by degree across Western history and in contemporary terms in the 'prison industrial' system. The place of animals in the social hierarchy of capitalist production is socially and historically contingent—in the colonial U.S. kidnapped Africans forced into slavery were considered both chattel property and their representation as politically designated persons in the U.S. Constitution was as three-fifths a person.

Slaves were 'product' as the 'property' of the slave 'owner,' the person who bought them. The labor of slaves was as producers whose product was the property of the slave owner. In the one-and-one-half centuries since slavery was formally ended a combination of racist legal, policing, judicial and incarceration practices were used to shift ownership of the product of the descendents of 'freed' slaves to connected capitalists outside of direct chattel property relations.

The 'innovation' of the for-profit prison industry is that by receiving payment for each incarcerated 'body' inmates are again 'product' outside of the labor they are required to produce and its product.

The place of factory farms in capitalist production comes through the motives of its actors, through the particular technologies used, through the relation of the 'factories' to the broader economy of animal exploitation and to the commodification of animals as 'products.' For most of history the relationship of people to animals stood outside the defining context of capitalist commodity.

Capitalist humanism—'rational' economic man as it evolved from Cartesian metaphysics, retained its division of the 'self' of deductive 'reason' from 'the world' in which animals (and persons, including this 'self') are considered to exist. The dividing line between 'human' and 'not human' finds gradation in capitalist strategies of classification.

'Labor' in 'developing countries' that produces much of the capitalist bounty seen in the West is placed in conditions between those of the 'developed' West and factory farms. Child labor, labor coerced through the engineered dependence of capitalist neo-imperialism and the reconstituted race-based pseudo-chattel relations of the prison industry in the U.S. are as much a part of contemporary capitalist production as are factory farms.

The criteria of division from full persons to gradations 'downward' — sentience, the use of tools, the ability to make plans, 'intelligence,' all have inglorious histories in strategies of imperial conquest, in the reassuring rationales Western empire offers its beneficiaries when its horrors are accidentally disclosed. Those offended by the relation made here between factory farms and slavery may well consider which of these criteria contributes to offense—then to consider the social history behind it.

It is the logic of capitalist production that led factory farms to 'market' prominence as the lowest cost agricultural producers. This logic favors those facilities that most effectively constrain, restrain and subdue animals to maximize the exact aspects of their being that are sent to market. In this world, efficient production has two components (1) the limitation through confinement, restraint and forced removal of any aspect of the animals' life that doesn't (2) promote growth of the animals' marketable parts and / or products.

Animals in this context are externally 'realized,' the breadth of their existence is determined by capitalist farmers and not by the animals themselves. The 'fact' of external realization here implies either an absence of intrinsic 'agency' on the part of the affected animals or the removal of this agency through the production process. To be clear, the logic of physical restraint and the promotion of the aspects of the animals to be 'realized' are economically 'rational' in the same sense as is applied to any capitalist enterprise.

'Workers' in the West have to a large extent internalized the capitalist ethos through the 'logic' of capitalist production. This internalization is the tool of self-restraint that 'frees' capitalists from need of external force to extract the labor needed for 'their' production. In fact, this internalization is so complete that the range of considered 'choice' is that which is put in front of Western 'labor.' Modern 'labor' works because the world was taken and divied up into 'property' before it was born. Material constraints such as need of food and shelter are put forward as psychic quantum because otherwise prior circumstance is visible as mode of coercion.

As evidence from contemporary capitalist production in geographies unaccustomed to its conventions suggests, coercive strategies long since rendered unnecessary through their successful instantiation in the West are still considered necessary outside of it. Modern factories have labor 'rationalized' down to thousandths of a second in remote, dissociated conditions where formal constraints on movements and capacity for social relations are 'reinforced' through physical force and engineered dependencies.

In this system animal lives are made 'modular' and the aspects that are suppressed or facilitated result from the capitalist calculus of what will 'earn' the most 'profit' for the 'producer.' Of note is that in fact the animals produce the products of factory farms. The same could be written of other agricultural 'products' but that is the point. The capitalist 'contribution' is through 'rational' organization, domination and control. Carrots or cattle might 'grow' in the wild or outside of capitalist production. But it is the 'system' of capitalist rationality—the 'rationality' of capitalist production, which confers-reduces the metaphysical equivalence of 'meat' or 'vegetable' to its product.

The capitalist frame converts its intended temporal existents into the psychic objects of 'commodity,' their equivalence in the metaphysical ether forced back onto 'the world.' The directionality of these 'objects' to application on / in 'the world' has no path in the other direction—from the world back 'up' to the metaphysical ether. 'Cooperative' theories of agriculture, those that have no basis in the hierarchy of metaphysical reasoning, can't 'compete' in agricultural markets because they are non-reductive—they don't originate from a commodity view and then set about producing their pre-supposition through force and coercion.

This idea of 'efficiency' as 'proved' by lowest cost production only works through tight circumscription of the cost calculus. Wars for resources and 'externalized' costs of production forced onto others are as much the 'product' of the factory farm as is 'meat.' Conversely, the need for state power to conceal the residual of capitalist production—the absolute horror of its 'rational' expression in the factory farm system, is evidence that 'the world' is proceeding from different premises. That the capitalist calculus doesn't count this horror does nothing to reduce its fact.

The public debate over the 'agency' of animals is suppressed—the increasingly repressive laws surrounding the distribution of images from factory farms are to remove evidence that animal agency remains an unsettled issue. And through inference the coherence of capital- ist humanism comes into question. The base criticism of the release of graphic images is that they produce 'visceral' responses; that they appeal to emotions when the logic of capitalist production is 'logical,' detached from emotions.

Ironically, the opposite is inferred back on animals, that they lack emo- tional lives and therefore what would be torture, deprivation and humil- iation to 'persons' has no impact on their well being. This 'modular' view of psychology—of distinct realms of the intellectual and the emotional and of their distribution in 'the world,' is wholly metaphysical. And even were this not the case, there is no basis in 'the world' for privileging one over the other.

Historically, the conceit evolved from Christian theology through Descartes that animals lack a 'soul.' 'Inside' the metaphysical construct is this soul reconstituted by Descartes as 'rational' actor on 'the world.' This is the basis for the metaphysical self that 'is' indubitable—timeless and universal, like its objects. But this onto-theology is hardly a 'rational' basis for the treatment of animals in capitalist production.

And the irony factor—that the goal of restricting information on the lives and conditions of animals in factory farms is to repress the very characteristic in people that is used to 'legitimate' the brutal treatment of animals, suggests moral ambiguity bordering on radical theoretical incoherence. In the absence of both plausible and clear division between 'intellect' and emotions and plausible rationale for privileging one over the other the visceral response to animal torture and cruelty is as 'valid' and 'true' as any other.

Conversely, the very idea of 'agency' is as imperial act, the imposition of a theoretical basis of differentiation to serve a purpose. The metaphysical partition is premised on a bundle of characteristics assumed to self-legitimate, first principles that confer privilege as well as the 'responsibility' of empire, the 'white man's burden,' of conquest for the alleged 'benefit' of others. The question of whether or not animals 'possess' agency depends on the terms of partition, on the strategies of legitimation that demarcate its social consequences.

'Granting' animals agency is to offer social privilege from the perspective of having it to grant. The literature on animal 'rights' takes this perspective as its point of departure, as grantors of imperial 'rights' in the service of beings that can't 'speak for themselves.' Deference to 'nature,' 'god' or any other 'objective' observer-powers as the basis of 'rights' requires overlooking the material absence of any such rights outside of the social power to enforce them.

And once social power enters the picture, of what conceivable relevance are 'rights?' The 'rights' achieved by the 'civil rights' movement in the U.S. would have been empty rhetoric if concrete changes in material conditions had not coincided. The vague 'fear' that animals too 'deserve' rights is behind the overkill of 'terrorism' laws applied to factory farms. Inferred is the imperial power to grant or not grant, the power over life and death and social conditions.

The broad circumstance of empire came through expression of social power, not through the 'rights' that 'nature' or 'god' grants to 'all human beings' that somehow are never enforced except through its expression. Through use of capitalist-state power to 'protect' capitalists against the circumstances of 'their' production factory farms exist on the side of this power against its detriments. In this way factory farm animals are placed on the outside of this power along side the overwhelming majority of the rest of us.

The goal of the factory farm 'system' is to produce 'uniform' products—a gallon of milk or a pound of hamburger, that are virtually indistinguishable from other 'like' products. Animal lives are reconstituted to resemble 'their' metaphysical 'objects' of 'meat,' 'milk' and 'food' as commodities unrelated to the beings that produced them. This process of abstraction is related to other capitalist production in all that traces of origination, of the social relations of production, are removed.

The meat and milk neatly packaged in stores gives no indication of which particular animals they were taken from, of the conditions of their lives or what their lives might have been like outside of 'object' in capitalist production. Some meat products are known to contain 'pieces' of a thousand or more animals and milk from different animals is combined and processed in huge vats.

This is the physical assertion of the metaphysical imperative that 'meat' is meat and 'milk' is milk unrelated to 'the world' from whence they came. The 'inputs' into this system, the animals, are confined, managed and handled so that their lives closely resemble the disposition of their corpses after they have been killed, the externally realized lives that become externally realized deaths.

This commodification is the theorized cleansing mechanism of capitalism, elevation from the 'clutter' of relationships and relatedness to the exchange of money for product that completes the transaction. Without the factory farm there is some reasonable likelihood that animals that are born will grow to 'produce' what to the capitalist are marketable parts in the context of fuller lives. And without the animals, there is no possibility that the factory farm would exist, and with it the factory farm capitalist.

The relation of Western economics to the conditions of capitalist production is roughly analogous to that of this economics to psychology. The conceit of 'complete information' is one of the central tenets of high-capitalist economics since the 1970s, the insistence that people know everything that need be known to make 'rational' economic decisions.

The 'information' of relevance excludes that with 'psychological' impact because psychology—the association of 'emotions' with rational 'thought objects,' renders economic outcomes indeterminate. Of relevance is that when this psychology, or 'emotional' reaction to information more broadly, is brought back in there is still 'rational' basis for full disclosure of the conditions of capitalist production.

Within the Western economic frame full disclosure of the treatment of animals from birth to their slaughter is 'information' in the economistic sense that it can be used to 'differentiate' between competing 'producers' and between eating 'meat' and other foods. Close confinement of animals, torture, toxic diets and heavy anti-biotic and hormone use has residual impact on the 'product' of factory farms.

Additionally, these conditions can be plausibly related to the broader social conditions of production—the treatment of animals has direct relation to our own treatment in capitalist production. It isn't much of a stretch to relate the increasing 'rationalization' of production in factory farms to the increasing rationalization of broad political economy through modes of surveillance, domination and control.

Factory farms have corollary with for-profit prisons, neo-imperial labor and environmental relations in economic production. The clear delineation between 'information' and psychological response Western economists claim is premised on an implausibly narrow concept of 'information.' Even within the Western frame a broader concept of 'rationality' reframes actual capitalist practice as neo-imperialist—based in naked power relations, rather than in 'market' outcomes.

The political 'left' has long had an ambiguous relationship with the treatment of animals and how to respond to it. This ambiguity results in part from the residual metaphysical humanism so deeply embedded in the Western psyche and partly in the social hierarchy that it implies. Stepping outside of metaphysical humanism doesn't create inclusive social relations, one that includes animals, but it does 'undo' exclusive relations premised on its divisions.

The challenge for the left is that staying within the metaphysical frame through 'competing' metaphysics leaves the 'self' of the capitalist worldview intact in support of 'its' humanism. 'Capitalism with a human face,' kinder and gentler capitalism, is theoretically incoherent within capitalist logic where the base premise is that we all benefit by acting on naked self-interest. Within this frame kindness and gentleness of the material sort only serve to reduce the circumstance of those they are intended to help.

Capitalism absolutely is applied Social Darwinism. Competing metaphysics can differ over the 'inside' of the 'human' self, 'creative man' versus 'economic man,' but the metaphysical construct leaves competing modes of exploitation from atomized, dissociated 'individuals,' not increased facilitation of creativity or social reconciliation.

If 'we' aren't of this world it is alien to us and we act 'on' it accordingly. Conversely, the treatment of people and animals in capitalist production across history and in current relations unites a broad swath of 'the world,' everything that is exploitable, in its 'use' value. Because of the totalizing onto-theological nature of capitalist theory the only effective theoretical challenges to it come from 'outside' of metaphysics. And once metaphysics is abandoned capitalist political economy remains to unite its 'objects' in exploitation.

The argument of 'class' as it might be applied to animals within the capitalist frame is competing metaphysics—most imperial strategies of economic exploitation have associated apologetics to explain why the exploited deserve their lot. Current 'trade' economics have full-blown explanations of how tech executives 'earned' their fortunes by exploiting historical circumstance to expropriate the labor of the people who make 'their' products.

Slavery had its defenders who put forward theories that slavery benefited the enslaved by exposing 'backward' peoples to the glories of white European culture. Surely defenders of factory farms could point to the abundance of food made 'available' to captive animals in their temperature-regulated cages as improvement over never having been bred and / or existing in the vagaries of the 'wild.'

Alternatively, within the idea of socially circumscribed economic class the animals in factory farms are exploited using rationales, technologies and strategies of domination and control that clearly unite their lot with that of tens, if not hundreds, of millions of people across the planet. Additionally, the alienation of / in capitalist product, the shoes made in sweatshops that sell for hundreds of dollars or the steak on the grocers shelf, function as commodity through the theorized benediction-like quality of 'trade.'

The social relations of production facilitate the 'system' of exploitation that hides all evidence of its basis. But this doesn't diminish its fact, nor does it alter its character. Abandoning metaphysics doesn't 'diminish' the theoretical persons of metaphysical humanism; it removes the frame used to justify the exploitation of actual persons to place it back in social struggle where it belongs. The question for the left is: are animals a 'class' of beings who can legitimately be exploited for their economic use value or is it the political economy of exploitation that is objected to?

Four or so decades back crude Marxian theories of class 'consciousness' had many on the left giving deference to working class attitudes toward animals. Again, the idea of consciousness as social partition has long imperial history. The Marxian innovation of giving a material-social basis to this consciousness can either be exclusive; in which case it quickly returns to imperial rationales for social partition, or it is inclusive through deference to social fact, to the facts of class belongingness and interests through shared social conditions.

Additionally, deference to 'consumer' attitudes, regardless of economic class, shares with Western economists the insistence that the use of psychology in advertising and other forms of economic coercion play little to no role in the formation of 'consciousness.' In the U.S. the Department of Agriculture has played the role of lead propagandist for industrial agriculture for the better part of a century.

This isn't to impose an alternative view, but rather to clear away the clutter to get to the metaphysical humanist core of any view that sees strong partition between persons and animals, particularly within the context of shared experience in capitalist exploitation. The working class that shops at Wal-Mart is welcomed to its self-defeating view of the sweatshop labor that brings it 'cheap' goods.

But that very same view reflected back on it is everywhere in evidence as a source of its own diminishment. 'Class' consciousness that retains the views of the U.S. Department of Agriculture, the Cattlemen's Beef Board, the capitalists behind the factory farm system and its bosses in capitalist enterprise is better described as class unconsciousness. This isn't to point a critical finger toward the working classes that retain these views, but rather to argue that they reflect political economy of radical alienation that is the base characteristic of capitalism.

The point is easily made that abandoning the clear lines of capitalist metaphysics opens up a lot of questions that aren't easily answered. If animals join persons in the class of beings exploited in capitalist political economy, wouldn't circumscription based on this criterion also include industrial agriculture broadly considered along with 'natural' resources and a wide swath of non-sentient entities? Absolutely.

The coal mined using 'mountain-top removal' in West Virginia, USA, isn't sentient but the practice only functions as capitalist production by assigning value to explicit 'product' and none to the broad social and environmental consequences of the practice. Dragnet fishing where a substantial proportion of the sea-creatures killed are thrown dead back into the ocean only counts its 'product' as that which finds its way to market.

Political economy that only counts what it wants to count leaves its residual—that which is left unaccounted for, in factual-material opposition to it. This isn't metaphysical opposition as the philosophers of passive post-modern 'democracy' might have it—it is circumscription as social act of the residual of capitalist production that is its social-material fact. Within this capitalist view we are all mountains to be decapitated, sea-creatures to be killed and our bodies disposed of as garbage and animals in the factory farm system to be confined, tortured and killed for our 'product.'

The differences that do exist are of degree, not type. Within the capitalist frame social partition that delimits exploitable from non-exploitable beings misunderstands the metaphysical construct—the worldly / otherworldly divide is of Western selves where the 'worldly' character of each and every self is exploitable. The alienation of the metaphysical construct is so radical that it has capitalists in theory acting on themselves as alien objects.

A central line of defense of industrial agriculture is to point to its engineered dependencies as fact of nature—how will 'we' feed all of these people at such low cost if it is ended? Left out of the consideration is the century or more of iterative instantiation into political economy that frames capitalist production as essential to existence.

The factory farm system of animals and animal products is phenomenally 'inefficient' in the social sense—the 'inputs' could be much more efficiently used to feed people directly rather than through 'meat' production. More broadly, were feeding people the goal of industrial agriculture the companies producing genetically modified 'suicide' seeds would be put out of business and their senior executives would be charged with crimes against humanity.

The low 'price' of industrial agriculture is in large measure a function of forcing its costs of production onto everyone but the capitalist. The miserable condition of animals in the factory farm system is by degree, but not type, different from that of labor in this same system. It is hardly coincidence that factory farms and meat 'packers' employ socially marginalized labor—undocumented immigrants and economically remote and therefore dependent workers, because of their economic fragility and associated willingness to work in miserable conditions for low wages.

Were these conditions evident in the 'product' of industrial agriculture 'consumers' would receive a container of misery, coercion, exploitation, environmental destruction and political-economic dysfunction along with the pesticides, hormones, antibiotics and 'suicide' seeds they already do get from industrial agriculture.

The appearance of 'necessity' crafted through this engineered dependence would be more plausible were it not for the expensive and persistent advertising of generic industrial agriculture such as 'meat' and dairy 'products' and the oh-so careful dissociation of them from the circumstances of their production through packaging and marketing.

There is little to no evidence of the lives and deaths of factory farm animals to be found in the plastic containers of 'meat' on grocers' shelves or in the pictures of sizzling hamburgers and steaks found in advertising. To be clear, these are every bit as much the 'product' that is produced as that found on the grocer's shelves or in the fast food hamburger.

Were the Western economist's conceit that advertising is the conveyance of product 'information' plausible these social facts would be as relevant to product comparison as any other. Conversely, food is a necessity making the imperial strategies of industrial agriculture—the creation of global dependencies through the destruction of indigenous agriculture and their replacement with subsidized industrial 'food', so dangerous.

The rapid rise of 'meat' consumption in the global East ties closely to the spread of capitalism, to the suddenly 'prosperous' being offered the chance to 'enjoy' the aspect of capitalist production that shows itself in 'product.' Left invisible and untold is that this same process of abstraction that makes 'meat' visible while hiding the misery, torture and death of factory farms 'works' equally as well for their very own products.

This isn't to overstate the case—plenty of information on the circumstances of animals in the factory farm system is available to those who seek it out. But to return to the AETA (above), the same public-private coalition whose agents are pushing strategies of engineered dependence in 'trade' agreements is intent on restricting these facts from being broadly distributed. It is the system of capitalist-state terrorism that AETA is designed to maintain against potential anti-terrorist actions against it.

The question of what to do about factory farms is more fundamentally about exploitative political economy? As part of the system of global capitalist production the basis of this system in exploitation through domination, control and economic expropriation needs to be put back to those who participate in it. Western economists have done an effective job of dissociating 'consumers' from their more relevant roles as producers.

The 'choice' of eating 'meat' is endorsement of this system that places those doing the eating as so much fodder for it themselves. 'Labor' in its various incarnations may not be served up as 'meat' on grocer's shelves, but by participating in exploitative political economy the lot of animals in factory farms is directly related to falling wages, looted pensions, jobs sent overseas and rising, persistent unemployment.

The lot of these animals is clearly not a fact of 'nature,' and neither is the social dysfunction of capitalism increasingly in evidence. The problem with addressing multiple narrow concerns that share common cause is that the cause simply shifts focus to other areas less resistant to exploitation. To the extent that labor unions were able to secure better wages and benefits, capitalists followed the imperial trail to overseas labor.

To the extent environmental regulations ever had impact capitalists shifted production to places that didn't have them. What AETA and the practice of kidnapping people and sending them elsewhere to be tortured and killed for political purposes, 'extraordinary rendition,' share is the idea of preventing disclosure of certain circumstances to avoid the consequences of doing so.

The dire circumstance of animals in the factory farm system is worthy of more direct comment. Once the metaphysical worldview is abandoned the relation of factory farms to the great atrocities of history becomes visible. If the capitalists of the factory farm system believe their treatment of animals is defensible then they should defend it rather than hide behind bogus terrorism laws and suppressed evidence.

Implied is that factory farms function as capitalist enterprise only by abstracting 'products' from their associated atrocities. Conversely, also implied is that the 'problem' these capitalists have with atrocities is their public disclosure, not their facts. The basis of capitalist political economy is as an atrocity generating system whose 'public' measure depends on the capacity to hide its 'private' measure.

If capitalists actually believed in capitalism they would put this 'private' measure forward for all to see. Inference from the fact of its existence is that the 'good' capitalism produces is more than is needed to 'justify' the bad. If 'meat' is justified then put the evidence, all of it, forward and let people decide for themselves. Until that time ending the factory farm system is a necessary step toward reconciliation with 'the world.' To be clear, it will not be voluntarily ended.

Zen and a Different Way of Being in the World

THE WESTERN TENDENCY TOWARD 'IDEALIST' UNDERSTANDING HAS LED
to insistence that alternative ways of existing be premised in 'ideas,' 'metaphysical' in the terms that have been laid out here. This is in large measure
attributable to the privilege that metaphysical understanding is granted
in the West and to the totalizing nature of Western metaphysics as geographical metaphor, as the 'place' where disembodied, dissociable and
distinct 'knowledge' resides.

This 'place' finds voice in the conceit that Western science, including
economics, is the accumulated knowledge of 'man.' The imperial premise
is brought to light in the overwhelming preponderance of actual persons
at present and across history that have little to no 'knowledge' of Western
science.

And even this formulation grants 'knowledge' in its metaphysical form
as shared space-access, the one-mind that so implausibly circumscribes
the 'man' of genocide, slavery, imperial conquest, regularly occurring
wars and the 'three-fifths' of a person slaves were designated in the U.S.
Constitution. As with mathematics, if the thought 'objects' of metaphysics are 'timeless and universal,' why aren't they 'known' across time and
invariant?

It is not incidental that the totalizing nature of Western metaphysics
finds its social form in the totalizing political economy of capitalism. The
base contradiction of 'shared' individual determination in metaphysical
language is reconstituted in the social institutions of Western capitalism
that are premised on the facilitation of 'individual' determination. Why
would social institutions exist at all if people determine themselves 'individually?'

The relation of the theoretical premises of capitalism to their 'fact'
embedded in the institutions of political economy of the West points to
a central challenge of existing differently—even if the premises were successfully done away with their embedded fact in political economy would
remain. This in turn points to the basic implausibility of metaphysical
reasoning. Historical embedding persists.

The political and economic theories of capitalist democracy are metaphysical 'impositions,' ideas worked through 'the mind' and imposed on 'the world' based on the conclusions drawn. They have basis in language, culture and history, but this circumscribes them in social life, not as the voice of a secular god—'nature,' they are put forward as.

The Western 'self' of capitalist democracy is metaphysical, the imposition of the metaphysical construct onto 'the world' under the premise that its fact in 'idea' is its fact in disembodied 'fact.' And because these thought 'objects' have been reconstituted in Western institutions and instantiated as 'identity' in Western culture there exists no 'clear ground' from which to launch alternatives to capitalist democracy.

Framed differently, the 'reactive' nature of proposed alternatives is a function of this hegemonic and totalizing character of Western political economy and not from a 'base' of competing ideas. As rough analog the saying we in the West are 'free' to do or say what we want has little meaning if we want to leap tall mountains in a single bound or tell the boss on whose good graces we are economically dependent that his or her children are ugly. Outside of the metaphysical ether history and culture have accumulated as developed political economy.

The social nature of metaphysical 'self-determination' can be conceived as paradox within the metaphysical frame—to the extent the internal 'dialogue' of the self is in a shared language it exists between people, not 'inside' of them. As shared language the 'origination' is social, not 'internal.' The likelihood of developing 'internal' language that could be shared faces the social-historical fact that languages are socially circumscribed—English speakers speak English and Portuguese speakers speak Portuguese.

Theories of 'natural' language face the same challenge, the tendency of people to speak the language they learned from others through the act of speaking. Theories of 'meta' language, timeless and universal 'rules' shared by all languages, require premises about what language 'is' that are interesting speculation, not 'fact' as given by the science that is claimed as mode of 'proof.' The point here is not to develop or regurgitate theories of language but rather to place the social nature of language against existing political economy—capitalism, premised on / in the asocial (anti-social) concept of language that is metaphysics.

In practical terms the idea of 'profit' in a theory of individually determined language—metaphysics, is fundamentally different from the idea in shared language where its meaning is between people rather than the individual 'possession' of each. As social act language is shared act much as capitalist production is social production undertaken within a theoretical-rhetorical frame of individual production.

To be clear, this isn't to argue that capitalist production be shared because the base premise is of 'private' circumscription of a shared act. The base premise is implausible by its fact as social production. Conversely, the very idea of metaphysical self-determination in the realms of language or economic production faces the same social-historical facts of shared language, culture, history and political economy.

Seen this way the 'paradox' of the social institutions of Western political economy existing to facilitate individual self-determination is reframed as strategies of social negotiation—again, self-determined 'individuals' don't need social institutions to 'facilitate' what they are already assumed to possess. This isn't to argue that the hegemonic character of capitalist metaphysics isn't hegemonic. It is to argue that through the more likely lens of social negotiation capitalism as embedded political economy is embedded assertion in this negotiation.

This may seem a roundabout way of getting to Zen as it might relate to different ways of being. The 'background' issues are necessary because it isn't oppositional metaphysics that is being proposed. The issue of capitalist political economy is its totalizing fact—the insistence that a narrow ideology circumscribe the realm of the possible through its totalizing logic and reconstitution in the social institutions of the West.

This ideology has material impact and it is the resulting set of social relations that are 'its' insistence. With forty thousand or however many years of 'human' history the capacity / trajectory / insistence for mass self-annihilation is but the age of this ideology. And no assertion of impending apocalypse is needed to tie theory to fact—it is the capitalist West that is so conspicuously incapable of reconciling its theory with its fact.

Catastrophic global warming is far more likely than not to be underway. Under what configuration of 'the world' is it 'worth' it to find out whether or not it is? The fear of nuclear annihilation has faded in recent decades but the capacity for it has gone nowhere. We in the West 'value' the 'goods' that capitalism produces while their production is leading to the mass extinction of everything that doesn't have a price tag attached to it.

It is the totalizing ideology of capitalism that has been reconstituted as totalizing political economy, not the 'idea' as it hangs in the ether of academic debate. This reconstitution is the material base from which different ways of being are forced to proceed. The Western conceit that 'different' being can proceed outside of it confuses metaphysical imposition with the beings doing the imposing.

The problem with simply abandoning metaphysics as a 'personal' act is that its social fact remains within totalizing political economy. The 'personal' of personal act is as reconstituted metaphysical 'self,' the 'personal' reconstitution of the 'self' of capitalist democracy in its 'act' of 'consumer choice.'

The capacity to live 'within' capitalist political economy while existing outside of it is paradox, the realm of the 'independently' wealthy whose wealth is the product of the 'system' now eschewed. This is to argue that Zen as it is laid out below is a political act. But to clear, this point is contextual, particular to the assertion of totalizing political economy, not 'nature.'

The question that follows critique of capitalism is: what are plausible alternatives to it? This is in part reaction to existing circumstance—the factual existence of capitalist political economy that is complex, interrelated, intrusive and deeply embedded. It is also in part because of the totalizing nature of the metaphysical frame of capitalist democracy that 'requires' oppositional metaphysics, 'solutions' that come from inside the frame because that is all that the people's of the West can 'see.'

This 'strategy' can be found in the alleged ideological opposition of capitalism to 'communism' when geography, culture and historical development—material conditions, go much farther in explaining the different experiences of the peoples who existed under these ideological 'umbrellas.' Much as political-economic actors today have the material base of existing relations as 'starting point,' the 'communist' governments in their various incarnations had the detritus of residual empires and the horrific land wars of Europe as the material base over which ideology was imposition of varying relation to the facts of history as they were lived.

Alternatively, without the circumscription of ideology Western capitalism was built on genocide, slavery, sequential imperial wars, environmental devastation and ongoing internal and external social repression. These are more than the unfortunate consequences of history—they are the fundament of Western political economy, its basis in visible wealth and strategies of social control under the implausible advertising slogan of 'freedom.'

In capitalist democracy the relation comes through the iterative reconstitution of capitalist theory as fact in history, through the instantiation of 'identity' as object of this theory. Oppositional metaphysics would impose a different identity as externally imposed 'self' circumscription. This conceit is the genesis of the 'invasion of the body snatchers' science fiction allegories of the 1950s and 1960s.

Misunderstood is that oppositional metaphysics would leave things pretty much where they already are with seven billion individual nation states of the 'self' at war with everything and everybody. If 'the problem' can be framed in terms of the alienation of these 'selves' from 'the world' then 'undoing' it is the path to reconciliation, to 'coming home' to ourselves and each other through coming home to 'the world.'

Conversely, unless the metaphysical frame is 'plausible' 'we' are already home, we just don't know it. Some understanding of this circumstance may already be 'intuited' in the broad search for 'deeper meaning' through religion. But here again, the otherworldly nature of religious meaning is broadly metaphysical—who cares about 'the world' we exist in when other unseen, unheard and unknown worlds are held out as 'home.' 'Meaning' outside of the material conditions to realize it places religion as close ally of the existing order. Zen as it is intended here bears no relation to conventional theology or 'religion' as it is generally conceived.

From 'within' the Marxian frame it is the anti-historical nature of capitalism and capitalist theory that is 'oppositional' in the sense of being implausible, not as oppositional metaphysics. Western metaphysical 'history' is anti-history, the 'view from nowhere' as 'detached' reporting of 'its' embedded 'facts.' In the Western sense history is 'written by the victors' while it is lived by everyone else.

The abstraction of history's 'facts' renders them metaphysical and therefore implausible. Marxian 'dialectics' applies a metaphysical structure to history without 'freezing' its objects in time and space. However, the structure itself is frozen. The typical critique of the metaphysical human-ism Marx put forward in his early writing, in the '1844 Manuscripts', leaves in place a metaphysical structure of history as general analog to the Western scientific 'project.'

Marx moved away from this early metaphysical humanism in his later writing. But as other than rhetorical device, the residual historical deter-minism of 'dialectic' is deference to a knowable 'tendency' of nature as 'external' object much as Darwin's 'evolution' that Marx admired. It is the sine wave of history applied to social struggle.

It is to place the question, as with that of 'dialectic,' into the realm of the temporal as social object. The 'immobility' of capitalism due to its atemporal 'core' strongly suggests that historical development away from it must be revolutionary because 'evolutionary' is fundamentally tempo-ral—the opposite of capitalist possibility. The return of antique capitalist theory in its most primitive form since the 1970s, and with it political economy, is evidence of this immobility.

The relation of a social philosophy impervious to either 'correction' or repair and its reconstituted fact in hegemonic political economy seeming-ly leaves very little room to maneuver. The totalizing nature of capitalist theory means that it is either taken as is or it is thrown onto the garbage heap without looking back.

This set up is necessary because it doesn't intuitively follow that the absence of judgment about 'the world' that is Zen has social consequence outside of opting out as religious sequestration. The question then is how does one maneuver in 'the world' without judgment? The answer is that one doesn't.

The question is of the nature of this judgment to be abandoned. Much as everyone who gets out of bed in the morning and puts one foot in front of another has 'faith' of one sort or another in embedded being—that 'the world' is there to 'catch' us, the absence of judgment meant here is metaphysical judgment, circumscription with the intent of privileging dissociated 'beings' over embedded existence.

'We' in the West already have the otherworldly nature of Cartesian metaphysics instantiated as hegemonic 'identity' if otherworldliness is the goal. 'We' already exist in the sequestration of the Western 'self.' Zen as it is meant here is to step across the metaphysical threshold to fully engage, to end this sequestration of the self.

Conversely, the Western self of capitalist democracy as theory of 'human' being is cartoon humanism, ethereal selves as 'consumers' of the social and environmental catastrophes we create. The rank implausibility of 'work' versus 'leisure' as life-choice within this humanism is only outdone by positing genocide and slavery as 'freedom.'

Zen is to clear away the clutter through re-engagement, to exist away from the totalizing hubris of metaphysical 'knowledge' as both determination and guide. And to be clear, it is not a singular view, a 'human' perspective. It is abandonment of this perspective as dissociated 'object' put forward with imperial intent. But again, embedded being does not take place in the metaphysical ether—abandonment of metaphysics isn't a taking away, it is a homecoming.

The post-modern philosophers who worked through the writing of Edmund Husserl and Martin Heidegger to come to broadly similar conclusions, Jacques Derrida and Jean-Francois Lyotard, were left with relatively little interesting to say about political economy. Martin Heidegger himself said that there might be very little left to say after metaphysics is abandoned. But outside of the idea of language as individual possession a different view emerges. It is more than a little ironic that post-modernism accompanied revival of the radical capitalist 'self' as consumers with self-determined 'choice.'

Zen is the complete and utter abandonment of metaphysics. But abandoning metaphysics is to remove implausible lines of division, not re-sequestration in some alternative ether of 'the mind.' Western imperialism, particularly in its high capitalist phases, has shown very little tendency to leave those who wish not to participate alone. In fact, capitalist democracy is metaphysical imperialism, the insistence, backed by coercive methods and force, that economic man is the atemporal core of human being and that participation in capitalist political economy will be either 'freely' chosen or imposed.

Confusion over this latter point comes through capitalist institutions that pose their socially created conditions as 'nature' against which capitalist democracy is the 'solution.' There is no 'neutral' base that leaves post-modern 'new' democratists, the 'selves' that emerge from a theorized absence of external circumscription, to their 'own' devices. Capitalism is premised on 'micro' narratives as consumer choice. Its 'meta' narrative is in this way posed as anti-ideology, as the 'system' of self-determination.

But as outlined above, through its metaphysical worldview and capitalist ideology embedded in social institutions, the micro-narratives that emerge are as tightly circumscribed as they might be through any totalitarian ideology.

In contrast to capitalist theory, most Marxian theory is 'workable' without metaphysics. While this likely won't move Marxian dogmatists, Marx's broad idea of social production[115] is analog to the idea of language as social production. To be clear, this idea of social language is to point to the implausibility of metaphysics as necessary starting point, not to suggest a new metaphysical starting point. To the argument that Marx made with 'social production,' and in contrast to dominant strains of philosophical post-modernism, the 'life of the mind' is socially embedded. It need not be perceived as such, hence capitalist theory and other theologies. But the idea of Zen as self-sequestration is its opposite once the metaphysical lines of division are dropped.

Another way to see this is that capitalism requires participation—without 'consumers' in the form of modern consumer 'culture,' any collective step away, even if in different directions, will face the full wrath of capitalist defense mechanisms very quickly. The point is well made that this would be true by degree of any concept of material being. This brings back the nature of capitalist 'freedom' in a world against which claims were laid long before we entered it. Once the metaphysical divisions are dropped to allow freedom from capitalism, from self-conception as a Western 'self' as Zen opens the possibility to, its institutional fact remains. The contradiction lies in the totalizing nature of the capitalist conceit that capitalism is a (the) 'natural' system of choice.

Perhaps this can be made clearer with an historical example. None of the world was 'owned' before the Anglo-European concept of ownership and property rights was imposed. What are today the Americas had indigenous peoples living 'on' and 'with' the land outside of this concept of owning it.

Choosing to step outside of, abandon if you will, the idea of ownership and property would have little to no impact on its broader social fact in Western political economy. Any move to affect this abandonment would be social—it would be between people who either through considered choice, or by simply no longer considering the premise, create different ways of existing socially.

Zen is often considered differently than it is put forward here. Interpreter of Zen for Westerners, D.T. Suzuki[117], addressed meditative Zen and the idea-practice of 'no-mind' in his correspondence with Martin Heidegger[119] and in other writing and came out on the side of non-metaphysical being rather than the more predominant 'no-mind'—a rough approximation of where it is taken here.

The difference is important and has analog is religious conceptions of Buddhism versus more philosophical conceptions. The basic tenets of Buddhism[121] like right livelihood are practical suggestions for living and life rather than rules as dogma handed down from a theorized otherworldly deity. The Zen concept of 'no-mind' more closely resembles a disciplined form of religious sequestration and as such has an implied social context.

Of current relevance is that Zen is social practice in addition to whatever else it might be. And 'practitioners' of Zen exist socially and utterly embedded in 'the world.' While an absence of metaphysical partition doesn't imply 'holism,' it is an absence of partition. The Western 'otherworldliness' of religious belief and metaphysical reasoning needn't be 'taken away' because it has no relevance in Zen.

This relates to the 'personal' decision to abandon metaphysics through the starting premise that it ever 'is / was.' The atemporal Western 'soul' as it evolved through Cartesian and capitalist metaphysics into 'rational' 'man' is serviceable as religious doctrine for those for whom it is serviceable. But its role in imperialist political economy is as social act, not personal religious sequestration.

What the clearing that is Zen makes visible is that capitalism is an imposition, a dim insistence that people 'accept' culturally and historically circumscribed religious precepts as they have been reconstituted in a wholly implausible 'science' of political economy. To be clear, this isn't to replace one insistence with another. It is to provide the clearing where imperial insistence has no place.

The starting position of this clearance is holding totalizing social philosophies as they are reconstituted in political economy at bay. To the new democratists—post-modernists, this means more than practicing 'democracy' locally; it means ending the totalizing political economy that is almost instantaneously re-consuming the democratic movements of recent history. And to be clear, metaphysical conceptions of the 'self' of

Western 'democracy' render its metaphysical incarnation the opposite of an absence of circumscription of Zen.

This latter point is a departure from much philosophical post-modernism. Martin Heidegger's contention[123] that there might not be much to say after abandoning metaphysics grants metaphysical 'space' to the role of language and leaves standing the reconstitution of metaphysical reasoning in 'assertive' political economy.

There is no 'requirement' that a 'social' theory of language or any other be put forward in 'opposition' to metaphysics except from 'within' the metaphysical frame. The idea that competing ideologies, 'meta-narratives,' even as hegemonic insistence, explain the great social catastrophes of the twentieth century takes metaphysical reasoning at face value.

This isn't to argue that ideas aren't important. It is to reiterate that the material circumstances as allegedly competing ideologies iterated 'through' them explain far more than does continents of 'true believers' launching holy wars against one another. The Cold War was used opportunistically by Western capitalists to spawn subversion, political coups, chaos through 'wars of attrition' and outright invasion to hide their interests behind the mystification of ideological difference.

The 'deeper' point of philosophical post-modernism that is also made here—that it was / is the totalizing nature of metaphysical reasoning that so contributes to imperial thinking, leaves its abandonment at the foot of 'personal' choice. Zen reframes the question from an absence of circumscription so that it is metaphysical reasoning that is the 'choice.' This is to launch a more radical questioning, one that, with the tenets of Buddhism again serving as analog, is willing to challenge the hegemonic core of the Western 'self' to achieve reconciliation with the world.

But as it is reconstituted in political economy, primarily in capitalist democracy, imperialism has no intention of simply going away. Much as material conditions provided a metaphorical distance between the broad frames of ideology and historically embedded circumstance in the Cold War, this historical embedding is present in existing political economy today.

Much of the Western view is of ideology metaphorically sitting 'atop' a human 'core.' As I've spent much of this book arguing, this 'core' is metaphysical humanism of which capitalism with homo economicus as its primary actor is the premier example. Without metaphysics and its otherworldly 'timeless and universal' atemporality no such humanism with its human 'core' is necessary. As clearing, Zen scrapes away this detritus to provide the possibility of reconciliation.

Ending ideology won't end historically embedded political economy. And in material terms, making the total product of capitalist democracy 'visible' and ending its social and environmental catastrophes is fundamental to the capacity for being. Once metaphysical otherworldliness is un-supposed this is the only world 'we've' got. Making capitalist imperialism 'stop' is not the same as imposing a competing form of imperialism.

What might this other, non-metaphysical world look like? The question as put forward is mis-framed—it requires the recovery of the metaphysical frame as mode of explanation complete with a 'view from nowhere' that reduces broad engagement to imperial 'virtues.' Alternatively, it would 'look' like what we make it. The 'practical' problem that should find some station with philosophical 'pragmatists' is that the existing ways we in 'the West' relate to 'the world' isn't 'working.'

The only 'solution' within the metaphysical frame is more metaphysics—more 'science' and more 'capitalism,' that bring with them more dysfunction. It is the specific mode of metaphysical alienation—acting 'on' 'the world' rather than 'in' it, that produces incapacity in capacity, the ability to act on the world but not-to-not act on it.

The solution to social catastrophes is to stop creating them. The solution to environmental catastrophes is to stop creating them. The 'imperative' driving these is socially given from particular political economy, not 'nature.' More broadly, the Western frame toward 'the world' is imperial, of 'conquering' nature. Well 'nature' has been pretty well conquered and the resulting state of affairs seems more of a problem than a 'solution.'

Different ways of relating to 'the world' don't carry with them metaphysical unity, the experience-being of 'man' as put forward by self-appointed spokespersons for 'god' or 'nature.' Likewise no 'timeless and universal' set of virtues that would drive alternate 'visions' of future 'being' is available outside of metaphysics.

So again, ending the imposition of the alleged virtues of capitalist democracy isn't to impose a competing set of virtues unless the goal is the rapid recovery of capitalist democracy—the imperial nature and metaphysical mode of doing so fuels the very same internal logic that leaves only 'its' own conclusions.

To be clear, this is different than concluding, as Martin Heidegger did, that there might be nothing left to say. It is to place the act of saying in 'the world' in a way that erases the logic of domination and control and with it the imperial tendencies behind social and environmental catastrophe. It is to refuse the capitalist assertion that its catastrophes exist behind an impenetrable wall and safely away from us.

Perceived dangers of this radical questioning take as their base proposition, their starting point, instantiated notions of the 'selves' doing the questioning. Once these selves are considered outside of their metaphysical frame what becomes apparent is that they aren't, and never were, what they are purported to be. The metaphysical frame is imperial insistence put forward as eternal truth. Any challenge to this insistence is radical questioning because it has already abandoned the realm of given answers.

Zen as this radical questioning is more likely to lead to social and worldly reconciliation than to nihilistic 'relativism' as is the commonly expressed fear. People who tread carefully because they have abandoned the clear conviction of imperial hubris are less likely than those supremely confident in misguided theology to act against 'the world.' Conversely, with climate crisis, nuclear weapons, never-ending wars and social pathologies the dominant themes of Western life, immovable adherence to this premise of 'core' selves seems the nihilistic conceit.

Revolution is the Solution

THE OFT POSITED CHOICE OF POLITICAL 'MOTION' IN THE WEST IS 'evolution or revolution,' incremental tendency one way or another in the broad trajectory of political economy or break, rupture and replacement? The question is superficially reasonable within the narrow theoretical frame of capitalist democracy. And it is a basic misunderstanding of circumstance outside of it.

Within the frame capitalist democracy is political economy 'designed' to facilitate social change through the principles that (1) a self-defined 'we' are all in this 'society' together, (2) this society is premised on the facilitation of self-determination and (3) social break and rupture are oppositional as assertion away from this 'we' and an imposition of some against the expressed self-determination of the many.

The 'self-evident' mode of social change from within is through consensus building—raise the set of relations at issue, propose alternative solutions and convince enough of the other 'we' mates in the marketplace of ideas to produce a political platform that embeds these changes into political economy.

From outside this frame the history of this 'we' is of opportunistic circumscription—The U.S. was founded in genocide against indigenous peoples and the overwhelming preponderance of 'our' history still has slavery as social fact. Today the U.S. has the highest incarceration rate, the proportion of the population in prison, in the world with the preponderance of those incarcerated being descendents of slaves and their state of incarceration being the 'freely determined' reconstitution of chattel relations as for-profit 'objects' in for-profit prisons.

The capacity for self-determination is from within the radical incoherence of the Western 'self' with the hypothesized realm being the 'unity' of 'man' and its social fact by degree race, class and gender as embedded in history through social repression. And the premise of break and rupture as assertive imposition takes existing political economy as 'neutral' ground, as the 'safe place' of being against which difference is detraction.

In fact, there is no such neutral ground and it is the totalizing hegemony of capitalist democracy that facilitates the illusion / delusion that there is. Existing political economy in the West is both assertion and imposition and its facts are wars for economic resources, external and internal social repression, increasing environmental catastrophe and the utter incapacity for resolution within existing political economy.

The factory farm system addressed above is both 'aspect' and broad metaphor for the political economy of capitalist democracy. It is a set of social relations theoretically legitimated as 'freedom' whose social fact is the freedom of residual and newly empowered plutocracy to place those who they can in imperial relation as 'use' value in their service.

The theorized human / not-human divide at work is the same social metaphysics behind several centuries of genocide, slavery, imperial conquest and existing class relations as reconstituted social fact. The factual political economy faced by increasing numbers in the West is by degree that of domination, control, extraction, surveillance, coercion and containment.

The difference by degree between the office worker, the incarcerated and the animals in factory farms is put forward as difference by type, as self-chosen metaphysical partition, when its social facts place vast majorities clearly on the 'losing' side of political economy as social 'objects' of economic expropriation and self-expropriation.

This confusion of degree and type finds social voice in the insistence of difference, that social inclusion / exclusion is both localized and binary—black-white, male-female, citizen-immigrant, etc. and that its posited boundaries are fact of 'nature' rather than of two centuries of imperial apologetics reconstituted in existing social relations. This degree as it is socially reconstituted produces difference in 'unity,' as socially 'legitimated' hierarchy, which appears as 'self-evident' partition and is put forward as 'natural' order.

Historical embedding, and with it 'place' in social partition, is recontextualized as capacity-choice, as the decision of any 'objective' observer whose 'objective' is place in the existing social order. This degree as difference finds displaced manufacturing workers shopping at Wal-Mart for 'bargains,' recently 'outsourced' suburbanites endorsing the looting of public pension plans and the descendents of former slaves supporting the murder of one-million or more Iraqis in a racist imperial war to secure oil for multi-national oil companies.

No 'revolutionary man' need be developed for social circumscription to define the realm of imposed facts, for 'unity' as imperial subjects to be found on the other side of the imperial partition. It is this imposition that is put forward as the 'neutral' ground against which refusal, resistance and rejection is 'revolutionary.'

The philosophical and political-economic critique of capitalism presented here is intended to clear away the clutter, to clear away the theoretical incapacitation presented by the metaphysical-dialectical requirement of 'opposition' that elevates capitalist political economy to more than social struggle accompanied by developed apologetics.

This critique of metaphysics shares space with philosophical post-modernism and its implied and asserted politics of studied humility and rejection of grand social theories. This 'humility' most recently found its concrete expression in the 'democratic revolutions' of North Africa and to equal extent, if to less effect, in the resurgence of interest in 'the West' in left-anarchism and the Marx-Bakunin[125] debate over the role of 'the state' in left revolutions.

These popular 'rebellions' are now in limbo with re-assertion of Western interests through the IMF, Western arms dealers and militaries and external support for governments subservient to the interests of the West. Apparently left unconsidered in this newfound humility are the differences between implicit acceptance of Western political economy and the capacity to exist outside its reach and the reach of other imperial tendencies.

The 'individual' capacity to do so is both utopian and remains wholly within the capitalist conceit of self-determination—it is the privilege of empire against its subjects. Post-metaphysical humility as a 'soft touch' in the world can only exist in the social clearing that makes it possible. Otherwise it is but a menu item within the totalizing reach of capitalist imperialism.

'Theoretical' rejection of grand social narratives does nothing to diminish them except to the extent their material reconstitution in the social institutions of political economy is effectively diminished. It is embedded social relations that facilitate which 'grand narratives' are put forward to serve as advertising slogans for the existing social order.

It is hardly a coincidence that the resurgence in social theories supporting imperial capitalist democracy was coincident with its resurgence in fact. With irony so apparent that postmodern icon Jacques Derrida had to recreate 'soft' Marxism[127] to fight the implication, the 'soft touch' of philosophical post-modernism was coincident with the 'hard touch' of capitalist resurgence.

This is to restate the point that capitalism is more than just political and economic imposition; it is the predominant counter-revolutionary force against pluralistic-democratic movements around the globe. The 'America' of democratist mythology was 'founded' as genocidal neo-imperialist plutocracy and deference paid it by pluralistic-democratic movements would be better spent understanding this history.

This includes those in the U.S. and the 'developed' West who find themselves increasingly on the wrong side of capitalist imposition. The so-called 'Twitter revolutions' came through the expropriated labor of the 'tech' industry, were mediated by the global telecommunications companies in the service of the NSA (National Security Agency), the CIA, the FBI, the DEA and local and sundry political operatives in the service of imperialist geopolitics. And the names, networks and content of 'revolutionary' communications were recorded for study and future disruptive actions.

Within the imperial realms circumscription of the proper 'objects' of democratic expression has assured that the outcomes of democratic 'choice' achieved only their intended outcomes for most of this history. The current state of 'representative' democracy in the U.S. is evidence of the economic basis of these 'political' parameters.

Hidden behind the rhetoric and machinations of the Cold War were the interests and motivations of Western industrialists and bankers who perpetuated it as an instrument of capitalist imperialism. Today Cold War revivalists wait at the ready to use renewed imperial tensions to shift attention away from the radical economic dysfunction increasingly in evidence in the West.

The contrived threat of anti-Western insurgency is repeatedly used to overthrow democratically elected governments to promote the interests of particular capitalists against those of pluralistic-democratic self-determination. This is to argue that capitalism and capitalists have in history been the greatest threats to revolutionary democratic movements. Theories that capitalism can be 'willed' away or that capitalists can be convinced through reasoned argument that 'its' political economy is a 'mistake' must confront this history.

The apparent paradox of revolution as opposition, defense or reaction gives undue deference to the internal logic of the metaphysical frame of capitalist imperialism—acting in the world is only 'reactive' within it or some other oppositional metaphysics. Capitalism is imperial assertion and stopping 'its' assertion, or any 'competing' imperial assertion, has meaning as social act, as an act 'between' people rather than 'by' them.

This isn't to assert a metaphysical 'holism' but rather to raise the question of social capacity. When considering this 'between' the question of 'its' realm is of both desire and capacity to participate. In 'practical' terms the late President of Venezuela, Hugo Chavez, faced generally analogous circumstance—internal plutocracy interested only in its plutocratic prerogative, external capitalist-imperialists, mainly in the U.S., interested in imperial imposition to control Venezuela's oil resources, and a large, wholly disenfranchised population that had no 'local' resources to create the clearing needed for pluralistic-democratic social relations to emerge.

Mr. Chavez won free and fair elections against well and externally funded opposition through his factual support for pluralistic-democratic institutions. With this support he was able to hold the forces of international capital at bay and in so doing facilitate the emergence of this social 'between' against capitalist-imperialist insistence.

Mr. Chavez's 'example' is put forward for several reasons including that the social 'clearing' he created was only 'oppositional' to the extent that he held Western imperialists and internal plutocrats at bay—he stopped them from forcing extractive, exploitative political economy onto people who lacked the social power to resist.

The social 'between' that brought Mr. Chavez to 'power' was reconstituted through the mechanism of 'state' to facilitate the development-emergence of the broader 'between' of pluralistic democracy as social fact, not as the improbable promise of the West.

The experience of Venezuelans with the clearing created through Hugo Chavez has implications for other recent pluralistic-democratic movements as well as for those increasingly on the outside of Western imperial power. The 'state' frame that Mr. Chavez used to benefit the Venezuelan people provided them the capacity for effective political action through its form and structure.

The question at present is whether enough of a clearing was created for it to persist against the determined predations of Western state interests in the service of Western capitalists. While history, culture, form and institutional structure may differ, the challenge for other pluralistic-democratic movements is that without the state 'frame' there is little capacity to hold external and internal imperial interests at bay. And within it the 'meta' frame as embedded political economy remains for these interests to re-assert themselves as is happening in Venezuela following Mr. Chavez's death.

To be clear, this is no assertion that pluralistic democracy is either the right or 'natural' form of political economy. And the irony factor that it is the long-held claim of the capitalist-democratic West that 'it' is the one true political economy of 'freedom' is put back against history and historical trajectory.

The social 'clearing' that Mr. Chavez created had / has the potential to facilitate the re-emergence of indigenous and sustainable political economy in Venezuela. Venezuela's resource 'curse' of oil has been a magnet for imperial predations for nearly a century now.

With no coherent plan or even convincing lip service for what to do about aggregating environmental catastrophes, the reason why the U.S. tried so insistently to destroy Mr. Chavez was to control Venezuela's oil. As is apparent in current trajectory, the only 'plan' the West will ever have to 'solve' its catastrophes is to leverage them through technology and hope that an improbable 'god' bails it out. The social 'clearing' that Mr. Chavez created need not have resulted in local pluralistic democracy in the Western conception to facilitate the re-emergence of sustainable political economy.

And what is demonstrated in the contrast between capitalist imposition and the creation of potentially sustainable political economy is the radical improbability that capitalist democracy will result in any kind of factual self-determination. The capacity for factual self-determination is a function of material conditions; not some ethereal 'feeling' that one is 'free.' The irony that capitalist metaphysical self-determination is by all appearances its opposite in fact raises the question of its persistence?

The question for the 'evolutionary' West is under what circumstances is reconciliation and resolution of the social and environmental catastrophes that capitalist imperialism creates possible? This is a question of both class-consciousness—the social 'chair' one occupies, and of circumscription of the 'facts' that enter this consciousness? This isn't a question of 'competing' political economy; it is of the fatal trajectory of Western capitalism.

The U.S. has 'limited' the greenhouse gas emissions 'it' reports in recent years by 'off-shoring' capitalist production. Relocating these emissions isn't reducing them. The claim is an environmental shell game, not resolution. The Internet, the Cartesian 'one-mind' of technocratic fantasy, is now wholly integrated as new and totalizing engineered dependence.

The move to 'squeeze' the newly dependent is underway with older channels of distribution disappeared in favor of those more amenable to coercive commercial-state power. The relation of science, technology and capitalist political economy through shared approach to 'the world' assures that these new technologies will be redirected to social control in the interests of their creators.

The mediation of ever more social relations through technology—through electronic media, is imposition posed as facilitation. To date the implications have not likely 'sunk in.' The theoretical incapacity for resolution, the 'internal' logic of capitalist metaphysics reified in these technologies, is reconstituted in their fact through control of context.

In the U.S. the Federal government is serving commercial interests by restricting dissemination of information about factory farm conditions through the use of 'anti' terrorism laws. The realm of these laws encompasses most large capitalist enterprises with now explicit conflation of state with commercial interests. Having largely destroyed alternative channels of communication, this one-mind knows where you live, where you work, who you communicate with, how much money is in your bank account, how you vote and who your family relations are.

Commercial and state interests watch and listen to you, your spouse, your children, your friends and your associates through any network portal at any time or even constantly without your / their knowledge or consent. 'Smart' algorithms decide what information is made available to you irrespective of the nature of your interest. Through restricting information only that which serves corporate-state interests now finds its way through the dominant media.

It is this unified imposition that circumscribes the realm of the imposed upon, not some 'natural' unified opposition. Criticism of grand (Meta) narratives proceeds from the premise that ideology is the basis of social difference rather than its product. Capitalist 'opposition' is to everything—life, the world and different conceptions of existing, due to its metaphysical structure, not from the perspective of 'competing' ideologies.

As within the capitalist metaphysical frame, people can 'internalize' its externally given imperatives to the extent they are even conscious of a choice. However, the material 'content' of this unified imposition includes social and environmental catastrophes as well as its 'facts' of imposition, the capitalist imperative reconstituted in institutions and social relations as factual political economy.

The reach and the effects of the environmental catastrophes related to global warming materially relate the lot of office workers to that of the incarcerated, to dead and dying oceans, to the animals in factory farms and to factory workers in China. The totalizing reach of the technologies of coercion, surveillance, domination and control may differ by degree but not by intent.

The threat of nuclear annihilation so receded in 'the Western mind' unites the potentially annihilated in catastrophe—why has the fear receded while the capacity is nowhere diminished? The totalizing reach of these technologies in the 'developed' West finds possible resolution in the poor neighborhoods of Caracas where social clearing was created, however fleetingly, through the combination of social intent and historical serendipity.

Because Western political economy is totalizing it is irresolvable. The irony-paradox that the rich who profit from causing global warming will also suffer its consequences illustrates this incapacity for resolution. Holding it at bay through use of existing and new social mechanisms as sustainable, functional political economy is recovered seems as promising a social goal as any.

This isn't to suggest that there is anything like a template for social engagement and recovery. The clearing that Hugo Chavez was able to create shares some tendencies that might facilitate a broader clearing.

The first is form and structure—the broad popular movement brought Mr. Chavez to power. But it was his ability to maintain and redirect it to create, rather than impose, the political-economic space where indigenous development and re-development is possible.

The post-modern democratist and anarcho-collectivist aversion to taking and maintaining state power faces the challenge of capitalist imposition and re-imposition of imperial relations. The state is a frame for holding this tendency at bay as much as it is a tool for promoting capitalist interests. But Venezuela isn't the U.S. and Egypt isn't the European Union. Imperial history persists, as do its premises of intent and legitimacy.

The challenge can be seen in the supporting paradigm that post-modernism provided the high capitalist resurgence of recent decades. 'Micronarratives' find their analog in (small) batch economic production. To the extent it is relevant, by staying within the tightly circumscribed, self-determined self of capitalist metaphysics anarchists run the risk of simply extending the realm of capitalist consumer choice to political economy. Any deep and potentially lasting challenge to capitalism has to address the conception of the Western 'self' that would also pry open the anarchist conception.

The internationalist strategies developed and used by the U.S. based Black Panthers in the 1960s and 1970s and by Hugo Chavez and the South American Bolivarians more recently are possible models for breaking with the West. Additionally, implied in expanded and more intrusive trade 'agreements' is both that Western capitalists have no intention of ending their imposition of imperial political economy and that the task has not yet been completed, at least to their reasoning.

This is partly a function of capitalist metaphysics, the permanent distance between the 'purity' of unbounded ideological hallucination and social fact. But it can also be seen in occasional disruptions like the rebellion by the Guatemalan peasantry against the forced imposition of industrial corn from the U.S. Capitalism finds its most committed adherents on the 'winning' side of imperial history. On the other 'side' of that one-sided worldview history and circumstance have left a greater distance between accedence and propensity for resistance.

The question Hugo Chavez opened up is: what do people need for factual self-determination? The answer back, at least as of now, has not been the 'stuff' of the West. The material needs Mr. Chavez did his best to fill were basic nutrition, health care, sanitation and education including adult literacy programs that left approximately the same percentage of Venezuelans functionally literate[129] as in the much 'richer' U.S.

The goal here isn't to develop a template but to argue for social possibility. For the reasons laid out above capitalism is totalizing, hegemonic political economy that is incapable of the self-reflection needed for self–correction. The historical contention of ideological opposition results almost entirely from the inability of capitalist ideologues to 'step out' of the metaphysical frame of capitalist theory.

Through paradox and theoretical incoherence capitalism is always and everywhere the anti-thesis of democracy as pluralistic self-determination. Despite the toxic trivialization of the terminology, the continued capacity for any sort of self-determination requires creating functional and sustainable political economy. This requires holding capitalist and quasi-capitalist imperialism at bay for long enough to recover sustainable ways of getting by.

As improbable as any and all of this may seem, so is much of a future if current trajectory is maintained. The circle capitalist imperialism has drawn around its 'objects' is broadly the 'we' who 'between' us might affect a different direction. As a citizen of the U.S., and with understanding that a lot of distance must be traversed before any of this is possible, a very partial list toward reconciliation is provided.

End the prison system, free all prisoners and provide those who need it with psychological, substance abuse and medical care for re-integration into social life.

End the factory farm system. Rehabilitate and free the animals that are currently held captive and require that all farming fully respect the capacity of animals to live rich, psychologically complex, socially realized lives.

Create a permanent government jobs program that provides all comers with a guaranteed job in socially beneficial production at a living wage that includes quality health care and pensions for workers and their families.

End the U.S. military and related industries while maintaining the capacity for mutual defense through a citizen army that draws from the families of the corporate-state plutocracy before the general population.

Demilitarize the police, take away their weapons and all coercive capacity and reorient their roles to community coordinators beginning with making sure that everyone is fed, housed and receives health care.

Create a single payer national health care program that provides all comers with quality health care that is fully funded through the Federal government.

Provide quality, federally funded public education from pre-school through graduate degree programs that is available to all.

The question of where the money would come from to fund these programs is answered:

Prisons are extremely expensive in both social and financial terms. The Western narrative of 'crime' partitions like actions under strategies of social repression. The prison system is race and class based and the most socially destructive acts remain far outside its realm. Ending the prison system would save lives, communities and money.

The factory farm system represents the least efficient expenditure of social resources possible. Ending it would end the social catastrophe that is the treatment of animals within it and it would free resources to be used to produce nutritious, less toxic food and would lower associated medical costs. Reconciliation with animals is a necessary step toward reconciliation with the world.

The savings from ending the military would fund this program and provide needed employment for those displaced in doing so. Those employed as government workers would pay taxes on their earnings in contrast to the army of unemployed and sub-employed that currently exists. Additionally, the social costs of unemployment would be eliminated.

The U.S. military is the most expensive and extractive in world history. Additionally, not counted in its 'costs' are the social and financial costs of its destructive actions. Having a contingent military of citizen soldiers for mutual defense would force capitalists dependent on imperial predations to pay closer to the true costs of their production.

As configured the police in the U.S. are an army working in the service of the rich. The contention that the police need to be armed is a function of their historic role of enforcing racist and classist laws to carry out social repression and to maintain a reserve army of desperate labor to subsidize capitalist 'profits.' Disarming the police and turning their function to social distribution would remove much of the tension that has led to the level of violence to which they are claimed to exist to respond to.

The U.S. currently has the most expensive health care system (per person) with close to the worst results of any 'developed' system. The current system is set up to facilitate cartel 'profits,' transfers to insurers and medical care providers based on monopoly power, and to provide only 'profitable' health care. Replacing this system with a national system would represent the largest reduction in government expenditures listed here and have the added benefit of greatly increasing the quality and availability of health care.

The same broad arguments that leave the U.S. with the most expensive health care system in the world coincident with the worst results are now being applied to public education. Privatization is the argument that capitalists motivated by profits are best at economic organization. But the profit motive has no public interest—profits can be more easily earned by looting public institutions than by effectively managing them. Without public expression of irony many of the same privateers who argue that educational achievement must be measured have given themselves decades before their efforts are measured. Using monopoly power to drive down costs doesn't produce profits in capitalist theory; it produces economic rents. As Social Security is far more efficient than private health insurance schemes, so is public education when those who seek to destroy it are kept at bay.

Finally, the West has had two or more decades to address the growing threat of environmental catastrophe with no meaningful movement toward resolution. Those who hope to 'save' capitalism can either save the material environment in which it exists or watch it end at their own hand. The contrived notion that 'radicals' will end the world places capitalism and capitalists at its very center.

Endnotes

The rationale for using web addresses as footnotes is that in most cases far greater detail relating the thinking behind the footnote to its 'object' can be found. The risk that some of the web addresses will be deleted is put against the increasing difficulty of finding physical copies of these sources other than on the Internet.

Notes

1. *http://moodle.eosmith.org/pluginfile.php/3436/mod_resource/ content/1/The%20Structure%20OF%20Scientific%20Revolutions%20 3rd%20ed%20-%20Thomas%20Kuhn.pdf*

2. See Edmund Husserl's *The Crisis of the European Sciences* and Martin Heidegger's *Being and Time* for fuller formulation of the problem with metaphysics. Arguments from philosophical post-modernism are irrelevent to this discussion.

3. *http://www.history.com/topics/new-deal*

4. *http://www.salon.com/2009/06/04/jimmy_carter_did_it/*

5. *http://www.nytimes.com/1982/10/18/opinion/volcker-s-monetar- ist-policy-painful-costly.html*

6. *http://www.youtube.com/watch?v=nwXF6UdkeI4* Robert McNamara in *The Fog Of War*

7. *http://www.washingtonpost.com/wp-srv/politics/special/clinton/ stories/scaifemain050299.htm*

8. *http://www.chomsky.info/interviews/197703--.htm*

9. *http://www.nytimes.com/2007/11/13/opinion/13herbert.html*

10. *http://www.thenation.com/article/173593/why-was-paul-krugman- so-wrong#*

11. *http://www.amazon.com/World-Depression-1929-1939-Charles- Kindleberger/dp/0520275853* Charles Kindleberger, *The World in*

Depression, provides an account of the economic impact of national debts following WWI.

12. *http://www.greenpeace.org/international/en/campaigns/oceans/pollu-tion/trash-vortex/* The term 'island' of garbage larger than Texas has been used but vortex seems the more accurate description

13. *http://www.scientificamerican.com/article/is-global-warming-happen-ing-faster-than-expected/*

14. *http://www.biologicaldiversity.org/programs/biodiversity/elements_of_biodiversity/extinction_crisis/*

15. *http://elsa.berkeley.edu/~saez/saez-UStopincomes-2012.pdf*

16. *http://www.nytimes.com/2014/09/22/us/us-ramping-up-major-renew-al-in-nuclear-arms.html?_r=0*

17. *http://www.ssc.wisc.edu/~walker/wp/wp-content/uploads/2012/09/Becker1993.pdf*

18. *http://en.wikipedia.org/wiki/Cultural_hegemony*

19. *http://www.gutenberg.org/files/32625/32625-pdf.pdf*

20. *http://www.econlib.org/library/Enc/bios/Friedman.html*

21. *http://www.econlib.org/library/Enc/bios/Smith.html*

22. *http://en.wikipedia.org/wiki/Animal_spirits_(Keynes)*

23. *http://www.chomsky.info/interviews/197703—.htm* Chomsky's view that multi-national oil companies were behind the embargo was widely reported at the time. Iran remained a U.S. client state until the late 1970s when the Iranian revolution ended the relationship.

24. *http://www.theguardian.com/business/2012/jun/11/why-our-food-is-making-us-fat* Richard Nixon was also one of the architects of the HMO model of health care that kept it 'private' meaning that profits are earned from the quantity of ill-health that can be engineered.

25. *http://www.thirdworldtraveler.com/Democracy/ConservThinkTanks.html*

26. *http://elsa.berkeley.edu/users/saez/saez-UStopincomes-2012.pdf*

27. *http://academic.evergreen.edu/g/grossmaz/interventions.html* most often claimed as 'defensive' interventions, the U.S. is among the most militarist empires in world history.

28. *http://www.cepr.net/documents/publications/dereg-timeline-2009-07. pdf* The effort to give connected bankers everything they thought they wanted was bi-partisan with Democrat Bill Clinton being fully complicit in major deregulation and Democrat Barack Obama doing everything within his power to both hide the bodies and to fully restore the most culpable bankers at public expense

29. *http://www.sfgate.com/news/article/Mexico-s-corn-farmers-see-their-livelihoods-2515188.php* The introduction of Monsanto's 'suicide' seeds in India, a play to monopolize food production, is related to the thousands of farmer suicides from the combination of financial stress from the higher costs of production and the 'financialization' of agriculture that forces agricultural producers into debt-based financing of production.

30. *http://www.umich.edu/~snre492/Jones/maquiladora.htm*

31. *http://www.npr.org/2013/12/26/257255787/wave-of-illegal-immigrants-gains-speed-after-nafta*

32. *http://en.wikipedia.org/wiki/Citizens_United_v._Federal_Election_Commission*

33. *http://www.archives.gov/exhibits/charters/constitution_transcript.html*

34. *http://www.constitution.org/jl/2ndtr05.htm* Both Locke and Smith posited deduced 'earlier' periods to naturalize then developing property relations. For a more convincing account see the later chapters in Marx's Capital, volume 1.

35. *http://geolib.com/smith.adam/won1-08.html*

36. *http://www.smithsonianmag.com/air/the-political-history-of-cap-and-trade-34711212/?no-ist*

37. *http://www.c2es.org/facts-figures/trends/co2-temp*

38. *http://elsa.berkeley.edu/users/saez/saez-UStopincomes-2012.pdf*

39. *http://en.wikipedia.org/wiki/Hydraulic_fracturing*

40. *http://www.britannica.com/EBchecked/topic/124443/cogito-ergo-sum* also see Heidegger's *History of the Concept of Time* and *Being and Time* for fuller explanations of the radical irrelevance of Descartes' question

41. *http://www.bls.gov/jlt/* the data is regularly released and is publicly available making the argument that unemployment results from disinterest in working the hallucination of extremely lazy ideologues

42. *http://moodle.eosmith.org/pluginfile.php/3436/mod_resource/content/1/ The%20Structure%20OF%20Scientific%20Revolutions%203rd%20 ed%20-%20Thomas%20Kuhn.pdf*

43. *http://faculty.knox.edu/fmcandre/allegory_cave.pdf*

44. *http://www.durt.info/2011Summer/texts/Husserl,%20Edmund%20 1970%20The%20Crisis%20of%20European%20Sciences%20and%20 Transcendental%20Phenomenology%20(excerpts,%20translation%20 by%20David%20Carr).pdf*

45. *http://religiousstudies.stanford.edu/WWW/Sheehan/pdf/heideg-ger_texts_online/1915%20CONCEPT%20OF%20TIME%20and%20 SCIENCE%20OF%20HISTORY.pdf* those with an interest in Heidegger may wish to read this prior to Being and Time to see the development of some of the ideas expressed there

46. *http://www.clas.ufl.edu/users/burt/spliceoflife/beingandtime.pdf* several translations are available as well as other PDF versions of this available on the Internet

47. *http://www.hist.umn.edu/shank/hist3282/Derrida_EndsofMan.pdf*

48. *http://www.marxists.org/archive/marx/works/1857/grundrisse/ch01.htm*

49. *http://www.jstor.org/discover/10.2307/20098902?uid=3739832&uid=212 9&uid=2&uid=70&uid=4&uid=3739256&sid=21103500338077*

50. *http://www.clas.ufl.edu/users/burt/spliceoflife/beingandtime.pdf* section 4

51. *http://www.historyisaweapon.com/defcon1/bernprop.html*

52. *http://www.military.com/ContentFiles/techtv_update_PSYOPS.htm*

53. *http://en.wikipedia.org/wiki/Luddite*

54. *http://www.econlib.org/library/Enc/SavingsandLoanCrisis.html*

55. *http://www.businessinsider.com/heres-why-the-dot-com-bubble-began-and-why-it-popped-2010-12*

56. *http://qje.oxfordjournals.org/content/124/4/1449.short* Sufi and Mian have written several seminal papers on the economic effects of the housing boom and bust.

57. *http://krugman.blogs.nytimes.com/2013/09/25/bubbles-regulation-and-secular-stagnation/* Krugman has written elsewhere of bubbles where related theories are developed

58. *http://en.wikipedia.org/wiki/Ag-gag*

59. *http://www.goodreads.com/quotes/624158-in-the-social-production-of-their-existence-men-inevitably-enter*

60. *http://www.buddhanet.net/pdf_file/manual_zen.pdf*

61. *http://www.egs.edu/library/martin-heidegger/biography/*

62. *http://www.chakraretreat.com/tenants-of-buddhism/*

63. *http://www.hist.umn.edu/shank/hist3282/Derrida_EndsofMan.pdf* I can't find the precise quote. Derrida does yeoman's work in this seminal essay. But I have clear memory of the content of the quote.

64. *https://www.marxists.org/reference/archive/bakunin/bio/robertson-ann.htm* also see Lenin's The State and Revolution for exposition of the 'structural' quandary that 'stateless' revolutions face

65. *http://www.salon.com/2013/04/28/grappling_with_specters_of_marx_partner/* See Derrida's Specters of Marx written at the peak of neo-capitalist revival theorizing.

66. *http://www.indexmundi.com/facts/venezuela/literacy-rate*

Made in the USA
San Bernardino, CA
22 September 2016